## Hume on Morality

*In every system of morality, which I have hitherto met with, I have always remark'd, that the author proceeds for some time in the ordinary way of reasoning, and establishes the being of a God, or makes observations concerning human affairs; when of a sudden I am surpriz'd to find, that instead of the usual copulations of propositions, is, and is not, I meet with no proposition that is not connected with an* ought, *or an* ought not. *This change is imperceptible; but is, however, of the last consequence. For as this* ought *or* ought not, *expresses some new relation or affirmation, 'tis necessary that it shou'd be observ'd and explain'd; and at the same time that a reason should be given for what seems altogether inconceivable, how this new relation can be a deduction from others which are entirely different from it. But as authors do not commonly use this precaution, I shall presume to recommend it to the readers; and am persuaded, that this small attention wou'd subvert all the vulgar systems of morality, and let us see, that the distinction of vice and virtue is not founded merely on the relations of objects, nor is perceiv'd by reason.*

—*from* A Treatise of Human Nature

Edited, with an Introduction by
# Alasdair
# MacIntyre

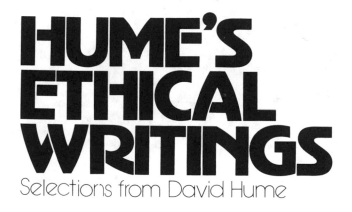

# HUME'S ETHICAL WRITINGS

Selections from David Hume

University of Notre Dame Press

Notre Dame                    London

Library of Congress Cataloging in Publication Data

Hume, David, 1711–1776.
  Hume's ethical writings.

  Reprint of the ed. published by Collier Books,
New York, which was issued in series: Collier
classics in the history of thought.
    1. Ethics—Collected works. I. MacIntyre,
Alasdair C. II. Title
[B1455.M22 1979]          171          79-1346
ISBN 0-268-01074-9
ISBN 0-268-01073-0 pbk.

Printed in the United States of America

# Contents

# EDITOR'S INTRODUCTION

# Introduction

AN INTRODUCTION should introduce. It should not be an attempt at a substitute for the book which it is introducing. So I shall not try here to summarise adequately the arguments which Hume uses in those parts of his writings which follow. I shall try rather to relate those arguments in a simple way to the general body of his work and to his life. The second task is necessary, if only because his style is so personal that you cannot confront the arguments and escape the man.

He had in one sense an uneventful life. He had a great liking for the "civilities and gay Company of Paris" and for their equivalents in the polite society of Edinburgh and London. These were the background to his constant philosophical and historical studies, apart from two interludes. In the earlier of these he served first as a staff officer in 1746 in the Mediterranean and after that as an aide-de-camp to General Sinclair at Vienna and Turin. In the later period he was first Secretary and then Chargé d'Affaires at the British Embassy in Paris in 1765-66, following this up with a spell as Under-Secretary of State in London. He was, as he said of himself in *My Own Life* (and it is a mark of Hume's rare objectivity that others said precisely the same) "a man of Mild Disposition, of Government of Temper, of an open, social and cheerful Humour, capable of Attachment, but little susceptible of Enmity, and of great Moderation in all my Passions. Even my Love of literary fame, my ruling Passion, never soured my humour, not withstanding my frequent Disappointments."

The disappointments were indeed frequent. His historical writings on the Tudor and Stuart monarchy caused clamour and controversy; his philosophical writings, notably controversial as they were, seemed at the time to pass almost unnoticed. "Never literary Attempt was more unfortunate than my Treatise of human Nature," he wrote of his first publication in 1738. "It fell *dead-born from the Press;* without reaching such distinction as even to excite a Murmur among the Zealots." And again, after remarking that the publication of his *Political Discourses* in 1752 was marked with immediate success, he has to add that "In the same Year was published at London my Enquiry concerning the Principles of Morals, which, in my own opinion (who ought not to judge on that subject) is of all my writings, historical, philosophical or literary, incomparably the best; It came unnoticed and unobserved into the World." If all this suggests a calm and engaging personality, it suggests no more than was constantly remarked upon by Hume's contemporaries. But there was deep in Hume a less often revealed and darker aspect of personality. To understand this we have to understand his background. He was born in 1711 "of a good Family both by Father and Mother. My Father's Family is a Branch of the Earl of Home's or Hume's; and my Ancestors had been Proprietors of the Estate, which my Brother possesses, for several Generations . . . My Family, however, was not rich . . ." His family belonged to the small gentry of Scotland at a time when that country both suffered from extremes of poverty and enjoyed what was for the age an exceptionally high degree of general culture. Scotland, in spite of its Calvinism, or perhaps rather because of it, was in many ways closer to Europe than to England; it was no exceptional thing for Hume to travel to Paris in 1734, to stay in France for three years and to write his first book, the *Treatise,* at La Flèche on the Loire, where he had the use of the library of the Jesuit college. It remains true that Hume had to pass from the narrow paths of a Presbyterian Calvinism, whose spirituality would often cast the shadows of a narrow, legalistic, and frightening deity, into the urbane, mannered rationalistic world of eighteenth-century letters. And this marks Hume for life. The shadows are never entirely removed. The sweetness of temper is interrupted by fears of depression and of a disordered mind. Hume is self-consciously aware of the influence of temperament upon outlook. He writes with autobiographical warrant when he says in the *Dialogues Concerning Natural Religion* (which were only published posthumously) that "when a man is in a cheerful disposition, he is fit for business or company or entertainment of any kind; and he naturally applies himself to these, and thinks not of religion. When melancholy, and dejected, he has nothing to do but brood upon the terrors of the invisible world, and to plunge himself still deeper in affliction. It may, indeed, happen, that after he has in his manner, engraved the religious opinions deep into his thought and imagination, there may arrive a change of health or circumstances, which may restore his good humour, and raising cheerful prospect of futurity, make him run into the other extreme of joy and triumph."

This psychological determinism is not restricted to religion. We have, in Hume's view, no alternative in any realm but to follow our natural propensities. This does not mean that rational argument and psychological nature always point in the same direction. Sceptical philosophical arguments may disquiet us by raising questions to which we can find no answer and our disquiet is to be removed not by counter-arguments, but only by the force of nature. "Nay, if we are philosophers, it ought only to be upon sceptical principles, and from an inclination, which we feel to employ ourselves after that manner. Where reason is lively and mixes itself with some propensity, it ought to be assented to. Where it does not, it never can have any title to operate upon us." The norm of reason then is the nature of the well-balanced, temperate individual; what scepticism in philosophy cannot justify, such as the form of inductive arguments or belief in personal identity, the force of nature supplies in us.

Hume is therefore predisposed to accept a view of moral beliefs as arising from our psychological make-up. This predisposition is very different from that of many other moral philosophers who have taken an apparently similar view. For they in taking this view have wanted to draw a sharp contrast between what they have seen as the objective, factual judgments of science and the subjective, non-factual judgments of morality. Hume indeed draws a sharp distinction between judgments as to matters of fact and moral judgments. But he does not draw it at this point. Indeed he could not. For if he makes moral judgments a matter of sentiment and feeling, so he does too with judgments upon matters of fact. When for example in the *Enquiry Concerning Human Understanding* he wishes to distinguish between factual belief and the mere entertainment in imagination of some fiction, he writes that "It follows, therefore, that the difference between *fiction* and *belief* lies in some sentiment or feeling, which is annexed to the latter, not to the former, and which depends not on the will, nor can be commanded at pleasure." Again a little later Hume writes that "it is evident that belief consists not in the peculiar nature or order of ideas, but in the *manner* of their conception, and in their *feeling* to the mind."

As to why Hume thought this, an account in his own words will be found in the companion volume to this, *On Human Nature and the Understanding,* edited by Antony Flew, and an excellent critical account will be found in *Hume's Philosophy of Belief* by Professor Flew (Routledge & Kegan Paul). But it is clear from these quotations alone that Hume cannot set out the distinctive character of moral judgments by saying that they arise from sentiment, for this, in his view, is true of all judgments.

Moral judgments cannot be factual, so Hume argues, on quite other grounds. They are not factual, because factual judgments cannot move us to action. Factual judgments are not practical, whereas this is the central function of moral judgments. Hume contrasts at this point reason and the passions. Reason is concerned either with relations of ideas (as in mathematics) or with matters of fact. Neither of these impels us to action. We are moved to act not by this or that being the case, but by the prospect of pleasure or pain from what is or will be the case. And not reason, but the passions are aroused by the prospect of pleasure or pain. Hume's psychologism leads him to speak as if what he is describing are the causes of movement in human beings; he may be plausibly rewritten (and at times indeed rewrites himself) so that what he asserts is not a thesis about the causes of behaviour, but one about the logic of practical argument. When Hume says that not reason but the passions move us to act, he may be read as asserting that from any number of premises of the form "Such-and-such is the case," where some relation of ideas or matter of fact is asserted, no conclusion of the form "So I ought to do so-and-so" or even of the form "So I will do so-and-so" follows. For such a conclusion to follow from such premises we need an additional premise of quite another kind, namely one presenting us with a prospect of pleasure or pain, one appealing to the passions.

In this assertion Hume is taking sides in a contemporary quarrel. He is espousing the cause of the moral sense theorists against that of the rationalists. Hume was especially influenced by Francis Hutcheson, who was Professor of Moral Philosophy at Glasgow when Hume was young, and who was the philosopher referred to when Hume wrote in 1748 that "a late Philosopher has taught us, by the most convincing Arguments, that Morality is nothing in the Abstract Nature of Things, but is entirely relative to the Sentiment or mental Taste of each particular Being; in the same Manner as the Distinctions of sweet and bitter, hot and cold, arise from the particular feeling of each Sense or Organ. Moral Perceptions therefore, ought not to be classed with the Operations of the Understanding, but with the Taste or Sentiments." The arguments, however, with which Hume supports this view are perhaps less interesting than the positions which he is attempting to destroy. For these are not only the positions of rationalist philosophers, such as Wollaston, who want to hold that vice and virtue are relations grasped by reason. Hume is equally concerned to make a case out against a theological ethics.

"I asked him," wrote Boswell when he visited Hume on his death-bed, "if he was not religious when he was young. He said he was, and he used to read the *Whole Duty of Man;* that he made an abstract from the Catalogue of vices at the end of it, and examined himself by this, leaving out Murder and Theft and such vices as he had no chance of committing, having no inclination to commit them." *The Whole Duty of*

*Man* was a seventeenth-century work of popular Protestant devotion. It is full of arguments to the effect that because God has done something, or given us something, therefore we ought to behave in some specific way. So its author can write that "whoever is in distress for any thing, wherewith I can supply him, that distress of his makes it a duty on me so to supply him and this in all kinds of events. Now the ground of its being a duty is that God hath given me abilities not only for their own use, but for the advantage and benefit of others. . . ." Hume sums up his case against such arguments in what is the best-known single passage in all his moral writings: "I cannot forbear adding to these reasonings an observation, which may, perhaps, be found of some importance. In every system of morality, which I have hitherto met with, I have always remark'd, that the author proceeds for some time in the ordinary way of reasoning, and establishes the being of a God, or makes observations concerning human affairs; when of a sudden I am surpriz'd to find, that instead of the usual copulations of propositions, *is*, and *is not*, I meet with no proposition that is not connected with an *ought*, or an *ought not*. This change is imperceptible; but is, however, of the last consequence. For as this *ought*, or *ought not*, expresses some new relation or affirmation, 'tis necessary that it shou'd be observ'd and explain'd; and at the same time that a reason should be given for what seems altogether inconceivable, how this new relation can be a deduction from others which are entirely different from it. But as authors do not commonly use this precaution, I shall presume to recommend it to the readers and am persuaded, that this small attention cou'd subvert all the vulgar systems of morality, and let us see, that the distinction of vice and virtue is not founded merely on the relations of objects, nor is perceiv'd by reason." (*Treatise* III, i,1.)

What then does Hume say positively about morality? In both the *Enquiry* and the *Treatise* he combines an appeal to feelings with a utilitarian interpretation of rules. "To have the sense of virtue is nothing but to *feel* a satisfaction of a particular kind from the contemplation of a character. The very *feeling* constitutes our praise or admiration." (*Treatise* III, i,2, p. 197.) When we apply moral rules and frame moral judgments we do so on the basis of the utility of the rules in question in bringing about what we desire or admire. This very simple framework of argument the *Treatise* shares with the *Enquiry*. But although both works rest morals on psychology, the psychology of the *Treatise* is both more interesting and more complex than that of the *Enquiry*. This can be brought out by comparing the following two quotations: "In general, it may be affirm'd, that there is no such passion in human minds, as the love of mankind, merely as such, independent of personal qualities, of services, or of relation to ourself." (*Treatise* III, ii,1, p. 207.) "It appears also, that, in our general approbation of characters and manners, the useful tendency of the social interests moves us not by any regards to self-interest, but has an influence much more universal and extensive. It appears that a tendency to public good, and to the promoting of peace, harmony, and order in society does always, by affecting the benevolent principles of our frame, engage us on the side of the social virtues." (*Enquiry* V, ii, p. 76.) That is, in the *Enquiry*, a native disposition to sympathy and benevolence is the effective basis of moral judgment and action. While in the *Treatise* there is a problem as to how, granted that by nature we are not disposed to the public good, we nonetheless have developed a morality in which the public good is given priority over the private. The difference between the two works brings out the range of questions which can be raised within a Humean framework. What they have in common brings out the basic weakness of all psychological theories in ethics.

This is that to say that moral judgments express a sentiment or feeling is vacuous and unhelpful. Of course they do. But what sentiment or feeling? We can find no useful definition of moral sentiment, except as that sentiment which is bound up with moral judgment. What it is that makes moral judgment and sentiment distinctive, what entitles them to the appellation "moral," what their relation is to other kinds of judgment and sentiment—to none of these questions do such theories return an answer. And if in the course of his argument Hume does return an answer to some of these questions, his answers are quite incidental to his psychologism.

What misleads Hume is that he sees feelings, sentiments, passions as given and unproblematic. We just have the feelings we have. "A passion is an original existence . . ." But feelings do not just happen; they are not sensations. They can be modified, criticised, rejected, developed and so on. Furthermore we do not identify feelings except in relation to wishes, aversions, hopes, beliefs and the like. Feeling and judgment cannot be identified apart; indeed this is why moral feeling is not something in terms of which moral judgment can be elucidated.

Moreover Hume's moral psychology—even in the *Treatise* —is itself far too simple. He neither allows for the complexity of human nature nor for its historical development. But what he does do is to hold on at all costs to the internal connection between morals and desires. He insists upon a non-theological morality. And he insists upon a morality intelligible against the background of human nature. In insisting upon these things he makes himself a necessary starting-point for later moral philosophy. Hume himself saw his moral investigations as part of a much larger project, the founding of "the science of man." He would have in a later age been the first to see the relevance of anthropology and of psychoanalysis to philosophical ethics.

He was ill for the last four years of his life. Shortly before his death he was visited by Boswell, who was greatly perturbed by Hume's cheerful and calm acceptance of death. Boswell could scarcely believe that a man with no belief in religion, and more especially no belief in an afterlife, should be so little disturbed. Hume indeed returned to the attack. "He then said flatly that the Morality of every Religion was bad, and, I really thought, was not jocular when he said 'that when he heard a man was religious, he concluded he was a rascal, though he had known some instances of very good men being religious.' This was just an extravagant reverse of the common remark as to Infidels."

Hume died in Edinburgh on August 25, 1776. "Upon the whole," wrote Adam Smith, "I have always considered him, both in his lifetime and since his death, as approaching as nearly to the idea of a perfectly wise and virtuous man, as perhaps the nature of human frailty will admit." Up to thirteen days before his death he was still at work; the last correction to the *Enquiry concerning the Principles of Morals* was made on that day. It was by that work and its companion *Enquiry* that he wished to be remembered. It therefore forms the central part of this selection. It is followed by the more important parts of the *Treatise* upon morals and by a variety of Hume's minor ethical writings. It will be obvious from this how I have had to oversimplify both exposition and criticism in this introduction; as to Hume's complexity the texts will speak for themselves.

ALASDAIR MacINTYRE

*August 1963*

# A Note on the Text

The *Enquiry,* as reprinted here, follows the text of the edition of 1777. Hume's disowning of the *Treatise* as representing his considered opinions does not in fact diminish its usefulness both in its parallels to and in its departures from the *Enquiry.* Of the essays, that of *Of the Original Contract* was inserted in a new edition of Hume's *Essays Moral and Political* in 1748; that *Of the Standard of Taste* originally appeared as part of *Four Dissertations* in 1757; and *Of Suicide* was published posthumously in 1784. In these latter writings I have followed everywhere the edition of T. H. Green and T. H. Grose, now nearly ninety years old, in which variant texts were collated. Later additions by Hume to an original text have all been preserved in the body of the text; phrases that were excluded have been given in footnotes. I have also included *A Dialogue,* published originally with the first edition of the *Enquiry* in 1751 and extracts from the *Dialogues Concerning Natural Religion,* posthumously published; for full information as to the original editions the reader is referred to the excellent *History of the Editions* in Green and Grose's first volume.

ENQUIRY

# ADVERTISEMENT TO THE COLLECTED ESSAYS

MOST OF THE PRINCIPLES, and reasonings, contained in this volume* were published in a work in three volumes, called *A Treatise of Human Nature:* A work which the Author had projected before he left College, and which he wrote and published not long after. But not finding it successful, he was sensible of his error in going to the press too early, and he cast the whole anew in the following pieces, where some negligences in his former reasoning and more in the expression, are, he hopes, corrected. Yet several writers, who have honoured the Author's philosophy with answers, have taken care to direct all their batteries against that juvenile work, which the Author never acknowledged, and have affected to triumph in any advantages, which, they imagined, they had obtained over it: A practice very contrary to all rules of candour and fair-dealing, and a strong instance of those polemical artifices, which a bigoted zeal thinks itself authorized to employ. Henceforth, the Author desires, that the following Pieces may alone be regarded as containing his philosophical sentiments and principles.

* This advertisement refers to Volume II of the posthumous edition of Hume's works, published in 1777, which, in addition to the *Enquiry Concerning the Principles of Morals,* includes *An Enquiry Concerning Human Understanding* and *A Dissertation on the Passions.*

# AN ENQUIRY CONCERNING THE PRINCIPLES OF MORALS

## Section I

## Of the General Principles of Morals

DISPUTES WITH MEN, pertinaciously obstinate in their principles, are, of all others, the most irksome; except, perhaps, those with persons, entirely disingenuous, who really do not believe the opinions they defend, but engage in the controversy, from affectation, from a spirit of opposition, or from a desire of showing wit and ingenuity, superior to the rest of mankind. The same blind adherence to their own arguments is to be expected in both; the same contempt of their antagonists; and the same passionate vehemence, in inforcing sophistry and falsehood. And as reasoning is not the source, whence either disputant derives his tenets; it is in vain to expect, that any logic, which speaks not to the affections, will ever engage him to embrace sounder principles.

Those who have denied the reality of moral distinctions, may be ranked among the disingenuous disputants; nor is it conceivable, that any human creature could ever seriously believe, that all characters and actions were alike entitled to the affection and regard of everyone. The difference, which nature has placed between one man and another, is so wide, and this difference is still so much farther widened, by education, example, and habit, that, where the opposite extremes come at once under our apprehension, there is no scepticism so scrupulous, and scarce any assurance so determined, as absolutely to deny all distinction between them. Let a man's insensibility be ever so great, he must often be touched with the images of Right and Wrong; and let his prejudices be ever so obstinate, he must observe, that others are susceptible of like impressions. The only way, therefore, of converting an antagonist of this kind, is to leave him to himself. For, finding that nobody keeps up the controversy with him, it is probable he will, at last, of himself, from mere weariness, come over to the side of common sense and reason.

There has been a controversy started of late, much better worth examination, concerning the general foundation of Morals; whether they be derived from Reason, or from Sentiment; whether we attain the knowledge of them by a chain of argument and induction, or by an immediate feeling and finer internal sense; whether, like all sound judgement of truth and falsehood, they should be the same to every rational intelligent being; or whether, like the perception of beauty and deformity, they be founded entirely on the particular fabric and constitution of the human species.

The ancient philosophers, though they often affirm, that virtue is nothing but conformity to reason, yet, in general, seem to consider morals as deriving their existence from taste and sentiment. On the other hand, our modern enquirers, though they also talk much of the beauty of virtue, and deformity of vice, yet have commonly endeavoured to account for these distinctions by metaphysical reasonings, and by deductions from the most abstract principles of the understanding. Such confusion reigned in these subjects, that an opposition of the greatest consequence could prevail between one system and another, and even in the parts of almost each individual system; and yet nobody, till very lately, was ever sensible of it. The elegant Lord Shaftesbury, who first gave occasion to remark this distinction, and who, in general, adhered to the principles of the ancients, is not, himself, entirely free from the same confusion.

It must be acknowledged, that both sides of the question are susceptible of specious arguments. Moral distinctions, it may be said, are discernible by pure *reason*: else, whence the many disputes that reign in common life, as well as in philosophy, with regard to this subject: the long chain of proofs often produced on both sides; the examples cited, the authorities appealed to, the analogies employed, the fallacies detected, the inferences drawn, and the several conclusions adjusted to their proper principles. Truth is disputable; not taste: what exists in the nature of things is the standard of our judgement; what each man feels within himself is the standard of sentiment. Propositions in geometry may be proved, systems in physics may be controverted; but the harmony of verse, the tenderness of passion, the brilliancy of wit, must give immediate pleasure. No man reasons concerning another's beauty; but frequently concerning the justice or injustice of his actions. In every criminal trial the first object of the prisoner is to disprove the facts alleged, and deny the actions imputed to him: the second to prove, that, even if these actions were real, they might be justified, as innocent and lawful. It is confessedly by deductions of the understanding, that the first point is ascertained: how can we suppose that a different faculty of the mind is employed in fixing the other?

On the other hand, those who would resolve all moral determinations into *sentiment*, may endeavour to show, that it is impossible for reason ever to draw conclusions of this nature. To virtue, say they, it belongs to be *amiable*, and vice *odious*. This forms their very nature or essence. But can reason or argumentation distribute these different epithets to any subjects, and pronounce beforehand, that this must produce love, and that hatred? Or what other reason can we ever assign for these affections, but the original fabric and formation of the human mind, which is naturally adapted to receive them?

The end of all moral speculations is to teach us our duty; and, by proper representations of the deformity of vice and beauty of virtue, beget correspondent habits, and engage us to avoid the one, and embrace the other. But is this ever to be expected from inferences and conclusions of the understanding, which of themselves have no hold of the affections or set in motion the active powers of men? They discover truths: but where the truths which they discover are indifferent, and beget no desire or aversion, they can have no influence on conduct and behaviour. What is honourable, what is fair, what is becoming, what is noble, what is generous, takes possession of the heart, and animates us to embrace and maintain it. What is intelligible, what is evident, what is probable, what is true, procures only the cool assent of the understanding; and gratifying a speculative curiosity, puts an end to our researches.

Extinguish all the warm feelings and prepossessions in favour of virtue, and all disgust or aversion to vice: render men totally indifferent towards these distinctions; and morality is no longer a practical study, nor has any tendency to regulate our lives and actions.

These arguments on each side (and many more might be produced) are so plausible, that I am apt to suspect, they may, the one as well as the other, be solid and satisfactory, and that *reason* and *sentiment* concur in almost all moral determinations and conclusions. The final sentence, it is probable, which pronounces characters and actions amiable or odious, praise-worthy or blameable; that which stamps on them the mark of honour or infamy, approbation or censure; that which renders morality an active principle and constitutes virtue our happiness, and vice our misery: it is probable, I say, that this final sentence depends on some internal sense or feeling, which nature has made universal in the whole species. For what else can have an influence of this nature? But in order to pave the way for such a sentiment, and give a proper discernment of its object, it is often necessary, we find, that much reasoning should precede, that nice distinctions be made, just conclusions drawn, distant comparisons formed, complicated relations examined, and general facts fixed and ascertained. Some species of beauty, especially the natural kinds, on their first appearance, command our affection and approbation; and where they fail of this effect, it is impossible for any reasoning to redress their influence, or adapt them better to our taste and sentiment. But in many orders of beauty, particularly those of the finer arts, it is requisite to employ much reasoning, in order to feel the proper sentiment; and a false relish may frequently be corrected by argument and reflection. There are just grounds to conclude, that moral beauty partakes much of this latter species, and demands the assistance of our intellectual faculties, in order to give it a suitable influence on the human mind.

But though this question, concerning the general principles of morals, be curious and important, it is needless for us, at present, to employ farther care in our researches concerning it. For if we can be so happy, in the course of this enquiry, as to discover the true origin of morals, it will then easily appear how far either sentiment or reason enters into all determinations of this nature.[1] In order to attain this purpose, we shall endeavour to follow a very simple method: we shall analyse that complication of mental qualities, which form what, in common life, we call Personal Merit: we shall consider every attribute of the mind, which renders a man an object either of esteem and affection, or of hatred and contempt; every habit or sentiment or faculty, which, if ascribed to any person, implies either praise or blame, and may enter into any panegyric or satire of his character and manners. The quick sensibility, which, on this head, is so universal among mankind, gives a philosopher sufficient assurance, that he can never be considerably mistaken in framing the catalogue, or incur any danger of misplacing the objects of his contemplation: he needs only enter into his own breast for a moment, and consider whether or not he should desire to have this or that quality ascribed to him, and whether such or such an imputation would proceed from a friend or an enemy. The very nature of language guides us almost infallibly in forming a judgement of this nature; and as every tongue possesses one set of words which are taken in a good sense, and another in the opposite, the least acquaintance with the idiom suffices, without any reasoning, to direct us in collecting and arranging the estimable or blameable qualities of men. The only object of reasoning is to discover the circumstances on both sides, which are common to these qualities; to observe that particular in which the estimable qualities agree on the one hand, and the blameable on the other; and thence to reach the foundation of ethics, and find those universal principles, from which all censure or approbation is ultimately derived. As this is a question of fact, not of abstract science, we can only expect success, by following the experimental method, and deducing general maxims from a comparison of particular

[1] See Appendix I.

instances. The other scientific method, where a general abstract principle is first established, and is afterwards branched out into a variety of inferences and conclusions, may be more perfect in itself, but suits less the imperfection of human nature, and is a common source of illusion and mistake in this as well as in other subjects. Men are not cured of their passion for hypotheses and systems in natural philosophy, and will hearken to no arguments but those which are derived from experience. It is full time they should attempt a like reformation in all moral disquisitions; and reject every system of ethics, however subtle or ingenious, which is not founded on fact and observation.

We shall begin our enquiry on this head by the consideration of the social virtues, Benevolence and Justice. The explication of them will probably give us an opening by which the others may be accounted for.

# Section II

## Of Benevolence

### Part I

It may be esteemed, perhaps, a superfluous task to prove, that the benevolent or softer affections are estimable; and wherever they appear, engage the approbation and good-will of mankind. The epithets *sociable, good-natured, humane, merciful, grateful, friendly, generous, beneficent,* or their equivalents, are known in all languages, and universally express the highest merit, which *human nature* is capable of attaining. Where these amiable qualities are attended with birth and power and eminent abilities, and display themselves in the good government or useful instruction of mankind, they seem even to raise the possessors of them above the rank of *human nature,* and make them approach in some measure to the divine. Exalted capacity, undaunted courage, prosperous success; these may only expose a hero or politician to the envy and ill-will of the public: but as soon as the praises are added of humane and beneficent; when instances are displayed of lenity, tenderness or friendship; envy itself is silent, or joins the general voice of approbation and applause.

When Pericles, the great Athenian statesman and general, was on his death-bed, his surrounding friends, deeming him now insensible, began to indulge their sorrow for their expiring patron, by enumerating his great qualities and successes, his conquests and victories, the unusual length of his administration, and his nine trophies erected over the enemies of the republic. *You forget,* cries the dying hero, who had heard all, *you forget the most eminent of my praises, while you dwell so much on those vulgar advantages, in which fortune had a principal share. You have not observed that no citizen has ever yet worne mourning on my account.*[1]

[1] Plut. in Pericle.

In men of more ordinary talents and capacity, the social virtues become, if possible, still more essentially requisite; there being nothing eminent, in that case, to compensate for the want of them, or preserve the person from our severest hatred, as well as contempt. A high ambition, an elevated courage, is apt, says Cicero, in less perfect characters, to degenerate into a turbulent ferocity. The more social and softer virtues are there chiefly to be regarded. These are always good and amiable.[2]

The principal advantage, which Juvenal discovers in the extensive capacity of the human species, is that it renders our benevolence also more extensive, and gives us larger opportunities of spreading our kindly influence than what are indulged to the inferior creation.[3] It must, indeed, be confessed, that by doing good only, can a man truly enjoy the advantages of being eminent. His exalted station, of itself but the more exposes him to danger and tempest. His sole prerogative is to afford shelter to inferiors, who repose themselves under his cover and protection.

But I forget, that it is not my present business to recommend generosity and benevolence, or to paint, in their true colours, all the genuine charms of the social virtues. These, indeed, sufficiently engage every heart, on the first apprehension of them; and it is difficult to abstain from some sally of panegyric, as often as they occur in discourse or reasoning. But our object here being more the speculative, than the practical part of morals, it will suffice to remark, (what will readily, I believe, be allowed) that no qualities are more intitled to the general good-will and approbation of mankind than beneficence and humanity, friendship and gratitude, natural affection and public spirit, or whatever proceeds from a tender sympathy with others, and a generous concern for our kind and species. These wherever they appear, seem to transfuse themselves, in a manner, into each beholder, and to call forth, in their own behalf, the same favourable and affectionate sentiments, which they exert on all around.

[2] Cic. de Officiis, lib. I.
[3] Sat. xv. 139 and seq.

## Part II

We may observe that, in displaying the praises of any humane, beneficent man, there is one circumstance which never fails to be amply insisted on, namely, the happiness and satisfaction, derived to society from his intercourse and good offices. To his parents, we are apt to say, he endears himself by his pious attachment and duteous care still more than by the connexions of nature. His children never feel his authority, but when employed for their advantage. With him, the ties of love are consolidated by beneficence and friendship. The ties of friendship approach, in a fond observance of each obliging office, to those of love and inclination. His domestics and dependants have in him a sure resource; and no longer dread the power of fortune, but so far as she exercises it over him. From him the hungry receive food, the naked clothing, the ignorant and slothful skill and industry. Like the sun, an inferior minister of providence he cheers, invigorates, and sustains the surrounding world.

If confined to private life, the sphere of his activity is narrower; but his influence is all benign and gentle. If exalted into a higher station, mankind and posterity reap the fruit of his labours.

As these topics of praise never fail to be employed, and with success, where we would inspire esteem for any one; may it not thence be concluded, that the utility, resulting from the social virtues, forms, at least, a *part* of their merit, and is one source of that approbation and regard so universally paid to them?

When we recommend even an animal or a plant as *useful* and *beneficial*, we give it an applause and recommendation suited to its nature. As, on the other hand, reflection on the baneful influence of any of these inferior beings always inspires us with the sentiment of aversion. The eye is pleased with the prospect of corn-fields and loaded vineyards; horses grazing, and flocks pasturing: but flies the view of briars and brambles, affording shelter to wolves and serpents.

A machine, a piece of furniture, a vestment, a house well

contrived for use and conveniency, is so far beautiful, and is contemplated with pleasure and approbation. An experienced eye is here sensible to many excellencies, which escape persons ignorant and uninstructed.

Can anything stronger be said in praise of a profession, such as merchandize or manufacture, than to observe the advantages which it procures to society; and is not a monk and inquisitor enraged when we treat his order as useless or pernicious to mankind?

The historian exults in displaying the benefit arising from his labours. The writer of romance alleviates or denies the bad consequences ascribed to his manner of composition.

In general, what praise is implied in the simple epithet *useful*! What reproach in the contrary!

Your Gods, says Cicero,[4] in opposition to the Epicureans, cannot justly claim any worship or adoration, with whatever imaginary perfections you may suppose them endowed. They are totally useless and inactive. Even the Egyptians, whom you so much ridicule, never consecrated any animal but on account of its utility.

The sceptics assert,[5] though absurdly, that the origin of all religious worship was derived from the utility of inanimate objects, as the sun and moon, to the support and well-being of mankind. This is also the common reason assigned by historians, for the deification of eminent heroes and legislators.[6]

To plant a tree, to cultivate a field, to beget children: meritorious acts, according to the religion of Zoroaster.

In all determinations of morality, this circumstance of public utility is ever principally in view; and wherever disputes arise, either in philosophy or common life, concerning the bounds of duty, the question cannot, by any means, be decided with greater certainty, than by ascertaining, on any side, the true interests of mankind. If any false opinion, embraced from appearances, has been found to prevail; as soon as farther experience and sounder reasoning have given us

[4] De Nat. Deor. lib. i.
[5] Sext. Emp. adversus Math. lib. viii.
[6] Diod. Sic. passim.

juster notions of human affairs, we retract our first sentiment, and adjust anew the boundaries of moral good and evil.

Giving alms to common beggars is naturally praised; because it seems to carry relief to the distressed and indigent: but when we observe the encouragement thence arising to idleness and debauchery, we regard that species of charity rather as a weakness than a virtue.

*Tyrannicide,* or the assassination of usurpers and oppressive princes, was highly extolled in ancient times; because it both freed mankind from many of these monsters, and seemed to keep the others in awe, whom the sword or poinard could not reach. But history and experience having since convinced us, that this practice increases the jealousy and cruelty of princes, a Timoleon and a Brutus, though treated with indulgence on account of the prejudices of their times, are now considered as very improper models for imitation.

Liberality in princes is regarded as a mark of beneficence, but when it occurs, that the homely bread of the honest and industrious is often thereby converted into delicious cates for the idle and the prodigal, we soon retract our heedless praises. The regrets of a prince, for having lost a day, were noble and generous: but had he intended to have spent it in acts of generosity to his greedy courtiers, it was better lost than misemployed after that manner.

Luxury, or a refinement on the pleasures and conveniencies of life, had not long been supposed the source of every corruption in government, and the immediate cause of faction, sedition, civil wars, and the total loss of liberty. It was, therefore, universally regarded as a vice, and was an object of declamation to all satirists, and severe moralists. Those, who prove, or attempt to prove, that such refinements rather tend to the increase of industry, civility, and arts regulate anew our *moral* as well as *political* sentiments, and represent, as laudable or innocent, what had formerly been regarded as pernicious and blameable.

Upon the whole, then, it seems undeniable, *that* nothing can bestow more merit on any human creature than the sentiment of benevolence in an eminent degree; and *that* a *part,* at least, of its merit arises from its tendency to promote the interests of our species, and bestow happiness on human society. We carry our view into the salutary consequences of such a character and disposition; and whatever has so benign an influence, and forwards so desirable an end, is beheld with complacency and pleasure. The social virtues are never regarded without their beneficial tendencies, nor viewed as barren and unfruitful. The happiness of mankind, the order of society, the harmony of families, the mutual support of friends, are always considered as the result of their gentle dominion over the breasts of men.

How considerable a *part* of their merit we ought to ascribe to their utility, will better appear from future disquisitions;[7] as well as the reason, why this circumstance has such a command over our esteem and approbation.[8]

[7] Sect. III and IV.
[8] Sect. V.

# Section III

## Of Justice

### Part I

That Justice is useful to society, and consequently that *part* of its merit, at least, must arise from that consideration, it would be a superfluous undertaking to prove. That public utility is the *sole* origin of justice, and that reflections on the beneficial consequences of this virtue are the *sole* foundation of its merit; this proposition, being more curious and important, will better deserve our examination and enquiry.

Let us suppose that nature has bestowed on the human race such profuse *abundance* of all *external* conveniencies, that, without any uncertainty in the event, without any care or industry on our part, every individual finds himself fully provided with whatever his most voracious appetites can want, or luxurious imagination wish or desire. His natural beauty, we shall suppose, surpasses all acquired ornaments: the perpetual clemency of the seasons renders useless all clothes or covering: the raw herbage affords him the most delicious fare; the clear fountain, the richest beverage. No laborious occupation required: no tillage: no navigation. Music, poetry, and contemplation form his sole business: conversation, mirth, and friendship his sole amusement.

It seems evident that, in such a happy state, every other social virtue would flourish, and receive tenfold increase; but the cautious, jealous virtue of justice would never once have been dreamed of. For what purpose make a partition of goods, where every one has already more than enough? Why give rise to property, where there cannot possibly be any injury? Why call this object *mine*, when upon the seizing of it by another, I need but stretch out my hand to possess myself to what is equally valuable? Justice, in that case, being totally

**35**

useless, would be an idle ceremonial, and could never possibly have place in the catalogue of virtues.

We see, even in the present necessitous condition of mankind, that, wherever any benefit is bestowed by nature in an unlimited abundance, we leave it always in common among the whole human race, and make no subdivisions of right and property. Water and air, though the most necessary of all objects, are not challenged as the property of individuals; nor can any man commit injustice by the most lavish use and enjoyment of these blessings. In fertile extensive countries, with few inhabitants, land is regarded on the same footing. And no topic is so much insisted on by those, who defend the liberty of the seas, as the unexhausted use of them in navigation. Were the advantages, procured by navigation, as inexhaustible, these reasoners had never had any adversaries to refute; nor had any claims ever been advanced of a separate, exclusive dominion over the ocean.

It may happen, in some countries, at some periods, that there be established a property in water, none in land;[1] if the latter be in greater abundance than can be used by the inhabitants, and the former be found, with difficulty, and in very small quantities.

Again; suppose, that, though the necessities of human race continue the same as at present, yet the mind is so enlarged, and so replete with friendship and generosity, that every man has the utmost tenderness for every man, and feels no more concern for his own interest than for that of his fellows; it seems evident, that the use of justice would, in this case, be suspended by such an extensive benevolence, nor would the divisions and barriers of property and obligation have ever been thought of. Why should I bind another, by a deed or promise, to do me any good office, when I know that he is already prompted, by the strongest inclination, to seek my happiness, and would, of himself, perform the desired service; except the hurt, he thereby receives, be greater than the benefit accruing to me? in which case, he knows, that, from my innate humanity and friendship, I should be the first

---

[1] Genesis, chaps. xiii and xxi.

to oppose myself to his imprudent generosity. Why raise landmarks between my neighbour's field and mine, when my heart has made no division between our interests; but shares all his joys and sorrows with the same force and vivacity as if originally my own? Every man, upon this supposition, being a second self to another, would trust all his interests to the discretion of every man; without jealousy, without partition, without distinction. And the whole human race would form only one family; where all would lie in common, and be used freely, without regard to property; but cautiously too, with as entire regard to the necessities of each individual, as if our own interests were most intimately concerned.

In the present disposition of the human heart, it would, perhaps, be difficult to find complete instances of such enlarged affections; but still we may observe, that the case of families approaches towards it; and the stronger the mutual benevolence is among the individuals, the nearer it approaches; till all distinction of property be, in a great measure, lost and confounded among them. Between married persons, the cement of friendship is by the laws supposed so strong as to abolish all division of possessions; and has often, in reality, the force ascribed to it. And it is observable, that, during the ardour of new enthusiasms, when every principle is inflamed into extravagance, the community of goods has frequently been attempted; and nothing but experience of its inconveniencies, from the returning or disguised selfishness of men, could make the imprudent fanatics adopt anew the ideas of justice and of separate property. So true is it, that this virtue derives its existence entirely from its necessary *use* to the intercourse and social state of mankind.

To make this truth more evident, let us reverse the foregoing suppositions; and carrying everything to the opposite extreme, consider what would be the effect of these new situations. Suppose a society to fall into such want of all common necessaries, that the utmost frugality and industry cannot preserve the greater number from perishing, and the whole from extreme misery; it will readily, I believe, be admitted, that the strict laws of justice are suspended, in such a pressing emergence, and give place to the stronger motives of necessity and self-preservation. Is it any crime, after a shipwreck, to seize whatever means or instrument of safety one can lay hold of, without regard to former limitations of property? Or if a city besieged were perishing with hunger; can we imagine, that men will see any means of preservation before them, and lose their lives, from a scrupulous regard to what, in other situations, would be the rules of equity and justice? The use and tendency of that virtue is to procure happiness and security, by preserving order in society: but where the society is ready to perish from extreme necessity, no greater evil can be dreaded from violence and injustice; and every man may now provide for himself by all the means, which prudence can dictate, or humanity permit. The public, even in less urgent necessities, opens granaries, without the consent of proprietors; as justly supposing, that the authority of magistracy may, consistent with equity, extend so far: but were any number of men to assemble, without the tie of laws or civil jurisdiction; would an equal partition of bread in a famine, though effected by power and even violence, be regarded as criminal or injurious?

Suppose likewise, that it should be a virtuous man's fate to fall into the society of ruffians, remote from the protection of laws and government; what conduct must he embrace in that melancholy situation? He sees such a desperate rapaciousness prevail; such a disregard to equity, such contempt of order, such stupid blindness to future consequences, as must immediately have the most tragical conclusion, and must terminate in destruction to the greater number, and in a total dissolution of society to the rest. He, meanwhile, can have no other expedient than to arm himself, to whomever the sword he seizes, or the buckler, may belong: To make provision of all means of defence and security: And his particular regard to justice being no longer of use to his own safety or that of others, he must consult the dictates of self-preservation alone, without concern for those who no longer merit his care and attention.

When any man, even in political society, renders himself

by his crimes, obnoxious to the public, he is punished by the laws in his goods and person; that is, the ordinary rules of justice are, with regard to him, suspended for a moment, and it becomes equitable to inflict on him, for the *benefit* of society, what otherwise he could not suffer without wrong or injury.

The rage and violence of public war; what is it but a suspension of justice among the warring parties, who perceive, that this virtue is now no longer of any *use* or advantage to them? The laws of war, which then succeed to those of equity and justice, are rules calculated for the *advantage* and *utility* of that particular state, in which men are now placed. And were a civilized nation engaged with barbarians, who observed no rules even of war, the former must also suspend their observance of them, where they no longer serve to any purpose; and must render every action or rencounter as bloody and pernicious as possible to the first aggressors.

Thus, the rules of equity or justice depend entirely on the particular state and condition in which men are placed, and owe their origin and existence to that utility, which results to the public from their strict and regular observance. Reverse, in any considerable circumstance, the condition of men: Produce extreme abundance or extreme necessity: Implant in the human breast perfect moderation and humanity, or perfect rapaciousness and malice: By rendering justice totally *useless*, you thereby totally destroy its essence, and suspend its obligation upon mankind.

The common situation of society is a medium amidst all these extremes. We are naturally partial to ourselves, and to our friends; but are capable of learning the advantage resulting from a more equitable conduct. Few enjoyments are given us from the open and liberal hand of nature; but by art, labour, and industry, we can extract them in great abundance. Hence the ideas of property become necessary in all civil society: Hence justice derives its usefulness to the public: And hence alone arises its merit and moral obligation.

These conclusions are so natural and obvious, that they have not escaped even the poets, in their descriptions of the felicity attending the golden age or the reign of Saturn. The seasons, in that first period of nature, were so temperate, if we credit these agreeable fictions, that there was no necessity for men to provide themselves with clothes and houses, as a security against the violence of heat and cold: The rivers flowed with wine and milk: The oaks yielded honey; and nature spontaneously produced her greatest delicacies. Nor were these the chief advantages of that happy age. Tempests were not alone removed from nature; but those more furious tempests were unknown to human breasts, which now cause such uproar, and engender such confusion. Avarice, ambition, cruelty, selfishness, were never heard of: Cordial affection, compassion, sympathy, were the only movements with which the mind was yet acquainted. Even the punctilious distinction of *mine* and *thine* was banished from among that happy race of mortals, and carried with it the very notion of property and obligation, justice and injustice.

This *poetical* fiction of the *golden age* is, in some respects, of a piece with the *philosophical* fiction of the *state of nature*; only that the former is represented as the most charming and most peaceable condition, which can possibly be imagined; whereas the latter is painted out as a state of mutual war and violence, attended with the most extreme necessity. On the first origin of mankind, we are told, their ignorance and savage nature were so prevalent, that they could give no mutual trust, but must each depend upon himself and his own force or cunning for protection and security. No law was heard of: No rule of justice known: No distinction of property regarded: Power was the only measure of right; and a perpetual war of all against all was the result of men's untamed selfishness and barbarity.[2]

[2] This fiction of a state of nature, as a state of war, was not first started by Mr. Hobbes, as is commonly imagined. Plato endeavours to refute an hypothesis very like it in the second, third, and fourth books de republica. Cicero, on the contrary, supposes it certain and universally acknowledged in the following passage. "Quis enim vestrum, judices, ignorat, ita naturam rerum tulisse, ut quodam tempore homines, nondum neque naturali neque civili jure descripto, fusi per agros ac dispersi vagarentur tantumque haberent quantum manu ac viribus, per caedem ac vulnera, aut eripere aut retinere potuissent? Qui igitur primi

Whether such a condition of human nature could ever exist, or if it did, could continue so long as to merit the appellation of a *state*, may justly be doubted. Men are necessarily born in a family-society, at least; and are trained up by their parents to some rule of conduct and behaviour. But this must be admitted, that, if such a state of mutual war and violence was ever real, the suspension of all laws of justice, from their absolute inutility, is a necessary and infallible consquence.

The more we vary our views of human life, and the newer and more unusual the lights are in which we survey it, the more shall we be convinced, that the origin here assigned for the virtue of justice is real and satisfactory.

Were there a species of creatures intermingled with men, which, though rational, were possessed of such inferior strength, both of body and mind, that they were incapable of all resistance, and could never, upon the highest provocation, make us feel the effects of their resentment; the necessary consequence, I think, is that we should be bound by the laws of humanity to give gentle usage to these creatures, but should not, properly speaking, lie under any restraint of justice with regard to them, nor could they possess any right or property, exclusive of such arbitrary lords. Our intercourse with them could not be called society, which supposes a degree of equality; but absolute command on the one side, and servile obedience on the other. Whatever we covet, they must instantly resign: Our permission is the only tenure, by which they hold their possessions: Our compassion and kindness the only check, by which they curb our lawless will: And as no incon-

---

virtute & consilio praestanti extiterunt, ii perspecto genere humanae docilitatis atque ingenii, dissipatos unum in locum congregarunt, eosque ex feritate illa ad justitiam ac mansuetudinem transduxerunt. Tum res ad communem utilitatem, quas publicas appellamus, tum conventicula hominum, quae postea civitates nominatae sunt, tum domicilia conjuncta, quas urbes dicamus, invento & divino & humano jure, moenibus sepserunt. Atque inter hanc vitam, perpolitam humanitate, & illam immanem, nihil tam interest quam JUS atque VIS. Horum utro uti nolimus, altero est utendum. Vim volumus extingui. Jus valeat necesse est, id est, judicia, quibus omne jus continetur. Judicia displicent, aut nulla sunt. Vis dominetur necesse est. Haec vident omnes." *Pro Sext.* §. 42.

venience ever results from the exercise of a power, so firmly established in nature, the restraints of justice and property, being totally *useless*, would never have place in so unequal a confederacy.

This is plainly the situation of men, with regard to animals; and how far these may be said to possess reason, I leave it to others to determine. The great superiority of civilized Europeans above barbarous Indians, tempted us to imagine ourselves on the same footing with regard to them, and made us throw off all restraints of justice, and even of humanity, in our treatment of them. In many nations, the female sex are reduced to like slavery, and are rendered incapable of all property, in opposition to their lordly masters. But though the males, when united, have in all countries bodily force sufficient to maintain this severe tyranny, yet such are the insinuation, address, and charms of their fair companions, that women are commonly able to break the confederacy, and share with the other sex in all the rights and privileges of society.

Were the human species so framed by nature as that each indivudal possessed within himself every faculty, requisite both for his own preservation and for the propagation of his kind: Were all society and intercourse cut off between man and man, by the primary intention of the supreme Creator: It seems evident, that so solitary a being would be as much incapable of justice, as of social discourse and conversation. Where mutual regards and forbearance serve to no manner of purpose, they would never direct the conduct of any reasonable man. The headlong course of the passions would be checked by no reflection on future consequences. And as each man is here supposed to love himself alone, and to depend only on himself and his own activity for safety and happiness, he would, on every occasion, to the utmost of his power, challenge the preference above every other being, to none of which he is bound by any ties, either of nature or of interest.

But suppose the conjunction of the sexes to be established in nature, a family immediately arises; and particular rules being found requisite for its subsistence, these are immediately embraced; though without comprehending the rest of mankind within their prescriptions. Suppose that several families unite together into one society, which is totally disjoined from all others, the rules, which preserve peace and order, enlarge themselves to the utmost extent of that society; but becoming then entirely useless, lose their force when carried one step farther. But again suppose, that several distinct societies maintain a kind of intercourse for mutual convenience and advantage, the boundaries of justice still grow larger, in proportion to the largeness of men's views, and the force of their mutual connexions. History, experience, reason sufficiently instruct us in this natural progress of human sentiments, and in the gradual enlargement of our regards to justice, in proportion as we become acquainted with the extensive utility of that virtue.

## Part II

If we examine the *particular* laws, by which justice is directed, and property determined; we shall still be presented with the same conclusion. The good of mankind is the only object of all these laws and regulations. Not only it is requisite, for the peace and interest of society, that men's possessions should be separated; but the rules, which we follow, in making the separation, are such as can best be contrived to serve farther the interests of society.

We shall suppose that a creature, possessed of reason, but unacquainted with human nature, deliberates with himself what rules of justice or property would best promote public interest, and establish peace and security among mankind: His most obvious thought would be, to assign the largest possessions to the most extensive virtue, and give every one the power of doing good, proportioned to his inclination. In a perfect theocracy, where a being, infinitely intelligent, governs by particular volitions, this rule would certainly have place, and might serve to the wisest purposes: But were mankind to execute such a law; so great is the uncertainty of merit, both from its natural obscurity, and from the self-conceit of each individual, that no determinate rule of conduct would ever result from it; and the total dissolution of society must be the immediate consequence. Fanatics may suppose, *that dominion is founded on grace*, and *that saints alone inherit the earth*; but the civil magistrate very justly puts these sublime theorists on the same footing with common robbers, and teaches them by the severest discipline, that a rule, which, in speculation, may seem the most advantageous to society, may yet be found, in practice, totally pernicious and destructive.

That there were *religious* fanatics of this kind in England, during the civil wars, we learn from history; though it is probable, that the obvious *tendency* of these principles excited such horror in mankind, as soon obliged the dangerous enthusiasts to renounce, or at least conceal their tenets. Perhaps the *levellers*, who claimed an equal distribution of property, were a kind of *political* fanatics, which arose from the religious species, and more openly avowed their pretensions; as carrying a more plausible appearance, of being practicable in themselves, as well as useful to human society.

It must, indeed, be confessed, that nature is so liberal to mankind, that, were all her presents equally divided among the species, and improved by art and industry, every individual would enjoy all the necessaries, and even most of the comforts of life; nor would ever be liable to any ills, but such as might accidentally arise from the sickly frame and constitution of his body. It must also be confessed, that, wherever we depart from this equality, we rob the poor of more satisfaction than we add to the rich, and that the slight gratification of a frivolous vanity, in one individual, frequently costs more than bread to many families, and even provinces. It may appear withal, that the rule of equality, as it would be highly *useful*, is not altogether *impracticable*; but has taken place, at least in an imperfect degree, in some republics; particularly that of Sparta; where it was attended, it is said, with the most beneficial consequences. Not to mention that the Agrarian laws, so frequently claimed in Rome, and carried into execution in many Greek cities, proceeded, all of them, from a general idea of the utility of this principle.

But historians, and even common sense, may inform us,

that, however specious these ideas of *perfect* equality may seem, they are really, at bottom, *impracticable*; and were they not so, would be extremely *pernicious* to human society. Render possessions ever so equal, men's different degrees of art, care, and industry will immediately break that equality. Or if you check these virtues, you reduce society to the most extreme indigence; and instead of preventing want and beggary in a few, render it unavoidable to the whole community. The most rigorous inquisition too is requisite to watch every inequality on its first appearance; and the most severe jurisdiction, to punish and redress it. But besides, that so much authority must soon degenerate into tyranny, and be exerted with great partialities; who can possibly be possessed of it, in such a situation as is here supposed? Perfect equality of possessions, destroying all subordination, weakens extremely the authority of magistracy, and must reduce all power nearly to a level, as well as property.

We may conclude, therefore, that, in order to establish law for the regulation of property, we must be acquainted with the nature and situation of man; must reject appearances, which may be false, though specious; and must search for those rules, which are, on the whole, most *useful* and *beneficial*. Vulgar sense and slight experience are sufficient for this purpose; where men give not way to too selfish avidity, or too extensive enthusiasm.

Who sees not, for instance, that whatever is produced or improved by a man's art or industry ought, for ever, to be secured to him, in order to give encouragement to such *useful* habits and accomplishments? That the property ought also to descend to children and relations, for the same *useful* purpose? That it may be alienated by consent, in order to beget that commerce and intercourse, which is so *beneficial* to human society? And that all contracts and promises ought carefully to be fulfilled, in order to secure mutual trust and confidence, by which the general *interest* of mankind is so much promoted?

Examine the writers on the laws of nature; and you will always find, that, whatever principles they set out with, they are sure to terminate here at last, and to assign, as the ultimate reason for every rule which they establish, the convenience and necessities of mankind. A concession thus extorted, in opposition to systems, has more authority than if it had been made in prosecution of them.

What other reason, indeed, could writers ever give, why this must be *mine* and that *yours*; since uninstructed nature surely never made any such distinction? The objects which receive those appellations are, of themselves, foreign to us; they are totally disjoined and separated from us; and nothing but the general interests of society can form the connexion.

Somtimes the interests of society may require a rule of justice in a particular case; but may not determine any particular rule, among several, which are all equally beneficial. In that case, the slightest *analogies* are laid hold of, in order to prevent that indifference and ambiguity, which would be the source of perpetual dissension. Thus possession alone, and first possession, is supposed to convey property, where no body else has any preceding claim and pretension. Many of the reasonings of lawyers are of this analogical nature, and depend on very slight connexions of the imagination.

Does any one scruple, in extraordinary cases, to violate all regard to the private property of individuals, and sacrifice to public interest a distinction, which had been established for the sake of that interest? The safety of the people is the supreme law: All other particular laws are subordinate to it, and dependent on it: And if, in the *common* course of things, they be followed and regarded; it is only because the public safety and interest *commonly* demand so equal and impartial an administration.

Sometimes both *utility* and *analogy* fail, and leave the laws of justice in total uncertainty. Thus, it is highly requisite, that prescription or long possession should convey property; but what number of days or months or years should be sufficient for that purpose, it is impossible for reason alone to determine. *Civil laws* here supply the place of the natural *code*, and assign different terms for prescription, according to the different *utilities*, proposed by the legislator. Bills of exchange and promissory notes, by the laws of most countries, prescribe sooner than bonds, and mortgages, and contracts of a more formal nature.

In general we may observe that all questions of property are subordinate to the authority of civil laws, which extend, restrain, modify, and alter the rules of natural justice, according to the particular *convenience* of each community. The laws have, or ought to have, a constant reference to the constitution of government, the manners, the climate, the religion, the commerce, the situation of each society. A late author of genius, as well as learning, has prosecuted this subject at large, and has established, from these principles, a system of political knowledge, which abounds in ingenious and brilliant thoughts, and is not wanting in solidity.[8]

*What is a man's property?* Anything which it is lawful for

---

[8] The author of *L'Esprit des Loix* [Montesquieu]. This illustrious writer, however, sets out with a different theory, and supposes all right to be founded on certain *rapports* or relations; which is a system, that, in my opinion, never will be reconciled with true philosophy. Father Malebranche, as far as I can learn, was the first that started this abstract theory of morals, which was afterwards adopted by Cudworth Clarke, and others; and as it excludes all sentiment, and pretends to found everything on reason, it has not wanted followers in this philosophic age. See Section I, Appendix I. With regard to justice, the virtue here treated of, the inference against this theory seems short and conclusive. Property is allowed to be dependent on civil laws; civil laws are allowed to have no other object, but the interest of society: This therefore must be allowed to be the sole foundation of property and justice. Not to mention, that our obligation itself to obey the magistrate and his laws is founded on nothing but the interests of society.

If the ideas of justice, sometimes, do not follow the dispositions of civil law; we shall find, that these cases, instead of objections, are confirmations of the theory delivered above. Where a civil law is so perverse as to cross all the interests of society, it loses all its authority, and men judge by the ideas of natural justice, which are conformable to those interests. Sometimes also civil laws, for useful purposes, require a ceremony or form to any deed; and where that is wanting, their decrees run contrary to the usual tenour of justice; but one who takes advantage of such chicanes, is not commonly regarded as an honest man. Thus, the interests of society require, that contracts be fulfilled; and there is not a more material article either of natural or civil justice: But the omission of a trifling circumstance will often, by law, invalidate a contract, *in foro humano*, but not *in foro conscientiae*, as divines express themselves. In these cases, the magistrate is supposed only to withdraw his power of enforcing the right, not to have altered the right. Where his intention extends to the right, and is conformable to the interests of society; it never fails to alter the right; a clear proof of the origin of justice and of property, as assigned above.

him, and for him alone, to use. *But what rule have we, by
which we can distinguish these objects?* Here we must have
recourse to statutes, customs, precedents, analogies, and a
hundred other circumstances; some of which are constant and
inflexible, some variable and arbitrary. But the ultimate point, in
which they all professedly terminate, is the interest and happiness of human society. Where this enters not into consideration, nothing can appear more whimsical, unnatural, and even
superstitious, than all or most of the laws of justice and of
property.

Those who ridicule vulgar superstitions, and expose the
folly of particular regards to meats, days, places, postures,
apparel, have an easy task; while they consider all the qualities and relations of the objects, and discover no adequate
cause for that affection or antipathy, veneration or horror,
which have so mighty an influence over a considerable part of
mankind. A Syrian would have starved rather than taste pigeon;
an Egyptian would not have approached bacon: But if these
species of food be examined by the senses of sight, smell, or
taste, or scrutinized by the sciences of chemistry, medicine, or
physics, no difference is ever found between them and any
other species, nor can that precise circumstance be pitched
on, which may afford a just foundation for the religious passion. A fowl on Thursday is lawful food; on Friday abominable: Eggs in this house and in this diocese, are permitted
during Lent; a hundred paces farther, to eat them is a
damnable sin. This earth or building, yesterday was profane;
to-day, by the muttering of certain words, it has become holy
and sacred. Such reflections as these, in the mouth of a philosopher, one may safely say, are too obvious to have any
influence; because they must always, to every man, occur at
first sight; and where they prevail not, of themselves, they are
surely obstructed by education, prejudice, and passion, not
by ignorance or mistake.

It may appear to a careless view, or rather a too abstracted reflection, that there enters a like superstition into all
the sentiments of justice; and that, if a man expose its object,
or what we call property, to the same scrutiny of sense and

science, he will not, by the most accurate enquiry, find any
foundation for the difference made by moral sentiment. I may
lawfully nourish myself from this tree; but the fruit of another of the same species, ten paces off, it is criminal for me
to touch. Had I worn this apparel an hour ago, I had merited
the severest punishment; but a man, by pronouncing a few
magical syllables, has now rendered it fit for my use and service. Were this house placed in the neighbouring territory, it
had been immoral for me to dwell in it; but being built on this
side the river, it is subject to a different municipal law, and
by its becoming mine I incur no blame or censure. The same
species of reasoning it may be thought, which so successfully
exposes superstition, is also applicable to justice; nor is it possible, in the one case more than in the other, to point out, in
the object, that precise quality or circumstance, which is the
foundation of the sentiment.

But there is this material difference between *superstition*
and *justice*, that the former is frivolous, useless, and burden-
some; the latter is absolutely requisite to the well-being of
mankind and existence of society. When we abstract from this
circumstance (for it is too apparent ever to be overlooked) it
must be confessed, that all regards to right and property, seem
entirely without foundation, as much as the grossest and most
vulgar superstition. Were the interests of society nowise concerned, it is as unintelligible why another's articulating certain
sounds implying consent, should change the nature of my
actions with regard to a particular object, as why the reciting
of a liturgy by a priest, in a certain habit and posture, should
dedicate a heap of brick and timber, and render it, thenceforth and for ever, sacred.[4]

[4] It is evident, that the will or consent alone never transfers property,
nor causes the obligation of a promise (for the same reasoning extends
to both) but the will must be expressed by words or signs, in order to
impose a tie upon any man. The expression being once brought in
as subservient to the will, soon becomes the principal part of the
promise; nor will a man be less bound by his word, though he secretly
give a different direction to his intention, and withhold the assent of
his mind. But though the expression makes, on most occasions, the
whole of the promise, yet it does not always so; and one who should
make use of any expression, of which he knows not the meaning, and

These reflections are far from weakening the obligations of justice, or diminishing anything from the most sacred attention to property. On the contrary, such sentiments must ac-

---

which he uses without any sense of the consequences, would not certainly be bound by it. Nay, though he know its meaning, yet if he use it in jest only, and with such signs as evidently show, that he has no serious intention of binding himself, he would not lie under any obligation of performance; but it is necessary, that the words be a perfect expression of the will, without any contrary signs. Nay, even this we must not carry so far as to imagine, that one, whom, by our quickness of understanding, we conjecture, from certain signs, to have an intention of deceiving us, is not bound by his expression or verbal promise, if we accept of it; but must limit this conclusion to those cases where the signs are of a different nature from those of deceit. All these contradictions are easily accounted for, if justice arise entirely from its usefulness to society; but will never be explained on any other hypothesis.

It is remarkable, that the moral decisions of the *Jesuits* and other relaxed casuists, were commonly formed in prosecution of some such subtilties of reasoning as are here pointed out, and proceed as much from the habit of scholastic refinement as from any corruption of the heart, if we may follow the authority of Mons. Bayle. See his Dictionary, article LOYOLA. And why has the indignation of mankind risen so high against these casuists; but because every one perceived, that human society could not subsist were such practices authorized, and that morals must always be handled with a view to public interest, more than philosophical regularity? If the secret direction of the intention, said every man of sense, could invalidate a contract; where is our security? And yet a metaphysical schoolman might think, that, where an intention was supposed to be requisite, if that intention really had not place, no consequence ought to follow, and no obligation be imposed. The casuistical subtilties may not be greater than the subtilties of lawyers, hinted at above; but as the former are *pernicious*, and the latter *innocent* and even *necessary*, this is the reason of the very different reception they meet with from the world.

It is a doctrine of the Church of Rome, that the priest, by a secret direction of his intention, can invalidate any sacrament. This position is derived from a strict and regular prosecution of the obvious truth, that empty words alone, without any meaning or intention in the speaker, can never be attended with any effect. If the same conclusion be not admitted in reasonings concerning civil contracts, where the affair is allowed to be of so much less consequence than the eternal salvation of thousands, it proceeds entirely from men's sense of the danger and inconvenience of the doctrine in the former case: And we may thence observe, that however positive, arrogant, and dogmatical any superstition may appear, it never can convey any thorough persuasion of the reality of its objects, or put them, in any degree, on a balance with the common incidents of life, which we learn from daily observation and experimental reasoning.

quire new force from the present reasoning. For what stronger foundation can be desired or conceived for any duty, than to observe, that human society, or even human nature, could not subsist without the establishment of it; and will still arrive at greater degrees of happiness and perfection, the more inviolable the regard is, which is paid to that duty?

The dilemma seems obvious: As justice evidently tends to promote public utility and to support civil society, the sentiment of justice is either derived from our reflecting on that tendency, or like hunger, thirst, and other appetites, resentment, love of life, attachment to offspring, and other passions, arises from a simple original instinct in the human breast, which nature has implanted for like salutary purposes. If the latter be the case, it follows, that property, which is the object of justice, is also distinguished by a simple original instinct, and is not ascertained by any argument or reflection. But who is there that ever heard of such an instinct? Or is this a subject in which new discoveries can be made? We may as well expect to discover, in the body, new senses, which had before escaped the observation of all mankind.

But farther, though it seems a very simple proposition to say, that nature, by an instinctive sentiment, distinguishes property, yet in reality we shall find, that there are required for that purpose ten thousand different instincts, and these employed about objects of the greatest intricacy and nicest discernment. For when a definition of *property* is required, that relation is found to resolve itself into any possession acquired by occupation, by industry, by prescription, by inheritance, by contract, &c. Can we think that nature, by an original instinct, instructs us in all these methods of acquisition?

These words too, inheritance and contract, stand for ideas infinitely complicated; and to define them exactly, a hundred volumes of laws, and a thousand volumes of commentators, have not been found sufficient. Does nature, whose instincts in men are all simple, embrace such complicated and artificial objects, and create a rational creature, without trusting anything to the operation of his reason?

But even though all this were admitted, it would not be

satisfactory. Positive laws can certainly transfer property. Is it by another original instinct, that we recognize the authority of kings and senates, and mark all the boundaries of their jurisdiction? Judges too, even though their sentence be erroneous and illegal, must be allowed, for the sake of peace and order, to have decisive authority, and ultimately to determine property. Have we original innate ideas of praetors and chancellors and juries? Who sees not, that all these institutions arise merely from the necessities of human society?

All birds of the same species in every age and country, built their nests alike: In this we see the force of instinct. Men, in different times and places, frame their houses differently: Here we perceive the influence of reason and custom. A like inference may be drawn from comparing the instinct of generation and the institution of property.

How great soever the variety of municipal laws, it must be confessed, that their chief out-lines pretty regularly concur; because the purposes, to which they tend, are everywhere exactly similar. In like manner, all houses have a roof and walls, windows and chimneys; though diversified in their shape, figure, and materials. The purposes of the latter, directed to the conveniencies of human life, discover not more plainly their origin from reason and reflection, than do those of the former, which point all to a like end.

I need not mention the variations, which all the rules of property receive from the finer turns and connexions of the imagination, and from the subtilties and abstractions of law-topics and reasonings. There is no possibility of reconciling this observation to the notion of original instincts.

What alone will beget a doubt concerning the theory, on which I insist, is the influence of education and acquired habits, by which we are so accustomed to blame injustice, that we are not, in every instance, conscious of any immediate reflection on the pernicious consequences of it. The views the most familiar to us are apt, for that very reason, to escape us; and what we have very frequently performed from certain motives, we are apt likewise to continue mechanically, without recalling, on every occasion, the reflections, which first determined us. The convenience, or rather necessity, which leads to justice is so universal, and everywhere points so much to the same rules, that the habit takes place in all societies; and it is not without some scrutiny, that we are able to ascertain its true origin. The matter, however, is not so obscure, but that even in common life we have every moment recourse to the principle of public utility, and ask, *What must become of the world, if such practices prevail? How could society subsist under such disorders?* Were the distinction or separation of possessions entirely useless, can any one conceive, that it ever should have obtained in society?

Thus we seem, upon the whole, to have attained a knowledge of the force of that principle here insisted on, and can determine what degree of esteem or moral approbation may result from reflections on public interest and utility. The necessity of justice to the support of society is the sole foundation of that virtue; and since no moral excellence is more highly esteemed, we may conclude that this circumstance of usefulness has, in general, the strongest energy, and most entire command over our sentiments. It must, therefore, be the source of a considerable part of the merit ascribed to humanity, benevolence, friendship, public spirit, and other social virtues of that stamp; as it is the sole source of the moral approbation paid to fidelity, justice, veracity, integrity, and those other estimable and useful qualities and principles. It is entirely agreeable to the rules of philosophy, and even of common reason; where any principle has been found to have a great force and energy in one instance, to ascribe to it a like energy in all similar instances. This indeed is Newton's chief rule of philosophizing.[5]

[5] Principia, Lib. iii.

## Section IV

## Of Political Society

Had every man sufficient *sagacity* to perceive, at all times, the strong interest which binds him to the observance of justice and equity, and *strength of mind* sufficient to persevere in a steady adherence to a general and a distant interest, in opposition to the allurements of present pleasure and advantage; there had never, in that case, been any such thing as government or political society, but each man, following his natural liberty, had lived in entire peace and harmony with all others. What need of positive law where natural justice is, of itself, a sufficient restraint? Why create magistrates, where there never arises any disorder or iniquity? Why abridge our native freedom, when, in every instance, the utmost exertion of it is found innocent and beneficial? It is evident, that, if government were totally useless, it never could have place, and that the sole foundation of the duty of allegiance is the *advantage*, which it procures to society, by preserving peace and order among mankind.

When a number of political societies are erected, and maintain a great intercourse together, a new set of rules are immediately discovered to be *useful* in that particular situation; and accordingly take place under the title of Laws of Nations. Of this kind are, the sacredness of the person of ambassadors, abstaining from poisoned arms, quarter in war, with others of that kind, which are plainly calculated for the *advantage* of states and kingdoms in their intercourse with each other.

The rules of justice, such as prevail among individuals, are not entirely suspended among political societies. All princes pretend a regard to the rights of other princes; and some, no doubt, without hypocrisy. Alliances and treaties are every day made between independent states, which would only be so much waste of parchment, if they were not found by experience to have *some* influence and authority. But here is the difference between kingdoms and individuals. Human nature cannot by any means subsist, without the association of individuals; and that association never could have place, were no regard paid to the laws of equity and justice. Disorder, confusion, the war of all against all, are the necessary consequences of such a licentious conduct. But nations can subsist without intercourse. They may even subsist, in some degree, under a general war. The observance of justice, though useful among them, is not guarded by so strong a necessity as among individuals; and the *moral obligation* holds proportion with the *usefulness*. All politicians will allow, and most philosophers, that reasons of state may, in particular emergencies, dispense with the rules of justice, and invalidate any treaty or alliance, where the strict observance of it would be prejudicial, in a considerable degree, to either of the contracting parties. But nothing less than the most extreme necessity, it is confessed, can justify individuals in a breach of promise, or an invasion of the properties of others.

In a confederated commonwealth, such as the Achaean republic of old, or the Swiss Cantons and United Provinces in modern times; as the league has here a peculiar *utility*, the conditions of union have a peculiar sacredness and authority, and a violation of them would be regarded as no less, or even as more criminal, than any private injury or injustice.

The long and helpless infancy of man requires the combination of parents for the subsistence of their young; and that combination requires the virtue of chastity or fidelity to the marriage bed. Without such a *utility*, it will readily be owned, that such a virtue would never have been thought of.[1]

---

[1] The only solution, which Plato gives to all the objections that might be raised against the community of women, established in his imaginary commonwealth, is Κάλλιστα γὰρ δὴ τοῦτο καὶ λέγεται καὶ λελέξεται, ὅτι τὸ μὲν ὠφέλιμον καλόν, τὸ δὲ βλαβερὸν αἰσχρόν. *Scite enim istud et dicitur et dicetur, Id quod utile sit honestum esse, quod autem inutile sit turpe esse.* De Rep. lib. v. p. 457. ex edit. Ser. And this maxim will admit of no doubt, where public utility is concerned; which is Plato's meaning. And indeed to what other purpose do all the ideas of chastity and modesty serve? *Nisi utile est quod faci-*

An infidelity of this nature is much more *pernicious* in *women* than in *men*. Hence the laws of chastity are much stricter over the one sex than over the other.

These rules have all a reference to generation; and yet women past child-bearing are no more supposed to be exempted from them than those in the flower of their youth and beauty. *General rules* are often extended beyond the principle whence they first arise; and this in all matters of taste and sentiment. It is a vulgar story at Paris, that, during the rage of the Mississippi, a hump-backed fellow went every day into the Rue de Quincempoix, where the stock-jobbers met in great crowds, and was well paid for allowing them to make use of his hump as a desk, in order to sign their contracts upon it. Would the fortune, which he raised by this expedient, make him a handsome fellow; though it be confessed, that personal beauty arises very much from ideas of utility? The imagination is influenced by associations of ideas; which, though they arise at first from the judgement, are not easily altered by every particular exception that occurs to us. To which we may add, in the present case of chastity, that the example of the old would be pernicious to the young; and that women, continually foreseeing that a certain time would bring them the liberty of indulgence, would naturally advance that period, and think more lightly of this whole duty, so requisite to society.

Those who live in the same family have such frequent opportunities of licence of this kind, that nothing could preserve purity of manners, were marriage allowed, among the nearest relations, or any intercourse of love between them ratified by law and custom. Incest, therefore, being *pernicious* in a superior degree, has also a superior turpitude and moral deformity annexed to it.

What is the reason, why, by the Athenian laws, one might

---

*mus, frustra est gloria,* says Phaedrus. Καλὸν τῶν βλαβερῶν οὐδέν, says Plutarch, *de vitioso pudore*. Nihil eorum quae damnosa sunt, pulchrum est. The same was the opinion of the Stoics. Φασὶν οὖν οἱ Στωικοὶ ἀγαθὸν εἶναι ὠφέλειαν ἢ οὐχ ἕτερον ὠφελείας, ὠφέλειαν μὲν λέγοντες τὴν ἀρετὴν καὶ τὴν σπουδαίαν πρᾶξιν. Sept. Emp. lib. iii. cap. 20.

marry a half-sister by the father, but not by the mother? Plainly this: The manners of the Athenians were so reserved, that a man was never permitted to approach the women's apartment, even in the same family, unless where he visited his own mother. His step-mother and her children were as much shut up from him as the women of any other family, and there was as little danger of any criminal correspondence between them. Uncles and nieces, for a like reason, might marry at Athens; but neither these, nor half-brothers and sisters, could contract that alliance at Rome, where the intercourse was more open between the sexes. Public utility is the cause of all these variations.

To repeat, to a man's prejudice, anything that escaped him in private conversation, or to make any such use of his private letters, is highly blamed. The free and social intercourse of minds must be extremely checked, where no such rules of fidelity are established.

Even in repeating stories, whence we can foresee no ill consequences to result, the giving of one's author is regarded as a piece of indiscretion, if not of immorality. These stories, in passing from hand to hand, and receiving all the usual variations, frequently come about to the persons concerned, and produce animosities and quarrels among people, whose intentions are the most innocent and inoffensive.

To pry into secrets, to open or even read the letters of others, to play the spy upon their words and looks and actions; what habits more inconvenient in society? What habits, of consequence, more blameable?

This principle is also the foundation of most of the laws of good manners; a kind of lesser morality, calculated for the ease of company and conversation. Too much or too little ceremony are both blamed, and everything, which promotes ease, without an indecent familiarity, is useful and laudable.

Constancy in friendships, attachments, and familiarities, is commendable, and is requisite to support trust and good correspondence in society. But in places of general, though casual concourse, where the pursuit of health and pleasure brings people promiscuously together, public conveniency has dispensed with this maxim; and custom there promotes an unreserved conversation for the time, by indulging the privilege of dropping afterwards every indifferent acquaintance, without breach of civility or good manners.

Even in societies, which are established on principles the most immoral, and the most destructive to the interests of the general society, there are required certain rules, which a species of false honour, as well as private interest, engages the members to observe. Robbers and pirates, it has often been remarked, could not maintain their pernicious confederacy, did they not establish a new distributive justice among themselves, and recall those laws of equity, which they have violated with the rest of mankind.

I hate a drinking companion, says the Greek proverb, who never forgets. The follies of the last debauch should be buried in eternal oblivion, in order to give full scope to the follies of the next.

Among nations, where an immoral gallantry, if covered with a thin veil of mystery, is, in some degree, authorized by custom, there immediately arise a set of rules, calculated for the conveniency of that attachment. The famous court or parliament of love in Provence formerly decided all difficult cases of this nature.

In societies for play, there are laws required for the conduct of the game; and these laws are different in each game. The foundation, I own, of such societies is frivolous; and the laws are, in a great measure, though not altogether, capricious and arbitrary. So far is there a material difference between them and the rules of justice, fidelity, and loyalty. The general societies of men are absolutely requisite for the subsistence of the species; and the public conveniency, which regulates morals, is inviolably established in the nature of man, and of the world, in which he lives. The comparison, therefore, in these respects, is very imperfect. We may only learn from it the necessity of rules, wherever men have any intercourse with each other.

They cannot even pass each other on the road without rules. Waggoners, coachmen, and postilions have principles, by which they give the way; and these are chiefly founded on mutual ease and convenience. Sometimes also they are arbitrary, at least dependent on a kind of capricious analogy like many of the reasonings of lawyers.[2]

To carry the matter farther, we may observe, that it is impossible for men so much as to murder each other without statutes, and maxims, and an idea of justice and honour. War has its laws as well as peace; and even that sportive kind of war, carried on among wrestlers, boxers, cudgel-players, gladiators, is regulated by fixed principles. Common interest and utility beget infallibly a standard of right and wrong among the parties concerned.

---

[2] That the lighter machine yield to the heavier, and, in machines of the same kind, that the empty yield to the loaded; this rule is founded on convenience. That those who are going to the capital take place of those who are coming from it; this seems to be founded on some idea of the dignity of the great city, and of the preference of the future to the past. From like reasons, among foot-walkers, the right-hand entitles a man to the wall, and prevents jostling, which peaceable people find very disagreeable and inconvenient.

# Section V

## Why Utility Pleases

### Part I

It seems so natural a thought to ascribe to their utility the praise, which we bestow on the social virtues, that one would expect to meet with this principle everywhere in moral writers, as the chief foundation of their reasoning and enquiry. In common life, we may observe, that the circumstance of utility is always appealed to; nor is it supposed, that a greater eulogy can be given to any man, than to display his usefulness to the public, and enumerate the services, which he has performed to mankind and society. What praise, even of an inanimate form, if the regularity and elegance of its parts destroy not its fitness for any useful purpose! And how satisfactory an apology for any disproportion or seeming deformity, if we can show the necessity of that particular construction for the use intended! A ship appears more beautiful to an artist, or one moderately skilled in navigation, where its prow is wide and swelling beyond its poop, than if it were framed with a precise geometrical regularity, in contradiction to all the laws of mechanics. A building, whose doors and windows were exact squares, would hurt the eye by that very proportion; as ill adapted to the figure of a human creature, for whose service the fabric was intended. What wonder then, that a man, whose habits and conduct are hurtful to society, and dangerous or pernicious to every one who has an intercourse with him, should, on that account, be an object of disapprobation, and communicate to every spectator the strongest sentiment of disgust and hatred.[1]

[1] We ought not to imagine, because an inanimate object may be useful as well as a man, that therefore it ought also, according to this system, to merit the appellation of *virtuous*. The sentiments, excited by utility, are, in the two cases, very different; and the one is mixed with affection, esteem, approbation, &c., and not the other. In like manner, an

But perhaps the difficulty of accounting for these effects of usefulness, or its contrary, has kept philosophers from admitting them into their systems of ethics, and has induced them rather to employ any other principle, in explaining the origin of moral good and evil. But it is no just reason for rejecting any principle, confirmed by experience, that we cannot give a satisfactory account of its origin, nor are able to resolve it into other more general principles. And if we would employ a little thought on the present subject, we need be at no loss to account for the influence of utility, and to deduce it from principles, the most known and avowed in human nature.

From the apparent usefulness of the social virtues, it has readily been inferred by sceptics, both ancient and modern, that all moral distinctions arise from education, and were, at first, invented, and afterwards encouraged, by the art of politicians, in order to render men tractable, and subdue their natural ferocity and selfishness, which incapacitated them for society. This principle, indeed, of precept and education, must so far be owned to have a powerful influence, that it may frequently increase or diminish, beyond their natural standard, the sentiments of approbation or dislike; and may even, in particular instances, create, without any natural principle, a new sentiment of this kind; as is evident in all super-

---

inanimate object may have good colour and proportions as well as a human figure. But can we ever be in love with the former? There are a numerous set of passions and sentiments, of which thinking rational beings are, by the original constitution of nature, the only proper objects: and though the very same qualities be transferred to an insensible, inanimate being, they will not excite the same sentiments. The beneficial qualities of herbs and minerals are, indeed, sometimes called their *virtues*; but this is an effect of the caprice of language, which ought not to be regarded in reasoning. For though there be a species of approbation attending even inanimate objects, when beneficial, yet this sentiment is so weak, and so different from that which is directed to beneficent magistrates or statesmen; that they ought not to be ranked under the same class or appellation.

A very small variation of the object, even where the same qualities are preserved, will destroy a sentiment. Thus, the same beauty, transferred to a different sex, excites no amorous passion, where nature is not extremely perverted.

stitious practices and observances: But that *all* moral affection or dislike arises from this origin, will never surely be allowed by any judicious enquirer. Had nature made no such distinction, founded on the original constitution of the mind, the words, *honourable* and *shameful, lovely* and *odious, noble* and *despicable,* had never had place in any language; nor could politicians, had they invented these terms, ever have been able to render them intelligible, or make them convey any idea to the audience. So that nothing can be more superficial than this paradox of the sceptics; and it were well, if, in the abstruser studies of logic and metaphysics, we could as easily obviate the cavils of that sect, as in the practical and more intelligible sciences of politics and morals.

The social virtues must, therefore, be allowed to have a natural beauty and amiableness, which, at first, antecedent to all precept or education, recommends them to the esteem of uninstructed mankind, and engages their affections. And as the public utility of these virtues is the chief circumstance, whence they derive their merit, it follows, that the end, which they have a tendency to promote, must be some way agreeable to us, and take hold of some natural affection. It must please, either from considerations of self-interest, or from more generous motives and regards.

It has often been asserted, that, as every man has a strong connexion with society, and perceives the impossibility of his solitary subsistence, he becomes, on that account, favourable to all those habits or principles, which promote order in society, and insure to him the quiet possession of so inestimable a blessing. As much as we value our own happiness and welfare, as much must we applaud the practice of justice and humanity, by which alone the social confederacy can be maintained, and every man reap the fruits of mutual protection and assistance.

This deduction of morals from self-love, or a regard to private interest, is an obvious thought, and has not arisen wholly from the wanton sallies and sportive assaults of the sceptics. To mention no others, Polybius, one of the gravest and most judicious, as well as most moral writers of antiquity, has assigned this selfish origin to all our sentiments of virtue.[2] But though the solid practical sense of that author, and his aversion to all vain subtilties, render his authority on the present subject very considerable; yet is not this an affair to be decided by authority, and the voice of nature and experience seems plainly to oppose the selfish theory.

We frequently bestow praise on virtuous actions, performed in very distant ages and remote countries; where the utmost subtilty of imagination would not discover any appearance of self-interest, or find any connexion of our present happiness and security with events so widely separated from us.

A generous, a brave, a noble deed, performed by an adversary, commands our approbation; while in its consequences it may be acknowledged prejudicial to our particular interest.

Where private advantage concurs with general affection for virtue, we readily perceive and avow the mixture of these distinct sentiments, which have a very different feeling and influence on the mind. We praise, perhaps, with more alacrity, where the generous humane action contributes to our particular interest: But the topics of praise, which we insist on, are very wide of this circumstance. And we may attempt to bring over others to our sentiments, without endeavouring to convince them, that they reap any advantage from the actions which we recommend to their approbation and applause.

Frame the model of a praiseworthy character, consisting of all the most amiable moral virtues: Give instances, in which these display themselves after an eminent and extraordinary manner: You readily engage the esteem and approbation of all your audience, who never so much as enquire in what age and country the person lived, who possessed these noble qualities: A circumstance, however, of all others, the most

---

[2] Undutifulness to parents is disapproved of by mankind, προορωμέ-νους τὸ μέλλον, καὶ συλλογιζομένους ὅτι τὸ παραπλήσιον ἑκάστοις αὐτῶν συγκυρήσει. Ingratitude for a like reason (though he seems there to mix a more generous regard) συναγανακτοῦντας μὲν τῷ πέλας, ἀναφέροντας δ' ἐπ' αὐτοὺς τὸ παραπλήσιον, ἐξ ὧν ὑπογίγνεταί τις ἔννοια παρ' ἑκάστῳ τῆς τοῦ καθή-κοντος δυνάμεως καὶ θεωρίας. Lib. vi. cap. 4 (ed. Gronovius). Perhaps the historian only meant, that our sympathy and humanity was more enlivened, by our considering the similarity of our case with that of the person suffering; which is a just sentiment.

material to self-love, or a concern for our own individual happiness.

Once on a time, a statesman, in the shock and contest of parties, prevailed so far as to procure, by his eloquence, the banishment of an able adversary; whom he secretly followed, offering him money for his support during his exile, and soothing him with topics of consolation in his misfortunes. *Alas!* cries the banished statesman, *with what regret must I leave my friends in this city, where even enemies are so generous!* Virtue, though in an enemy, here pleased him: And we also give it the just tribute of praise and approbation; nor do we retract these sentiments, when we hear, that the action passed at Athens, about two thousand years ago, and that the persons names were Eschines and Demosthenes.

*What is that to me?* There are few occasions, when this question is not pertinent: And had it that universal, infallible influence supposed, it would turn into ridicule every composition, and almost every conversation, which contain any praise or censure of men and manners.

It is but a weak subterfuge, when pressed by these facts and arguments, to say, that we transport ourselves, by the force of imagination, into distant ages and countries, and consider the advantage, which we should have reaped from these characters, had we been contemporaries, and had any commerce with the persons. It is not conceivable, how a *real* sentiment or passion can ever arise from a known *imaginary* interest; especially when our *real* interest is still kept in view, and is often acknowledged to be entirely distinct from the imaginary, and even sometimes opposite to it.

A man, brought to the brink of a precipice, cannot look down without trembling; and the sentiment of *imaginary* danger actuates him, in opposition to the opinion and belief of *real* safety. But the imagination is here assisted by the presence of a striking object; and yet prevails not, except it be also aided by novelty, and the unusual appearance of the object. Custom soon reconciles us to heights and precipices, and wears off these false and delusive terrors. The reverse is observable in the estimates which we form of characters and manners; and the more we habituate ourselves to an accurate scrutiny of morals, the more delicate feeling do we acquire of the most minute distinctions between vice and virtue. Such frequent occasion, indeed, have we, in common life, to pronounce all kinds of moral determinations, that no object of this kind can be new or unusual to us; nor could any *false* views or prepossessions maintain their ground against an experience, so common and familiar. Experience being chiefly what forms the associations of ideas, it is impossible that any association could establish and support itself, in direct opposition to that principle.

Usefulness is agreeable, and engages our approbation. This is a matter of fact, confirmed by daily observation. But, *useful?* For what? For somebody's interest, surely. Whose interest then? Not our own only: For our approbation frequently extends farther. It must, therefore, be the interest of those, who are served by the character or action approved of; and these we may conclude, however remote, are not totally indifferent to us. By opening up this principle, we shall discover one great source of moral distinctions.

## Part II

Self-love is a principle in human nature of such extensive energy, and the interest of each individual is, in general, so closely connected with that of the community, that those philosophers were excusable, who fancied that all our concern for the public might be resolved into a concern for our own happiness and preservation. They saw every moment, instances of approbation or blame, satisfaction or displeasure towards characters and actions; they denominated the objects of these sentiments, *virtues*, or *vices*; they observed, that the former had a tendency to increase the happiness, and the latter the misery of mankind; they asked, whether it were possible that we could have any general concern for society, or any disinterested resentment of the welfare or injury of others; they found it simpler to consider all these sentiments as modifications of self-love; and they discovered a pretence, at least, for this unity of principle, in that close union of interest, which is so observable between the public and each individual.

But notwithstanding this frequent confusion of interests, it is easy to attain what natural philosophers, after Lord Bacon, have affected to call the *experimentum crucis*, or that experiment which points out the right way in any doubt or ambiguity. We have found instances, in which private interest was separate from public; in which it was even contrary: And yet we observed the moral sentiment to continue, notwithstanding this disjunction of interests. And wherever these distinct interests sensibly concurred, we always found a sensible increase of the sentiment, and a more warm affection to virtue, and detestation of vice, or what we properly call, *gratitude* and *revenge*. Compelled by these instances, we must renounce the theory, which accounts for every moral sentiment by the principle of self-love. We must adopt a more public affection, and allow, that the interests of society are not, even on their own account, entirely indifferent to us. Usefulness is only a tendency to a certain end; and it is a contradiction in terms, that anything pleases as means to an end, where the end itself no wise affects us. If usefulness, therefore, be a source of moral sentiment, and if this usefulness be not always considered with a reference to self; it follows, that everything, which contributes to the happiness of society, recommends itself directly to our approbation and good-will. Here is a principle, which accounts, in great part, for the origin of morality: And what need we seek for abstruse and remote systems, when there occurs one so obvious and natural?[3]

---

[3] It is needless to push our researches so far as to ask, why we have humanity or a fellow-feeling with others. It is sufficient, that this is experienced to be a principle in human nature. We must stop somewhere in our examination of causes; and there are, in every science, some general principles, beyond which we cannot hope to find any principle more general. No man is absolutely indifferent to the happiness and misery of others. The first has a natural tendency to give pleasure; the second, pain. This every one may find in himself. It is not probable, that these principles can be resolved into principles more simple and universal, whatever attempts may have been made to that purpose. But if it were possible, it belongs not to the present subject; and we may here safely consider these principles as original: happy, if we can render all the consequences sufficiently plain and perspicuous!

Have we any difficulty to comprehend the force of humanity and benevolence? Or to conceive, that the very aspect of happiness, joy, prosperity, gives pleasure; that of pain, suffering, sorrow, communicates uneasiness? The human countenance, says Horace,[4] borrows smiles or tears from the human countenance. Reduce a person to solitude, and he loses all enjoyment, except either of the sensual or speculative kind; and that because the movements of his heart are not forwarded by correspondent movements in his fellow-creatures. The signs of sorrow and mourning, though arbitrary, affect us with melancholy; but the natural symptoms, tears and cries and groans, never fail to infuse compassion and uneasiness. And if the effects of misery touch us in so lively a manner; can we be supposed altogether insensible or indifferent towards its causes; when a malicious or treacherous character and behaviour are presented to us?

We enter, I shall suppose, into a convenient, warm, well-contrived apartment: We necessarily receive a pleasure from its very survey; because it presents us with the pleasing ideas of ease, satisfaction, and enjoyment. The hospitable, good-humoured, humane landlord appears. This circumstance surely must embellish the whole; nor can we easily forbear reflecting, with pleasure, on the satisfaction which results to every one from his intercourse and good-offices.

His whole family, by the freedom, ease, confidence, and calm enjoyment, diffused over their countenances, sufficiently express their happiness. I have a pleasing sympathy in the prospect of so much joy, and can never consider the source of it, without the most agreeable emotions.

He tells me, that an oppressive and powerful neighbour had attempted to dispossess him of his inheritance, and had long disturbed all his innocent and social pleasures. I feel an immediate indignation arise in me against such violence and injury.

But it is no wonder, he adds, that a private wrong should proceed from a man, who had enslaved provinces, depopu-

---

[4] "Uti ridentibus arrident, ita flentibus adflent
Humani vultus."—Hor.

lated cities, and made the field and scaffold stream with human blood. I am struck with horror at the prospect of so much misery, and am actuated by the strongest antipathy against its author.

In general, it is certain, that, wherever we go, whatever we reflect on or converse about, everything still presents us with the view of human happiness or misery, and excites in our breast a sympathetic movement of pleasure or uneasiness. In our serious occupations, in our careless amusements, this principle still exerts its active energy.

A man who enters the theatre, is immediately struck with the view of so great a multitude, participating of one common amusement; and experiences, from their very aspect, a superior sensibility or disposition of being affected with every sentiment, which he shares with his fellow-creatures.

He observes the actors to be animated by the appearance of a full audience, and raised to a degree of enthusiasm, which they cannot command in any solitary or calm moment.

Every movement of the theatre, by a skilful poet, is communicated, as it were by magic, to the spectators; who weep, tremble, resent, rejoice, and are inflamed with all the variety of passions, which actuate the several personages of the drama.

Where any event crosses our wishes, and interrupts the happiness of the favourite characters, we feel a sensible anxiety and concern. But where their sufferings proceed from the treachery, cruelty, or tyranny of an enemy, our breasts are affected with the liveliest resentment against the author of these calamities.

It is here esteemed contrary to the rules of art to represent anything cool and indifferent. A distant friend, or a confidant, who has no immediate interest in the catastrophe, ought, if possible, to be avoided by the poet; as communicating a like indifference to the audience, and checking the progress of the passions.

Few species of poetry are more entertaining than *pastoral*; and every one is sensible, that the chief source of its pleasure arises from those images of a gentle and tender tranquillity, which it represents in its personages, and of which it communicates a like sentiment to the reader. Sannazarius, who transferred the scene to the sea-shore, though he presented the most magnificent object in nature, is confessed to have erred in his choice. The idea of toil, labour, and danger, suffered by the fishermen, is painful; by an unavoidable sympathy, which attends every conception of human happiness or misery.

When I was twenty, says a French poet, Ovid was my favourite: Now I am forty, I declare for Horace. We enter, to be sure, more readily into sentiments, which resemble those we feel every day: But no passion, when well represented, can be entirely indifferent to us; because there is none, of which every man has not, within him, at least the seeds and first principles. It is the business of poetry to bring every affection near to us by lively imagery and representation, and make it look like truth and reality: A certain proof, that, wherever that reality is found, our minds are disposed to be strongly affected by it.

Any recent event or piece of news, by which the fate of states, provinces, or many individuals is affected, is extremely interesting even to those whose welfare is not immediately engaged. Such intelligence is propagated with celerity, heard with avidity, and enquired into with attention and concern. The interest of society appears, on this occasion, to be in some degree the interest of each individual. The imagination is sure to be affected; though the passions excited may not always be so strong and steady as to have great influence on the conduct and behaviour.

The perusal of a history seems a calm entertainment; but would be no entertainment at all, did not our hearts beat with correspondent movements to those which are described by the historian.

Thucydides and Guicciardin support with difficulty our attention; while the former describes the trivial rencounters of the small cities of Greece, and the latter the harmless wars of Pisa. The few persons interested and the small interest fill not the imagination, and engage not the affections. The deep distress of the numerous Athenian army before Syracuse; the danger which so nearly threatens Venice; these excite compassion; these move terror and anxiety.

The indifferent, uninteresting style of Suetonius, equally with the masterly pencil of Tacitus, may convince us of the cruel depravity of Nero or Tiberius: But what a difference of sentiment! While the former coldly relates the facts; and the latter sets before our eyes the venerable figures of a Soranus and a Thrasea, intrepid in their fate, and only moved by the melting sorrows of their friends and kindred. What sympathy then touches every human heart! What indignation against the tyrant, whose causeless fear or unprovoked malice gave rise to such detestable barbarity!

If we bring these subjects nearer: If we remove all suspicion of fiction and deceit: What powerful concern is excited, and how much superior, in many instances, to the narrow attachments of self-love and private interest! Popular sedition, party zeal, a devoted obedience to factious leaders; these are some of the most visible, though less laudable effects of this social sympathy in human nature.

The frivolousness of the subject too, we may observe, is not able to detach us entirely from what carries an image of human sentiment and affection.

When a person stutters, and pronounces with difficulty, we even sympathize with this trivial uneasiness, and suffer for him. And it is a rule in criticism, that every combination of syllables or letters, which gives pain to the organs of speech in the recital, appears also from a species of sympathy harsh and disagreeable to the ear. Nay, when we run over a book with our eye, we are sensible of such unharmonious composition; because we still imagine, that a person recites it to us, and suffers from the pronunciation of these jarring sounds. So delicate is our sympathy!

Easy and unconstrained postures and motions are always beautiful: An air of health and vigour is agreeable: Clothes which warm, without burthening the body; which cover, without imprisoning the limbs, are well-fashioned. In every judgement of beauty, the feelings of the person affected enter into consideration, and communicate to the spectator similar touches of pain or pleasure.[5] What wonder, then, if we can pronounce no judgment concerning the character and conduct of men, without considering the tendencies of their actions, and the happiness or misery which thence arises to society? What association of ideas would ever operate, were that principle here totally unactive.[6]

If any man from a cold insensibility, or narrow selfishness of temper, is unaffected with the images of human happiness or misery, he must be equally indifferent to the images of vice and virtue: As, on the other hand, it is always found, that a warm concern for the interests of our species is attended with a delicate feeling of all moral distinctions; a strong resentment of injury done to men; a lively approbation of their welfare. In this particular, though great superiority is observable of one man above another; yet none are so entirely indifferent to the interest of their fellow-creatures, as to perceive no distinctions of moral good and evil, in consequence of the different tendencies of actions and principles. How, indeed, can we suppose it possible in any one, who wears a human heart, that if there be subjected to his censure, one character or system of conduct, which is beneficial, and an-

[5] "Decentior equus cujus astricta sunt ilia; sed idem velocior. Pulcher aspectu sit athleta, cujus lacertos exercitatio expressit; idem certamini paratior. Nunquam enim *species* ab *utilitate* dividitur. Sed hoc quidem discernere modici judicii est."—Quintilian, *Inst.* lib. viii. cap. 3.

[6] In proportion to the station which a man possesses, according to the relations in which he is placed; we always expect from him a greater or less degree of good, and when disappointed, blame his inutility; and much more do we blame him, if any ill or prejudice arise from his conduct and behaviour. When the interests of one country interfere with those of another, we estimate the merits of a statesman by the good or ill, which results to his own country from his measures and counsels, without regard to the prejudice which he brings on its enemies and rivals. His fellow-citizens are the objects, which lie nearest the eye, while we determine his character. And as nature has implanted in every one a superior affection to his own country, we never expect any regard to distant nations, where a competition arises. Not to mention, that, while every man consults the good of his own community, we are sensible, that the general interest of mankind is better promoted, than by any loose indeterminate views to the good of a species, whence no beneficial action could ever result, for want of a duly limited object, on which they could exert themselves.

other which is pernicious to his species or community, he will not so much as give a cool preference to the former, or ascribe to it the smallest merit or regard? Let us suppose such a person ever so selfish; let private interest have ingrossed ever so much his attention; yet in instances, where that is not concerned, he must unavoidably feel *some* propensity to the good of mankind, and make it an object of choice, if everything else be equal. Would any man, who is walking along, tread as willingly on another's gouty toes, whom he has no quarrel with, as on the hard flint and pavement? There is here surely a difference in the case. We surely take into consideration the happiness and misery of others, in weighing the several motives of action, and incline to the former, where no private regards draw us to seek our own promotion or advantage by the injury of our fellow-creatures. And if the principles of humanity are capable, in many instances, of influencing our actions, they must, at all times, have *some* authority over our sentiments, and give us a general approbation of what is useful to society, and blame of what is dangerous or pernicious. The degrees of these sentiments may be the subject of controversy; but the reality of their existence, one should think, must be admitted in every theory or system.

A creature, absolutely malicious and spiteful, were there any such in nature, must be worse than indifferent to the images of vice and virtue. All his sentiments must be inverted, and directly opposite to those, which prevail in the human species. Whatever contributes to the good of mankind, as it crosses the constant bent of his wishes and desires, must produce uneasiness and disapprobation; and on the contrary, whatever is the source of disorder and misery in society, must, for the same reason, be regarded with pleasure and complacency. Timon, who probably from his affected spleen more than any inveterate malice, was denominated the manhater, embraced Alcibiades with great fondness. *Go on my boy!* cried he, *acquire the confidence of the people: You will one day, I foresee, be the cause of great calamities to them.*[7] Could we

[7] Plutarch *in vita Alc.*

admit the two principles of the Manicheans, it is an infallible consequence, that their sentiments of human actions, as well as of everything else, must be totally opposite, and that every instance of justice and humanity, from its necessary tendency, must please the one deity and displease the other. All mankind so far resemble the good principle, that, where interest or revenge or envy perverts not our disposition, we are always inclined, from our natural philanthropy, to give the preference to the happiness of society, and consequently to virtue above its opposite. Absolute, unprovoked, disinterested malice has never perhaps place in any human breast; or if it had, must there pervert all the sentiments of morals, as well as the feelings of humanity. If the cruelty of Nero be allowed entirely voluntary, and not rather the effect of constant fear and resentment; it is evident that Tigellinus, preferably to Seneca or Burrhus, must have possessed his steady and uniform approbation.

A statesman or patriot, who serves our own country in our own time, has always a more passionate regard paid to him, than one whose beneficial influence operated on distant ages or remote nations; where the good, resulting from his generous humanity, being less connected with us, seems more obscure, and affects us with a less lively sympathy. We may own the merit to be equally great, though our sentiments are not raised to an equal height, in both cases. The judgement here corrects the inequalities of our internal emotions and perceptions; in like manner, as it preserves us from error, in the several variations of images, presented to our external senses. The same object, at a double distance, really throws on the eye a picture of but half the bulk; yet we imagine that it appears of the same size in both situations; because we know that on our approach to it, its image would expand on the eye, and that the difference consists not in the object itself, but in our position with regard to it. And, indeed, without such a correction of appearances, both in internal and external sentiment, men could never think or talk steadily on any subject; while their fluctuating situations produce a continual variation on objects, and throw them into such different and contrary lights and positions.[8]

The more we converse with mankind, and the greater social intercourse we maintain, the more shall we be familiarized to these general preferences and distinctions, without which our conversation and discourse could scarcely be rendered intelligible to each other. Every man's interest is peculiar to himself, and the aversions and desires, which result from it, cannot be supposed to affect others in a like degree. General language, therefore, being formed for general use, must be moulded on some more general views, and must affix the epithets of praise or blame, in conformity to sentiments, which arise from the general interests of the community. And if these sentiments, in most men, be not so strong as those, which have a reference to private good; yet still they must make some distinction, even in persons the most depraved and selfish; and must attach the notion of good to a beneficent conduct, and of evil to the contrary. Sympathy, we shall allow, is much fainter than our concern for ourselves, and sympathy with persons remote from us much fainter than that with persons near and contiguous; but for this very reason it is necessary for us, in our calm judgements and discourse concerning the characters of men, to neglect all these differences, and render our sentiments more public and social. Besides, that we ourselves often change our situation in this particular, we every day meet with persons who are in a situation different

[8] For a like reason, the tendencies of actions and characters, not their real accidental consequences, are alone regarded in our moral determinations or general judgements; though in our real feeling or sentiment, we cannot help paying greater regard to one whose station, joined to virtue, renders him really useful to society, than to one, who exerts the social virtues only in good intentions and benevolent affections. Separating the character from the fortune, by an easy and necessary effort of thought, we pronounce these persons alike, and give them the same general praise. The judgement corrects or endeavours to correct the appearance: But is not able entirely to prevail over sentiment.

Why is this peach-tree said to be better than that other; but because it produces more or better fruit? And would not the same praise be given it, though snails or vermin had destroyed the peaches, before they came to full maturity? In morals too, is not *the tree known by the fruit?* And cannot we easily distinguish between nature and accident, in the one case as well as in the other?

from us, and who could never converse with us were we to remain constantly in that position and point of view, which is peculiar to ourselves. The intercourse of sentiments, therefore, in society and conversation, makes us form some general unalterable standard, by which we may approve or disapprove of characters and manners. And though the heart takes not part entirely with those general notions, nor regulates all its love and hatred by the universal abstract differences of vice and virtue, without regard to self, or the persons with whom we are more intimately connected; yet have these moral differences a considerable influence, and being sufficient, at least for discourse, serve all our purposes in company, in the pulpit, on the theatre, and in the schools.[9]

Thus, in whatever light we take this subject, the merit, ascribed to the social virtues, appears still uniform, and arises chiefly from that regard, which the natural sentiment of benevolence engages us to pay to the interests of mankind and society. If we consider the principles of the human make, such as they appear to daily experience and observation, we must, *a priori*, conclude it impossible for such a creature as man to be totally indifferent to the well or ill-being of his fellow-creatures, and not readily, of himself, to pronounce, where nothing gives him any particular bias, that what promotes their happiness is good, what tends to their misery is evil, without any farther regard or consideration. Here then are the faint rudiments, at least, or outlines, of a *general* distinction between actions; and in proportion as the humanity of the person is supposed to encrease, his connexion with those who are injured or benefited, and his lively conception of their misery or happiness; his consequent censure or approbation acquires proportionable vigour. There is no necessity,

[9] It is wisely ordained by nature, that private connexions should commonly prevail over universal views and considerations; otherwise our affections and actions would be dissipated and lost, for want of a proper limited object. Thus a small benefit done to ourselves, or our near friends, excites more lively sentiments of love and approbation than a great benefit done to a distant commonwealth: But still we know here, as in all the senses, to correct these inequalities by reflection, and retain a general standard of vice and virtue, founded chiefly on general usefulness.

that a generous action, barely mentioned in an old history or remote gazette, should communicate any strong feelings of applause and admiration. Virtue, placed at such a distance, is like a fixed star, which, though to the eye of reason it may appear as luminous as the sun in his meridian, is so infinitely removed as to affect the senses, neither with light nor heat. Bring this virtue nearer, by our acquaintance or connexion with the persons, or even by an eloquent recital of the case; our hearts are immediately caught, our sympathy enlivened, and our cool approbation converted into the warmest sentiments of friendship and regard. These seem necessary and infallible consequences of the general principles of human nature, as discovered in common life and practice.

Again; reverse these views and reasonings: Consider the matter *a posteriori*; and weighing the consequences, enquire if the merit of social virtue be not, in a great measure, derived from the feelings of humanity, with which it affects the spectators. It appears to be matter of fact, that the circumstance of *utility*, in all subjects, is a source of praise and approbation: That it is constantly appealed to in all moral decisions concerning the merit and demerit of actions: That it is the *sole* source of that high regard paid to justice, fidelity, honour, allegiance, and chastity: That it is inseparable from all the other social virtues, humanity, generosity, charity, affability, lenity, mercy, and moderation: And, in a word, that it is a foundation of the chief part of morals, which has a reference to mankind and our fellow-creatures.

It appears also, that, in our general approbation of characters and manners, the useful tendency of the social virtues moves us not by any regards to self-interest, but has an influence much more universal and extensive. It appears that a tendency to public good, and to the promoting of peace, harmony, and order in society, does always, by affecting the benevolent principles of our frame, engage us on the side of the social virtues. And it appears, as an additional confirmation, that these principles of humanity and sympathy enter so deeply into all our sentiments, and have so powerful an influence, as may enable them to excite the strongest censure and applause. The present theory is the simple result of all these inferences, each of which seems founded on uniform experience and observation.

Were it doubtful, whether there were any such principle in our nature as humanity or a concern for others, yet when we see, in numberless instances, that whatever has a tendency to promote the interests of society, is so highly approved of, we ought thence to learn the force of the benevolent principle; since it is impossible for anything to please as means to an end, where the end is totally indifferent. On the other hand, were it doubtful, whether there were, implanted in our nature, any general principle of moral blame and approbation, yet when we see, in numberless instances, the influence of humanity, we ought thence to conclude, that it is impossible, but that everything which promotes the interest of society must communicate pleasure, and what is pernicious give uneasiness. But when these different reflections and observations concur in establishing the same conclusion, must they not bestow an undisputed evidence upon it?

It is however hoped, that the progress of this argument will bring a farther confirmation of the present theory, by showing the rise of other sentiments of esteem and regard from the same or like principles.

# Section VI

## Of Qualities Useful to Ourselves

### Part I

It seems evident, that where a quality or habit is subjected to our examination, if it appear in any respect prejudicial to the person possessed of it, or such as incapacitates him for business and action, it is instantly blamed, and ranked among his faults and imperfections. Indolence, negligence, want of order and method, obstinacy, fickleness, rashness, credulity; these qualities were never esteemed by any one indifferent to a character; much less, extolled as accomplishments or virtues. The prejudice, resulting from them, immediately strikes our eye, and gives us the sentiment of pain and disapprobation.

No quality, it is allowed, is absolutely either blameable or praise-worthy. It is all according to its degree. A due medium, says the Peripatetics, is the characteristic of virtue. But this medium is chiefly determined by utility. A proper celerity, for instance, and dispatch in business, is commendable. When defective, no progress is ever made in the execution of any purpose: When excessive, it engages us in precipitate and ill-concerted measures and enterprises: By such reasonings, we fix the proper and commendable mediocrity in all moral and prudential disquisitions; and never lose view of the advantages, which result from any character or habit.

Now as these advantages are enjoyed by the person possessed of the character, it can never be *self-love* which renders the prospect of them agreeable to us, the spectators, and prompts our esteem and approbation. No force of imagination can convert us into another person, and make us fancy, that we, being that person, reap benefit from those valuable qualities, which belong to him. Or if it did, no celerity of imagination could immediately transport us back, into ourselves, and make us love and esteem the person, as different from us. Views and sentiments, so opposite to known truth and to each other, could never have place, at the same time, in the same person. All suspicion, therefore, of selfish regards, is here totally excluded. It is a quite different principle, which actuates our bosom, and interests us in the felicity of the person whom we contemplate. Where his natural talents and acquired abilities give us the prospect of elevation, advancement, a figure in life, prosperous success, a steady command over fortune, and the execution of great or advantageous undertakings; we are struck with such agreeable images, and feel a complacency and regard immediately arise towards him. The ideas of happiness, joy, triumph, prosperity, are connected with every circumstance of his character, and diffuse over our minds a pleasing sentiment of sympathy and humanity.[1]

Let us suppose a person originally framed so as to have no manner of concern for his fellow-creatures, but to regard the happiness and misery of all sensible beings with greater indifference than even two contiguous shades of the same colour. Let us suppose, if the prosperity of nations were laid on the one hand, and their ruin on the other, and he were desired to choose; that he would stand like the schoolman's ass, irresolute and undetermined, between equal motives; or rather, like the same ass between two pieces of wood or marble, without any inclination or propensity to either side.

[1] One may venture to affirm, that there is no human creature, to whom the appearance of happiness (where envy or revenge has no place) does not give pleasure, that of misery, uneasiness. This seems inseparable from our make and constitution. But they are only the more generous minds, that are thence prompted to seek zealously the good of others, and to have a real passion for their welfare. With men of narrow and ungenerous spirits, this sympathy goes not beyond a slight feeling of the imagination, which serves only to excite sentiments of complacency or censure, and makes them apply to the object either honourable or dishonourable appellations. A griping miser, for instance, praises extremely *industry* and *frugality* even in others, and sets them, in his estimation, above all the other virtues. He knows the good that results from them, and feels that species of happiness with a more lively sympathy, than any other you could represent to him; though perhaps he would not part with a shilling to make the fortune of the industrious man, whom he praises so highly.

The consequence, I believe, must be allowed just, that such a person, being absolutely unconcerned, either for the public good of a community or the private utility of others, would look on every quality, however pernicious, or however beneficial, to society, or to its possessor, with the same indifference as on the most common and uninteresting object.

But if, instead of this fancied monster, we suppose a *man* to form a judgement or determination in the case, there is to him a plain foundation of preference, where everything else is equal; and however cool his choice may be, if his heart be selfish, or if the persons interested be remote from him; there must still be a choice or distinction between what is useful, and what is pernicious. Now this distinction is the same in all its parts, with the *moral distinction*, whose foundation has been so often, and so much in vain, enquired after. The same endowments of the mind, in every circumstance, are agreeable to the sentiment of morals and to that of humanity; the same temper is susceptible of high degrees of the one sentiment and of the other; and the same alteration in the objects, by their nearer approach or by connexions, enlivens the one and the other. By all the rules of philosophy, therefore, we must conclude, that these sentiments are originally the same; since, in each particular, even the most minute, they are governed by the same laws, and are moved by the same objects.

Why do philosophers infer, with the greatest certainty, that the moon is kept in its orbit by the same force of gravity, that makes bodies fall near the surface of the earth, but because these effects are, upon computation, found similar and equal? And must not this argument bring as strong conviction, in moral as in natural disquisitions?

To prove, by any long detail, that all the qualities, useful to the possessor, are approved of, and the contrary censured, would be superfluous. The least reflection on what is every day experienced in life, will be sufficient. We shall only mention a few instances, in order to remove, if possible, all doubt and hesitation.

The quality, the most necessary for the execution of any useful enterprise, is discretion; by which we carry on a safe intercourse with others, give due attention to our own and to their character, weigh each circumstance of the business which we undertake, and employ the surest and safest means for the attainment of any end or purpose. To a Cromwell, perhaps, or a De Retz, discretion may appear an alderman-like virtue, as Dr. Swift calls it; and being incompatible with those vast designs, to which their courage and ambition prompted them, it might really, in them, be a fault or imperfection. But in the conduct of ordinary life, no virtue is more requisite, not only to obtain success, but to avoid the most fatal miscarriages and disappointments. The greatest parts without it, as observed by an elegant writer, may be fatal to their owner; as Polyphemus, deprived of his eye, was only the more exposed, on account of his enormous strength and stature.

The best character, indeed, were it not rather too perfect for human nature, is that which is not swayed by temper of any kind; but alternately employs enterprise and caution, as each is *useful* to the particular purpose intended. Such is the excellence which St. Evremond ascribes to Mareschal Turenne, who displayed every campaign, as he grew older, more temerity in his military enterprises; and being now, from long experience, perfectly acquainted with every incident in war, he advanced with greater firmness and security, in a road so well known to him. Fabius, says Machiavel, was cautious; Scipio enterprising: And both succeeded, because the situation of the Roman affairs, during the command of each, was peculiarly adapted to his genius; but both would have failed, had these situations been reversed. He is happy, whose circumstances suit his temper; but he is more excellent, who can suit his temper to any circumstances.

What need is there to display the praises of industry, and to extol its advantages, in the acquisition of power and riches, or in raising what we call a *fortune* in the world? The tortoise, according to the fable, by his perseverance, gained the race of the hare, though possessed of much superior swiftness. A man's time, when well husbanded, is like a cultivated field, of which a few acres produce more of what is useful to life, than extensive provinces, even of the richest soil, when over-run with weeds and brambles.

But all prospect of success in life, or even of tolerable subsistence, must fail, where a reasonable frugality is wanting. The heap, instead of encreasing, diminishes daily, and leaves its possessor so much more unhappy, as, not having been able to confine his expences to a large revenue, he will still less be able to live contentedly on a small one. The souls of men, according to Plato,[2] inflamed with impure appetites, and losing the body, which alone afforded means of satisfaction, hover about the earth, and haunt the places, where their bodies are deposited; possessed with a longing desire to recover the lost organs of sensation. So may we see worthless prodigals, having consumed their fortune in wild debauches, thrusting themselves into every plentiful table, and every party of pleasure, hated even by the vicious, and despised even by fools.

The one extreme of frugality is *avarice*, which, as it both deprives a man of all use of his riches, and checks hospitality and every social enjoyment, is justly censured on a double account. *Prodigality*, the other extreme, is commonly more hurtful to a man himself; and each of these extremes is blamed above the other, according to the temper of the person who censures, and according to his greater or less sensibility to pleasure, either social or sensual.

Qualities often derive their merit from complicated sources. *Honesty, fidelity, truth*, are praised for their immediate tendency to promote the interests of society; but after those virtues are once established upon this foundation, they are also considered as advantageous to the person himself, and as the source of that trust and confidence, which can alone give a man any consideration in life. One becomes contemptible, no less than odious, when he forgets the duty, which, in this particular, he owes to himself as well as to society.

Perhaps, this consideration is one *chief* source of the high blame, which is thrown on any instance of failure among

[2] *Phaedo.*

women in point of *chastity*. The greatest regard, which can be acquired by that sex, is derived from their fidelity; and a woman becomes cheap and vulgar, loses her rank, and is exposed to every insult, who is deficient in this particular. The smallest failure is here sufficient to blast her character. A female has so many opportunities of secretly indulging these appetites, that nothing can give us security but her absolute modesty and reserve; and where a breach is once made, it can scarcely ever be fully repaired. If a man behave with cowardice on one occasion, a contrary conduct reinstates him in his character. But by what action can a woman, whose behaviour has once been dissolute, be able to assure us, that she has formed better resolutions, and has self-command enough to carry them into execution?

All men, it is allowed, are equally desirous of happiness; but few are successful in the pursuit: One considerable cause is the want of strength of mind, which might enable them to resist the temptation of present ease or pleasure, and carry them forward in the search of more distant profit and enjoyment. Our affections, on a general prospect of their objects, form certain rules of conduct, and certain measures of preference of one above another: and these decisions, though really the result of our calm passions and propensities, (for what else can pronounce any object eligible or the contrary?) are yet said, by a natural abuse of terms, to be the determinations of pure *reason* and reflection. But when some of these objects approach nearer to us, or acquire the advantages of favourable lights and positions, which catch the heart or imagination; our general resolutions are frequently confounded, a small enjoyment preferred, and lasting shame and sorrow entailed upon us. And however poets may employ their wit and eloquence, in celebrating present pleasure, and rejecting all distant views to fame, health, or fortune; it is obvious, that this practice is the source of all dissoluteness and disorder, repentance and misery. A man of a strong and determined temper adheres tenaciously to his general resolutions, and is neither seduced by the allurements of pleasure, nor terrified by the menaces of pain; but keeps still in view those distant pursuits, by which he, at once, ensures his happiness and his honour.

Self-satisfaction, at least in some degree, is an advantage, which equally attends the fool and the wise man: But it is the only one; nor is there any other circumstance in the conduct of life, where they are upon an equal footing. Business, books, conversation; for all of these, a fool is totally incapacitated, and except condemned by his station to the coarsest drudgery, remains a *useless* burthen upon the earth. Accordingly, it is found, that men are extremely jealous of their character in this particular; and many instances are seen of profligacy and treachery, the most avowed and unreserved; none of bearing patiently the imputation of ignorance and stupidity. Dicaearchus, the Macedonian general, who, as Polybius tells us,[3] openly erected one altar to impiety, another to injustice, in order to bid defiance to mankind; even he, I am well assured, would have started at the epithet of *fool*, and have meditated revenge for so injurious an appellation. Except the affection of parents, the strongest and most indissoluble bond in nature, no connexion has strength sufficient to support the disgust arising from this character. Love itself, which can subsist under treachery, ingratitude, malice, and infidelity, is immediately extinguished by it, when perceived and acknowledged; nor are deformity and old age more fatal to the dominion of that passion. So dreadful are the ideas of an utter incapacity for any purpose or undertaking, and of continued error and misconduct in life!

When it is asked, whether a quick or a slow apprehension be most valuable? Whether one, that, at first view, penetrates far into a subject, but can perform nothing upon study; or a contrary character, which must work out everything by dint of application? Whether a clear head or a copious invention? Whether a profound genius or a sure judgement? In short, what character, or peculiar turn of understanding, is more excellent than another? It is evident, that we can answer none of these questions, without considering which of

[3] Lib. xvii. cap. 35.

those qualities capacitates a man best for the world, and carries him farthest in any undertaking.

If refined sense and exalted sense be not so *useful* as common sense, their rarity, their novelty, and the nobleness of their objects make some compensation, and render them the admiration of mankind: As gold, though less serviceable than iron, acquires from its scarcity a value which is much superior.

The defects of judgement can be supplied by no art or invention; but those of memory frequently may, both in business and in study, by method and industry, and by diligence in committing everything to writing; and we scarcely ever hear a short memory given as a reason for a man's failure in any undertaking. But in ancient times, when no man could make a figure without the talent of speaking, and when the audience were too delicate to bear such crude, undigested harangues as our extemporary orators offer to public assemblies; the faculty of memory was then of the utmost consequence, and was accordingly much more valued than at present. Scarce any great genius is mentioned in antiquity, who is not celebrated for this talent; and Cicero enumerates it among the other sublime qualities of Caesar himself.[4]

Particular customs and manners alter the usefulness of qualities: they also alter their merit. Particular situations and accidents have, in some degree, the same influence. He will always be more esteemed, who possesses those talents and accomplishments, which suit his station and profession, than he whom fortune has misplaced in the part which she has assigned him. The private or selfish virtues are, in this respect, more arbitrary than the public and social. In other respects they are, perhaps, less liable to doubt and controversy.

In this kingdom, such continued ostentation, of late years, has prevailed among men in *active* life with regard to *public spirit*, and among those in *speculative* with regard to *benevolence*; and so many false pretensions to each have been, no doubt, detected, that men of the world are apt, without any bad intention, to discover a sullen incredulity on the head of

---

[4] Fuit in illo ingenium, ratio, memoria, literae, cura, cogitatio, diligentia, &c. Philip. 2.

those moral endowments, and even sometimes absolutely to deny their existence and reality. In like manner I find, that, of old, the perpetual cant of the *Stoics* and *Cynics* concerning *virtue*, their magnificent professions and slender performances, bred a disgust in mankind; and Lucian, who, though licentious with regard to pleasure, is yet in other respects a very moral writer, cannot sometimes talk of virtue, so much boasted, without betraying symptoms of spleen and irony.[5] But surely this peevish delicacy, whence-ever it arises, can never be carried so far as to make us deny the existence of every species of merit, and all distinction of manners and behaviour. Besides *discretion, caution, enterprise, industry, assiduity, frugality, economy, good-sense, prudence, discernment*; besides these endowments, I say, whose very names force an avowal of their merit, there are many others, to which the most determined scepticism cannot for a moment refuse the tribute of praise and approbation. *Temperance, sobriety, patience, constancy, perseverance, forethought, considerateness, secrecy, order, insinuation, address, presence of mind, quickness of conception, facility of expression*; these, and a thousand more of the same kind, no man will ever deny to be excellencies and perfections. As their merit consists in their tendency to serve the person, possessed of them, without any magnificent claim to public and social desert, we are the less jealous of their pretensions, and readily admit them into the catalogue of laudable qualities. We are not sensible that, by this concession, we have paved the way for all the other moral excellencies, and cannot consistently hesitate any longer, with regard to disinterested benevolence, patriotism, and humanity.

It seems, indeed, certain, that first appearances are here, as usual, extremely deceitful, and that it is more difficult, in a speculative way, to resolve into self-love the merit which we ascribe to the selfish virtues above mentioned, than that even of the social virtues, justice and beneficence. For this

---

[5] Ἀρετήν τινα, καὶ ἀσώματα, καὶ λήρους μεγάλη τῇ φωνῇ ξυνειρόντων. Luc. Timon. 9. Again, Καὶ συναγαγόντες (οἱ φιλόσοφοι) εὐεξαπάτητα μειράκια τήν τε πολυθρύλητον ἀρετὴν τραγῳδοῦσι. Icaro-men. In another place, Ἡ ποῦ γὰρ ἐστιν ἡ πολυθρύλητος ἀρετή, καὶ φύσις, καὶ εἱμαρμένη, καὶ τύχη, ἀνυπόστατα καὶ κενὰ πραγμάτων ὀνόματα; Deor. Concil. 13.

latter purpose, we need but say, that whatever conduct promotes the good of the community is loved, praised, and esteemed by the community, on account of that utility and
interest, of which every one partakes; and though this affection and regard be, in reality, gratitude, not self-love, yet a
distinction, even of this obvious nature, may not readily be
made by superficial reasoners; and there is room, at least, to
support the cavil and dispute for a moment. But as qualities,
which tend only to the utility of their possessor, without any
reference to us, or to the community, are yet esteemed and
valued; by what theory or system can we account for this
sentiment from self-love, or deduce it from that favourite
origin? There seems here a necessity for confessing that the
happiness and misery of others are not spectacles entirely
indifferent to us; but that the view of the former, whether in
its causes or effects, like sunshine or the prospect of well-
cultivated plains (to carry our pretensions no higher), communicates a secret joy and satisfaction; the appearance of the
latter, like a lowering cloud or barren landscape, throws a
melancholy damp over the imagination. And this concession
being once made, the difficulty is over; and a natural unforced
interpretation of the phenomena of human life will afterwards, we may hope, prevail among all speculative enquirers.

## Part II

It may not be improper, in this place, to examine the
influence of bodily endowments, and of the goods of fortune,
over our sentiments of regard and esteem, and to consider
whether these phenomena fortify or weaken the present theory.
It will naturally be expected, that the beauty of the body, as is
supposed by all ancient moralists, will be similar, in some respects, to that of the mind; and that every kind of esteem,
which is paid to a man, will have something similar in its
origin, whether it arise from his mental endowments, or from
the situation of his exterior circumstances.

It is evident, that one considerable source of *beauty* in all
animals is the advantage which they reap from the particular
structure of their limbs and members, suitably to the particu-

lar manner of life, to which they are by nature destined. The just proportions of a horse, described by Xenophon and Virgil, are the same that are received at this day by our modern jockeys; because the foundation of them is the same, namely, experience of what is detrimental or useful in the animal.

Broad shoulders, a lank belly, firm joints, taper legs; all these are beautiful in our species, because signs of force and vigour. Ideas of utility and its contrary, though they do not entirely determine what is handsome or deformed, are evidently the source of a considerable part of approbation or dislike.

In ancient times, bodily strength and dexterity, being of greater *use* and importance in war, was also much more esteemed and valued, than at present. Not to insist on Homer and the poets, we may observe, that historians scruple not to mention *force of body* among the other accomplishments even of Epaminondas, whom they acknowledge to be the greatest hero, statesman, and general of all the Greeks.[6] A like praise is given to Pompey, one of the greatest of the Romans.[7] This instance is similar to what we observed above with regard to memory.

What derision and contempt, with both sexes, attend *impotence*; while the unhappy object is regarded as one deprived of so capital a pleasure in life, and at the same time, as disabled from communicating it to others. *Barrenness* in women, being also a species of *inutility*, is a reproach, but not in the same degree: of which the reason is very obvious, according to the present theory.

There is no rule in painting or statuary more indispensible than that of balancing the figures, and placing them with the

[6] *Cum alacribus, saltu; cum velocibus, cursu; cum validis recte certabat.* Sallust apud Veget.

[7] Diodorus Siculus, lib. xv. It may not be improper to give the character of Epaminondas, as drawn by the historian, in order to show the ideas of perfect merit, which prevailed in those ages. In other illustrious men, says he, you will observe, that each possessed some one shining quality, which was the foundation of his fame: In Epaminondas all the *virtues* are found united; force of body, eloquence of expression, vigour of mind, contempt of riches, gentleness of disposition, and *what is chiefly to be regarded*, courage and conduct in war.

greatest exactness on their proper centre of gravity. A figure, which is not justly balanced, is ugly; because it conveys the disagreeable ideas of fall, harm, and pain.[8]

A disposition or turn of mind, which qualifies a man to rise in the world and advance his fortune, is entitled to esteem and regard, as has already been explained. It may, therefore, naturally be supposed, that the actual possession of riches and authority will have a considerable influence over these sentiments.

Let us examine any hypothesis by which we can account for the regard paid to the rich and powerful; we shall find none satisfactory, but that which derives it from the enjoyment communicated to the spectator by the images of prosperity, happiness, ease, plenty, authority, and the gratification of every appetite. Self-love, for instance, which some affect so much to consider as the source of every sentiment, is plainly insufficient for this purpose. Where no good-will or friendship appears, it is difficult to conceive on what we can found our hope of advantage from the riches of others; though we naturally respect the rich, even before they discover any such favourable disposition towards us.

We are affected with the same sentiments, when we lie so much out of the sphere of their activity, that they cannot even be supposed to possess the power of serving us. A prisoner of war, in all civilized nations, is treated with a regard suited to his condition; and riches, it is evident, go far towards fixing the condition of any person. If birth and quality enter

[8] All men are equally liable to pain and disease and sickness; and may again recover health and ease. These circumstances, as they make no distinction between one man and another, are no source of pride or humility, regard or contempt. But comparing our own species to superior ones, it is a very mortifying consideration, that we should all be so liable to diseases and infirmities; and divines accordingly employ this topic, in order to depress self-conceit and vanity. They would have more success, if the common bent of our thoughts were not perpetually turned to compare ourselves with others. The infirmities of old age are mortifying; because a comparison with the young may take place. The king's evil is industriously concealed, because it affects others, and is often transmitted to posterity. The case is nearly the same with such diseases as convey any nauseous or frightful images; the epilepsy, for instance, ulcers, sores, scabs, &c.

for a share, this still affords us an argument to our present purpose. For what is it we call a man of birth, but one who is descended from a long succession of rich and powerful ancestors, and who acquires our esteem by his connexion with persons whom we esteem? His ancestors, therefore, though dead, are respected, in some measure, on account of their riches; and consequently, without any kind of expectation.

But not to go so far as prisoners of war or the dead, to find instances of this disinterested regard for riches; we may only observe, with a little attention, those phenomena which occur in common life and conversation. A man, who is himself, we shall suppose, of a competent fortune, and of no profession, being introduced to a company of strangers, naturally treats them with different degrees of respect, as he is informed of their different fortunes and conditions; though it is impossible that he can so suddenly propose, and perhaps he would not accept of, any pecuniary advantage from them. A traveller is always admitted into company, and meets with civility, in proportion as his train and equipage speak him a man of great or moderate fortune. In short, the different ranks of men are, in a great measure, regulated by riches; and that with regard to superiors as well as inferiors, strangers as well as acquaintance.

What remains, therefore, but to conclude, that, as riches are desired for ourselves only as the means of gratifying our appetites, either at present or in some imaginary future period, they beget esteem in others merely from their having that influence. This indeed is their very nature or offence: they have a direct reference to the commodities, conveniencies, and pleasures of life. The bill of a banker, who is broke, or gold in a desert island, would otherwise be full as valuable. When we approach a man who is, as we say, at his ease, we are presented with the pleasing ideas of plenty, satisfaction, cleanliness, warmth; a cheerful house, elegant furniture, ready service, and whatever is desirable in meat, drink, or apparel. On the contrary, when a poor man appears, the disagreeable images of want, penury, hard labour, dirty furniture, coarse or ragged clothes, nauseous meat and distasteful liquor, im-

mediately strike our fancy. What else do we mean by saying
that one is rich, the other poor? And as regard or contempt
is the natural consequence of those different situations in life,
it is easily seen what additional light and evidence this throws
on our preceding theory, with regard to all moral distinctions.[9]

A man who has cured himself of all ridiculous prepossessions, and is fully, sincerely, and steadily convinced, from
experience as well as philosophy, that the difference of fortune
makes less difference in happiness than is vulgarly imagined;
such a one does not measure out degrees of esteem according
to the rent-rolls of his acquaintance. He may, indeed, externally pay a superior deference to the great lord above the
vassal; because riches are the most convenient, being the most
fixed and determinate, source of distinction. But his internal
sentiments are more regulated by the personal characters of
men, than by the accidental and capricious favours of fortune.

In most countries of Europe, family, that is, hereditary
riches, marked with titles and symbols from the sovereign,
is the chief source of distinction. In England, more regard
is paid to present opulence and plenty. Each practice has its
advantages and disadvantages. Where birth is respected, unactive, spiritless minds remain in haughty indolence, and
dream of nothing but pedigrees and genealogies: the generous
and ambitious seek honour and authority, and reputation and
favour. Where riches are the chief idol, corruption, venality,
rapine prevail: arts, manufactures, commerce, agriculture

[9] There is something extraordinary, and seemingly unaccountable in
the operation of our passions, when we consider the fortune and situation of others. Very often another's advancement and prosperity
produces envy, which has a strong mixture of hatred, and arises chiefly
from the comparison of ourselves with the person. At the very same
time, or at least in very short intervals, we may feel the passion of
respect, which is a species of affection or good-will, with a mixture of
humility. On the other hand, the misfortunes of our fellows often
cause pity, which has in it a strong mixture of good-will. This sentiment
of pity is nearly allied to contempt, which is a species of dislike, with
a mixture of pride. I only point out these phenomena, as a subject of
speculation to such as are curious with regard to moral enquiries. It is
sufficient for the present purpose to observe in general, that power and
riches commonly cause respect, poverty and meanness contempt, though
particular views and incidents may sometimes raise the passions of
envy and of pity.

flourish. The former prejudice, being favourable to military virtue, is more suited to monarchies. The latter, being the chief spur to industry, agrees better with a republican government. And we accordingly find that each of these forms of government, by varying the *utility* of those customs, has commonly a proportionable effect on the sentiments of mankind.

# Section VII

## Of Qualities Immediately Agreeable to Ourselves

Whoever has passed an evening with serious melancholy people, and has observed how suddenly the conversation was animated, and what sprightliness diffused itself over the countenance, discourse, and behaviour of every one, on the accession of a good-humoured, lively companion; such a one will easily allow that cheerfulness carries great merit with it, and naturally conciliates the good-will of mankind. No quality, indeed, more readily communicates itself to all around; because no one has a greater propensity to display itself, in jovial talk and pleasant entertainment. The flame spreads through the whole circle; and the most sullen and morose are often caught by it. That the melancholy hate the merry, even though Horace says it, I have some difficulty to allow; because I have always observed that, where the jollity is moderate and decent, serious people are so much the more delighted, as it dissipates the gloom with which they are commonly oppressed, and gives them an unusual enjoyment.

From this influence of cheerfulness, both to communicate itself and to engage approbation, we may perceive that there is another set of mental qualities, which, without any utility or any tendency to farther good, either of the community or of the possessor, diffuse a satisfaction on the beholders, and procure friendship and regard. Their immediate sensation, to the person possessed of them, is agreeable. Others enter into the same humour, and catch the sentiment, by a contagion or natural sympathy; and as we cannot forbear loving whatever pleases, a kindly emotion arises towards the person who communicates so much satisfaction. He is a more animating spectacle; his presence diffuses over us more serene complacency and enjoyment; our imagination, entering into his feelings and disposition, is affected in a more agreeable manner than if a melancholy, dejected, sullen, anxious temper were presented to us. Hence the affection and probation which attend the former: the aversion and disgust, with which we regard the latter.[1]

Few men would envy the character which Caesar gives of Cassius:

> He loves no play,
> As thou do'st, Anthony: he hears no music:
> Seldom he smiles; and smiles in such a sort,
> As if he mock'd himself, and scorn'd his spirit
> That could be mov'd to smile at any thing.

Not only such men, as Caesar adds, are commonly *dangerous*, but also, having little enjoyment within themselves, they can never become agreeable to others, or contribute to social entertainment. In all polite nations and ages, a relish for pleasure, if accompanied with temperance and decency, is esteemed a considerable merit, even in the greatest men; and becomes still more requisite in those of inferior rank and character. It is an agreeable representation, which a French writer gives of the situation of his own mind in this particular, *Virtue I love*, says he, *without austerity: Pleasure without effeminacy: And life, without fearing its end.*[2]

Who is not struck with any signal instance of greatness of mind or dignity of character; with elevation of sentiment, disdain of slavery, and with that noble pride and spirit, which arises from conscious virtue? The sublime, says Longinus, is often nothing but the echo or image of magnanimity;

---

[1] There is no man, who, on particular occasions, is not affected with all the disagreeable passions, fear, anger, dejection, grief, melancholy, anxiety, &c. But these, so far as they are natural, and universal, make no difference between one man and another, and can never be the object of blame. It is only when the disposition gives a *propensity* to any of these disagreeable passions, that they disfigure the character, and by giving uneasiness, convey the sentiment of disapprobation to the spectator.

[2] "J'aime la vertu, sans rudesse;
J'aime le plaisir, sans molesse;
J'aime la vie, et n'en crains point la fin."—*St. Evremond.*

and where this quality appears in any one, even though a syllable be not uttered, it excites our applause and admiration; as may be observed of the famous silence of Ajax in the Odyssey, which expresses more noble disdain and resolute indignation than any language can convey.[3]

*Were I* Alexander, said Parmenio, *I would accept of these offers made by* Darius. *So would I too*, replied Alexander, *were I* Parmenio. This saying is admirable, says Longinus, from a like principle.[4]

*Go!* cries the same hero to his soldiers, when they refused to follow him to the Indies, *go tell your countrymen, that you left* Alexander *completing the conquest of the world.* "Alexander," said the Prince of Condé, who always admired this passage, "abandoned by his soldiers, among barbarians, not yet fully subdued, felt in himself such a dignity and right of empire, that he could not believe it possible that any one would refuse to obey him. Whether in Europe or in Asia, among Greeks or Persians, all was indifferent to him: wherever he found men, he fancied he should find subjects."

The confidant of Medea in the tragedy recommends caution and submission; and enumerating all the distresses of that unfortunate heroine, asks her, what she has to support her against her numerous and implacable enemies. *Myself*, replies she; *Myself I say, and it is enough.* Boileau justly recommends this passage as an instance of true sublime.[5]

When Phocion, the modest, the gentle Phocion, was led to execution, he turned to one of his fellow-sufferers, who was lamenting his own hard fate, *Is it not glory enough for you*, says he, *that you die with* Phocion?[6]

Place in opposition the picture which Tacitus draws of Vitellius, fallen from empire, prolonging his ignominy from a wretched love of life, delivered over to the merciless rabble; tossed, buffeted, and kicked about; constrained, by their holding a poinard under his chin, to raise his head, and expose

[3] Cap. 9.
[4] Idem.
[5] Réflexion 10 sur Longin.
[6] Plutarch in Phoc.

himself to every contumely. What abject infamy! What low humilation! Yet even here, says the historian, he discovered some symptoms of a mind not wholly degenerate. To a tribune, who insulted him, he replied, *I am still your emperor*.[7]

We never excuse the absolute want of spirit and dignity of character, or a proper sense of what is due to one's self, in society and the common intercourse of life. This vice constitutes what we properly call *meanness*; when a man can submit to the basest slavery, in order to gain his ends; fawn upon those who abuse him; and degrade himself by intimacies and familiarities with undeserving inferiors. A certain degree of generous pride or self-value is so requisite, that the absence of it in the mind displeases, after the same manner as the want of a nose, eye, or any of the most material feature of the face or member of the body.[8]

The utility of courage, both to the public and to the person possessed of it, is an obvious foundation of merit. But to any one who duly considers of the matter, it will appear that this quality has a peculiar lustre, which it derives wholly from itself, and from that noble elevation inseparable from it. Its figure, drawn by painters and by poets, displays, in each feature, a sublimity and daring confidence; which catches the eye, engages the affections, and diffuses, by sympathy, a like sublimity of sentiment over every spectator.

[7] Tacit. hist. lib. iii. The author entering upon the narration, says, *Laniata veste, foedum spectaculum ducebatur, multis increpantibus, nullo inlacrimante:* deformitas exitus misericordiam abstulerat. To enter thoroughly into this method of thinking, we must make allowance for the ancient maxims, that no one ought to prolong his life after it became dishonourable; but, as he had always a right to dispose of it, it then became a duty to part with it.
[8] The absence of virtue may often be a vice; and that of the highest kind; as in the instance of ingratitude, as well as meanness. Where we expect a beauty, the disappointment gives an uneasy sensation, and produces a real deformity. An abjectness of character, likewise, is disgustful and contemptible in another view. Where a man has no sense of value in himself, we are not likely to have any higher esteem of him. And if the same person, who crouches to his superiors, is insolent to his inferiors (as often happens), this contrariety of behaviour, instead of correcting the former vice, aggravates it extremely by the addition of a vice still more odious. See Sect. VIII.

Under what shining colours does Demosthenes[9] represent Philip; where the orator apologizes for his own administration, and justifies that pertinacious love of liberty, with which he had inspired the Athenians. "I beheld Philip," says he, "he with whom was your contest, resolutely, while in pursuit of empire and dominion, exposing himself to every wound; his eye gored, his neck wrested, his arm, his thigh pierced, what ever part of his body fortune should seize on, that cheerfully relinquishing; provided that, with what remained, he might live in honour and renown. And shall it be said that he, born in Pella, a place heretofore mean and ignoble, should be inspired with so high an ambition and thirst of fame: while you, Athenians, &c." These praises excite the most lively admiration; but the views presented by the orator, carry us not, we see, beyond the hero himself, nor ever regard the future advantageous consequences of his valour.

The martial temper of the Romans, inflamed by continual wars, had raised their esteem of courage so high, that, in their language, it was called *virtue*, by way of excellence and of distinction from all other moral qualities. The Suevi, in the opinion of Tacitus,[10] *dressed their hair with a laudable intent: not for the purpose of loving or being loved; they adorned themselves only for their enemies, and in order to appear more terrible.* A sentiment of the historian, which would sound a little oddly in other nations and other ages.

The Scythians, according to Herodotus,[11] after scalping their enemies, dressed the skin like leather, and used it as a towel; and whoever had the most of those towels was most esteemed among them. So much had martial bravery, in that nation, as well as in many others, destroyed the sentiments of humanity; a virtue surely much more useful and engaging.

It is indeed observable, that, among all uncultivated nations, who have not as yet had full experience of the advantages attending beneficence, justice, and the social virtues, courage

[9] De Corona.
[10] De moribus Germ.
[11] Lib. iv.

is the predominant excellence; what is most celebrated by poets, recommended by parents and instructors, and admired by the public in general. The ethics of Homer are, in this particular, very different from those of Fénélon, his elegant imitator; and such as were well suited to an age, when one hero, as remarked by Thucydides,[12] could ask another, without offence, whether he were a robber or not. Such also very lately was the system of ethics which prevailed in many barbarous parts of Ireland; if we may credit Spenser, in his judicious account of the state of that kingdom.[13]

Of the same class of virtues with courage is that undisturbed philosophical tranquillity, superior to pain, sorrow, anxiety, and each assault of adverse fortune. Conscious of his own virtue, say the philosophers, the sage elevates himself above every accident of life; and securely placed in the temple of wisdom, looks down on inferior mortals engaged in pursuit of honours, riches, reputation, and every frivolous enjoyment. These pretensions, no doubt, when stretched to the utmost, are by far too magnificent for human nature. They carry, however, a grandeur with them, which seizes the spectator, and strikes him with admiration. And the nearer we can approach in practice to this sublime tranquillity and indifference (for we must distinguish it from a stupid insensibility), the more secure enjoyment shall we attain within ourselves, and the more greatness of mind shall we discover to the world. The philosophical tranquillity may, indeed, be considered only as a branch of magnanimity.

Who admires not Socrates; his perpetual serenity and contentment, amidst the greatest poverty and domestic vexations; his resolute contempt of riches, and his magnanimous care of preserving liberty, while he refused all assistance from his

---

[12] Lib. i.

[13] It is a common use, says he, amongst their gentlemen's sons, that, as soon as they are able to use their weapons, they strait gather to themselves three or four stragglers or kern, with whom wandering a while up and down idly the country, taking only meat, he at last falleth into some bad occasion, that shall be offered; which being once made known, he is thenceforth counted a man of worth, in whom there is courage.

friends and disciples, and avoided even the dependence of an obligation? Epictetus had not so much as a door to his little house or hovel; and therefore, soon lost his iron lamp, the only furniture which he had worth taking. But resolving to disappoint all robbers for the future, he supplied its place with an earthen lamp, of which he very peacefully kept possession ever after.

Among the ancients, the heroes in philosophy, as well as those in war and patriotism, have a grandeur and force of sentiment, which astonishes our narrow souls, and is rashly rejected as extravagant and supernatural. They, in their turn, I allow, would have had equal reason to consider as romantic and incredible, the degree of humanity, clemency, order, tranquillity, and other social virtues, to which, in the administration of government, we have attained in modern times, had any one been then able to have made a fair representation of them. Such is the compensation, which nature, or rather education, has made in the distribution of excellencies and virtues, in those different ages.

The merit of benevolence, arising from its utility, and its tendency to promote the good of mankind, has been already explained, and is, no doubt, the source of a *considerable* part of that esteem, which is so universally paid to it. But it will also be allowed, that the very softness and tenderness of the sentiment, its engaging endearments, its fond expressions, its delicate attentions, and all that flow of mutual confidence and regard, which enters into a warm attachment of love and friendship: it will be allowed, I say, that these feelings, being delightful in themselves, are necessarily communicated to the spectators, and melt them into the same fondness and delicacy. The tear naturally starts in our eye on the apprehension of a warm sentiment of this nature: our breast heaves, our heart is agitated, and every humane tender principle of our frame is set in motion, and gives us the purest and most satisfactory enjoyment.

When poets form descriptions of Elysian fields, where the blessed inhabitants stand in no need of each other's assistance, they yet represent them as maintaining a constant intercourse of love and friendship, and sooth our fancy with the pleasing image of these soft and gentle passions. The idea of tender tranquillity in a pastoral Arcadia is agreeable from a like principle, as has been observed above.[14]

Who would live amidst perpetual wrangling, and scolding, and mutual reproaches? The roughness and harshness of these emotions disturb and displease us: we suffer by contagion and sympathy; nor can we remain indifferent spectators, even though certain that no pernicious consequences would ever follow from such angry passions.

As a certain proof that the whole merit of benevolence is not derived from its usefulness, we may observe, that in a kind way of blame, we say, a person is *too good*; when he exceeds his part in society, and carries his attention for others beyond the proper bounds. In like manner, we say a man is *too high-spirited, too intrepid, too indifferent about fortune*: reproaches, which really, at bottom, imply more esteem than many panegyrics. Being accustomed to rate the merit and demerit of characters chiefly by their useful or pernicious tendencies, we cannot forbear applying the epithet of blame, when we discover a sentiment, which rises to a degree, that is hurtful; but it may happen, at the same time, that its noble elevation, or its engaging tenderness so seizes the heart, as rather to increase our friendship and concern for the person.[15]

The amours and attachments of Harry the IVth of France, during the civil wars of the league, frequently hurt his interest and his cause; but all the young, at least, and amorous, who can sympathize with the tender passions, will allow that this very weakness, for they will readily call it such, chiefly endears that hero, and interests them in his fortunes.

The excessive bravery and resolute inflexibility of Charles the XIIth ruined his own country, and infested all his neighbours; but have such splendour and greatness in their appear-

---

[14] Sect. V. Part II.

[15] Cheerfulness could scarce admit of blame from its excess, were it not that dissolute mirth, without a proper cause or subject, is a sure symptom and characteristic of folly, and on that account disgustful.

ance, as strikes us with admiration; and they might, in some degree, be even approved of, if they betrayed not sometimes too evident symptoms of madness and disorder.

The Athenians pretended to the first invention of agriculture and of laws: and always valued themselves extremely on the benefit thereby procured to the whole race of mankind. They also boasted, and with reason, of their warlike enterprises; particularly against those innumerable fleets and armies of Persians, which invaded Greece during the reigns of Darius and Xerxes. But though there be no comparison in point of utility, between these peaceful and military honours; yet we find, that the orators, who have writ such elaborate panegyrics on that famous city, have chiefly triumphed in displaying the warlike achievements. Lysias, Thucydides, Plato, and Isocrates discover, all of them, the same partiality; which, though condemned by calm reason and reflection, appears so natural in the mind of man.

It is observable, that the great charm of poetry consists in lively pictures of the sublime passions, magnanimity, courage, disdain of fortune; or those of the tender affections, love and friendship; which warm the heart, and diffuse over it similar sentiments and emotions. And though all kinds of passion, even the most disagreeable, such as grief and anger, are observed, when excited by poetry, to convey a satisfaction, from a mechanism of nature, not easy to be explained: Yet those more elevated or softer affections have a peculiar influence, and please from more than one cause or principle. Not to mention that they alone interest us in the fortune of the persons represented, or communicate any esteem and affection for their character.

And can it possibly be doubted, that this talent itself of poets, to move the passions, this pathetic and sublime of sentiment, is a very considerable merit; and being enhanced by its extreme rarity, may exalt the person possessed of it, above every character of the age in which he lives? The prudence, address, steadiness, and benign government of Augustus, adorned with all the splendour of his noble birth and imperial crown, render him but an unequal competitor for fame with

Virgil, who lays nothing into the opposite scale but the divine beauties of his poetical genius.

The very sensibility to these beauties, or a delicacy of taste, is itself a beauty in any character; as conveying the purest, the most durable, and most innocent of all enjoyments.

These are some instances of the several species of merit, that are valued for the immediate pleasure which they communicate to the person possessed of them. No views of utility or of future beneficial consequences enter into this sentiment of approbation; yet is it of a kind similar to that other sentiment, which arises from views of a public or private utility. The same social sympathy, we may observe, or fellow-feeling with human happiness or misery, gives rise to both; and this analogy, in all the parts of the present theory, may justly be regarded as a confirmation of it.

# Section VIII

## Of Qualities Immediately Agreeable to Others[1]

As the mutual shocks, in *society*, and the oppositions of interest and self-love have constrained mankind to establish the laws of *justice*, in order to preserve the advantages of mutual assistance and protection: in like manner, the eternal contrarieties, in *company*, of men's pride and self-conceit, have introduced the rules of Good Manners or Politeness, in order to facilitate the intercourse of minds, and an undisturbed commerce and conversation. Among well-bred people, a mutual deference is affected; contempt of others disguised; authority concealed; attention given to each in his turn; and an easy stream of conversation maintained, without vehemence, without interruption, without eagerness for victory, and without any airs of superiority. These attentions and regards are immediately *agreeable* to others, abstracted from any consideration of utility or beneficial tendencies: they conciliate affection, promote esteem, and extremely enhance the merit of the person who regulates his behaviour by them.

Many of the forms of breeding are arbitrary and casual; but the thing expressed by them is still the same. A Spaniard goes out of his own house before his guest, to signify that he leaves him master of all. In other countries, the landlord walks out last, as a common mark of deference and regard.

But, in order to render a man perfect *good company*, he must have Wit and Ingenuity as well as good manners. What wit is, it may not be easy to define; but it is easy surely

---

[1] It is the nature and, indeed, the definition of virtue, that it is *a quality of the mind agreeable to or approved of by every one who considers or contemplates it*. But some qualities produce pleasure, because they are useful to society, or useful or agreeable to the person himself; others produce it more immediately, which is the case with the class of virtues here considered.

to determine that it is a quality immediately *agreeable* to others, and communicating, on its first appearance, a lively joy and satisfaction to every one who has any comprehension of it. The most profound metaphysics, indeed, might be employed in explaining the various kinds and species of wit; and many classes of it, which are now received on the sole testimony of taste and sentiment, might, perhaps, be resolved into more general principles. But this is sufficient for our present purpose, that it does affect taste and sentiment, and bestowing an immediate enjoyment, is a sure source of approbation and affection.

In countries where men pass most of their time in conversation, and visits, and assemblies, these *companionable* qualities, so to speak, are of high estimation, and form a chief part of personal merit. In countries where men live a more domestic life, and either are employed in business, or amuse themselves in a narrower circle of acquaintance, the more solid qualities are chiefly regarded. Thus, I have often observed, that, among the French, the first questions with regard to a stranger are, *Is he polite? Has he wit?* In our own country, the chief praise bestowed is always that of a *good-natured, sensible fellow.*

In conversation, the lively spirit of dialogue is *agreeable,* even to those who desire not to have any share in the discourse: hence the teller of long stories, or the pompous declaimer, is very little approved of. But most men desire likewise their turn in the conversation, and regard, with a very evil eye, that *loquacity* which deprives them of a right they are naturally so jealous of.

There is a sort of harmless *liars,* frequently to be met with in company, who deal much in the marvellous. Their usual intention is to please and entertain; but as men are most delighted with what they conceive to be truth, these people mistake extremely the means of pleasing, and incur universal blame. Some indulgence, however, to lying or fiction is given in *humorous* stories; because it is there really agreeable and entertaining, and truth is not of any importance.

Eloquence, genius of all kinds, even good sense, and sound

reasoning, when it rises to an eminent degree, and is employed upon subjects of any considerable dignity and nice discernment; all these endowments seem immediately agreeable, and have a merit distinct from their usefulness. Rarity, likewise, which so much enhances the price of every thing, must set an additional value on these noble talents of the human mind.

Modesty may be understood in different senses, even abstracted from chastity, which has been already treated of. It sometimes means that tenderness and nicety of honour, that apprehension of blame, that dread of intrusion or injury towards others, that Pudor, which is the proper guardian of every kind of virtue, and a sure preservative against vice and corruption. But its most usual meaning is when it is opposed to *impudence* and *arrogance*, and expresses a diffidence of our own judgement, and a due attention and regard for others. In young men chiefly, this quality is a sure sign of good sense; and is also the certain means of augmenting that endowment, by preserving their ears open to instruction, and making them still grasp after new attainments. But it has a further charm to every spectator; by flattering every man's vanity, and presenting the appearance of a docile pupil, who receives, with proper attention and respect, every word they utter.

Men have, in general, a much greater propensity to overvalue than undervalue themselves; notwithstanding the opinion of Aristotle.[2] This makes us more jealous of the excess on the former side, and causes us to regard, with a peculiar indulgence, all tendency to modesty and self-diffidence; as esteeming the danger less of falling into any vicious extreme of that nature. It is thus in countries where men's bodies are apt to exceed in corpulency, personal beauty is placed in a much greater degree of slenderness, than in countries where that is the most usual defect. Being so often struck with instances of one species of deformity, men think they can never keep at too great a distance from it, and wish always to have a leaning to the opposite side. In like manner, were the door opened to self-praise, and were Montaigne's maxim observed, that one should say as frankly, *I have sense, I have learning,*

[2] Ethic. ad Nicomachum.

*I have courage, beauty, or wit,* as it is sure we often think so; were this the case, I say, every one is sensible that such a flood of impertinence would break in upon us, as would render society wholly intolerable. For this reason custom has established it as a rule, in common societies, that men should not indulge themselves in self-praise, or even speak much of themselves; and it is only among intimate friends or people of very manly behaviour, that one is allowed to do himself justice. Nobody finds fault with Maurice, Prince of Orange, for his reply to one who asked him, whom he esteemed the first general of the age, *The marquis of Spinola,* said he, *is the second.* Though it is observable, that the self-praise implied is here better implied, than if it had been directly expressed, without any cover or disguise.

He must be a very superficial thinker, who imagines that all instances of mutual deference are to be understood in earnest, and that a man would be more esteemable for being ignorant of his own merits and accomplishments. A small bias towards modesty, even in the internal sentiment, is favourably regarded, especially in young people; and a strong bias is required in the outward behaviour; but this excludes not a noble pride and spirit, which may openly display itself in its full extent, when one lies under calumny or oppression of any kind. The generous contumacy of Socrates, as Cicero calls it, has been highly celebrated in all ages; and when joined to the usual modesty of his behaviour, forms a shining character. Iphicrates, the Athenian, being accused of betraying the interests of his country, asked his accused, *Would you,* says he, *have, on a like occasion, been guilty of that crime? By no means,* replied the other. *And can you then imagine,* cried the hero, *that* Iphicrates *would be guilty?*[3] In short, a generous spirit and self-value, well founded, decently disguised, and courageously supported under distress and calumny, is a great excellency, and seems to derive its merit from the noble elevation of its sentiment, or its immediate agreeableness to its possessor. In ordinary characters, we approve of a bias towards modesty, which is a quality immediately agreeable to others: the vicious excess of the former virtue, namely, inso-

[3] Quinctil. lib. v. cap. 12.

lence or haughtiness, is immediately disagreeable to others; the excess of the latter is so to the possessor. Thus are the boundaries of these duties adjusted.

A desire of fame, reputation, or a character with others, is so far from being blameable, that it seems inseparable from virtue, genius, capacity, and a generous or noble disposition. An attention even to trivial matters, in order to please, is also expected and demanded by society; and no one is surprised, if he find a man in company to observe a greater elegance of dress and more pleasant flow of conversation, than when he passes his time at home, and with his own family. Wherein, then, consists Vanity, which is so justly regarded as a fault or imperfection. It seems to consist chiefly in such an intemperate display of our advantages, honours, and accomplishments; in such an importunate and open demand of praise and admiration, as is offensive to others, and encroaches too far on *their* secret vanity and ambition. It is besides a sure symptom of the want of true dignity and elevation of mind, which is so great an ornament in any character. For why that impatient desire of applause; as if you were not justly entitled to it, and might not reasonably expect that it would for ever attend you? Why so anxious to inform us of the great company which you have kept; the obliging things which were said to you; the honours, the distinctions which you met with; as if these were not things of course, and what we could readily, of ourselves, have imagined, without being told of them?

Decency, or a proper regard to age, sex, character, and station in the world, may be ranked among the qualities which are immediately agreeable to others, and which, by that means, acquire praise and approbation. An effeminate behaviour in a man, a rough manner in a woman; these are ugly because unsuitable to each character, and different from the qualities which we expect in the sexes. It is as if a tragedy abounded in comic beauties, or a comedy in tragic. The disproportions hurt the eye, and convey a disagreeable sentiment to the spectators, the source of blame and disapprobation. This is that *indecorum*, which is explained so much at large by Cicero in his Offices.

Among the other virtues, we may also give Cleanliness a

place; since it naturally renders us agreeable to others, and is no inconsiderable source of love and affection. No one will deny, that a negligence in this particular is a fault; and as faults are nothing but smaller vices, and this fault can have no other origin than the uneasy sensation which it excites in others; we may, in this instance, seemingly so trivial, clearly discover the origin of moral distinctions, about which the learned have involved themselves in such mazes of perplexity and error.

But besides all the *agreeable* qualities, the origin of whose beauty we can, in some degree, explain and account for, there still remains something mysterious and inexplicable, which conveys an immediate satisfaction to the spectator, but how, or why, or for what reason, he cannot pretend to determine. There is a manner, a grace, an ease, a genteelness, an I-know-not-what, which some men possess above others, which is very different from external beauty and comeliness, and which, however, catches our affection almost as suddenly and powerfully. And though this *manner* be chiefly talked of in the passion between the sexes, where the concealed magic is easily explained, yet surely much of it prevails in all our estimation of characters, and forms no inconsiderable part of personal merit. This class of accomplishments, therefore, must be trusted entirely to the blind, but sure testimony of taste and sentiment; and must be considered as a part of ethics, left by nature to baffle all the pride of philosophy, and make her sensible of her narrow boundaries and slender acquisitions.

We approve of another, because of his wit, politeness, modesty, decency, or any agreeable quality which he possesses; although he be not of our acquaintance, nor has ever given us any entertainment, by means of these accomplishments. The idea, which we form of their effect on his acquaintance, has an agreeable influence on our imagination, and gives us the sentiment of approbation. This principle enters into all the judgements which we form concerning manners and characters.

# Section IX

## Conclusion

### Part I

It may justly appear surprising that any man in so late an age, should find it requisite to prove, by elaborate reasoning, that Personal Merit consists altogether in the possession of mental qualities, *useful* or *agreeable* to the *person himself* or to *others*. It might be expected that this principle would have occurred even to the first rude, unpractised enquirers concerning morals, and been received from its own evidence, without any argument or disputation. Whatever is valuable in any kind, so naturally classes itself under the division of *useful* or *agreeable*, the *utile* or the *dulce*, that it is not easy to imagine why we should ever seek further, or consider the question as a matter of nice research or inquiry. And as every thing useful or agreeable must possess these qualities with regard either to the *person himself* or to *others*, the complete delineation or description of merit seems to be performed as naturally as a shadow is cast by the sun, or an image is reflected upon water. If the ground, on which the shadow is cast, be not broken and uneven; nor the surface from which the image is reflected, disturbed and confused; a just figure is immediately presented, without any art or attention. And it seems a reasonable presumption, that systems and hypotheses have perverted our natural understanding, when a theory, so simple and obvious, could so long have escaped the most elaborate examination.

But however the case may have fared with philosophy, in common life these principles are still implicitly maintained; nor is any other topic of praise or blame ever recurred to, when we employ any panegyric or satire, any applause or censure of human action and behaviour. If we observe men, in every intercourse of business or pleasure, in every discourse and conversation, we shall find them nowhere, except in the schools, at any loss upon this subject. What so natural, for instance, as the following dialogue? You are very happy, we shall suppose one to say, addressing himself to another, that you have given your daughter to Cleanthes. He is a man of honour and humanity. Every one, who has any intercourse with him, is sure of *fair* and *kind* treatment.[1] I congratulate you too, says another, on the promising expectations of this son-in-law; whose assiduous application to the study of the laws, whose quick penetration and early knowledge both of men and business, prognosticate the greatest honours and advancement.[2] You surprise me, replies a third, when you talk of Cleanthes as a man of business and application. I met him lately in a circle of the gayest company, and he was the very life and soul of our conversation: so much wit with good manners; so much gallantry without affectation; so much ingenious knowledge so genteelly delivered, I have never before observed in any one.[3] You would admire him still more, says a fourth, if you knew him more familiarly. That cheerfulness, which you might remark in him, is not a sudden flash struck out by company: it runs through the whole tenor of his life, and preserves a perpetual serenity on his countenance, and tranquillity in his soul. He has met with severe trials, misfortunes as well as dangers; and by his greatness of mind, was still superior to all of them.[4] The image, gentlemen, which you have here delineated of Cleanthes, cried I, is that of accomplished merit. Each of you has given a stroke of the pencil to his figure; and you have unawares exceeded all the pictures drawn by Gratian or Castiglione. A philosopher might select this character as a model of perfect virtue.

And as every quality which is useful or agreeable to ourselves or others is, in common life, allowed to be a part of personal merit; so no other will ever be received, where men judge of things by their nautral, unprejudiced reason, without

---

[1] Qualities useful to others.
[2] Qualities useful to the person himself.
[3] Qualities immediately agreeable to others.
[4] Qualities immediately agreeable to the person himself.

the delusive glosses of superstition and false religion. Celibacy, fasting, penance, mortification, self-denial, humility, silence, solitude, and the whole train of monkish virtues; for what reason are they everywhere rejected by men of sense, but because they serve to no manner of purpose; neither advance a man's fortune in the world, nor render him a more valuable member of society: neither qualify him for the entertainment of company, nor increase his power of self-enjoyment? We observe, on the contrary, that they cross all these desirable ends; stupify the understanding and harden the heart, obscure the fancy and sour the temper. We justly, therefore, transfer them to the opposite column, and place them in the catalogue of vices; nor has any superstition force sufficient among men of the world, to pervert entirely these natural sentiments. A gloomy, hair-brained enthusiast, after his death, may have a place in the calendar; but will scarcely ever be admitted, when alive, into intimacy and society, except by those who are as delirious and dismal as himself.

It seems a happiness in the present theory, that it enters not into that vulgar dispute concerning the *degrees* of benevolence or self-love, which prevail in human nature; a dispute which is never likely to have any issue, both because men, who have taken part, are not easily convinced, and because the phenomena, which can be produced on either side, are so dispersed, so uncertain, and subject to so many interpretations, that it is scarcely possible accurately to compare them, or draw from them any determinate inference or conclusion. It is sufficient for our present purpose, if it be allowed, what surely, without the greatest absurdity cannot be disputed, that there is some benevolence, however small, infused into our bosom; some spark of friendship for human kind; some particle of the dove kneaded into our frame, along with the elements of the wolf and serpent. Let these generous sentiments be supposed ever so weak; let them be insufficient to move even a hand or finger of our body, they must still direct the determinations of our mind, and where everything else is equal, produce a cool preference of what is useful and serviceable to mankind, above what is pernicious and dangerous. A *moral distinction*, therefore, immediately arises; a general sentiment of blame and approbation; a tendency, however faint, to the objects of the one, and a proportionable aversion to those of the other. Nor will those reasoners, who so earnestly maintain the predominant selfishness of human kind, be any wise scandalized at hearing of the weak sentiments of virtue implanted in our nature. On the contrary, they are found as ready to maintain the one tenet as the other; and their spirit of satire (for such it appears, rather than of corruption) naturally gives rise to both opinions; which have, indeed, a great and almost an indissoluble connexion together.

Avarice, ambition, vanity, and all passions vulgarly, though improperly, comprised under the denomination of *self-love*, are here excluded from our theory concerning the origin of morals, not because they are too weak, but because they have not a proper direction for that purpose. The notion of morals implies some sentiment common to all mankind, which recommends the same object to general approbation, and makes every man, or most men, agree in the same opinion or decision concerning it. It also implies some sentiment, so universal and comprehensive as to extend to all mankind, and render the actions and conduct, even of the persons the most remote, an object of applause or censure, according as they agree or disagree with that rule of right which is established. These two requisite circumstances belong alone to the sentiment of humanity here insisted on. The other passions produce in every breast, many strong sentiments of desire and aversion, affection and hatred; but these neither are felt so much in common, nor are so comprehensive, as to be the foundation of any general system and established theory of blame or approbation.

When a man denominates another his *enemy*, his *rival*, his *antagonist*, his *adversary*, he is understood to speak the language of self-love, and to express sentiments, peculiar to himself, and arising from his particular circumstances and situation. But when he bestows on any man the epithets of *vicious* or *odious* or *depraved*, he then speaks another language, and expresses sentiments, in which he expects all his audience are to concur with him. He must here, therefore, depart from his private and particular situation, and must choose a point of view, common to him with others; he must move some universal principle of the human frame, and touch a string to which all mankind have an accord and symphony. If he mean, therefore,. to express that this man possesses qualities, whose tendency is pernicious to society, he has chosen this common point of view, and has touched the principle of humanity, in which every man, in some degree, concurs. While the human heart is compounded of the same elements as at present, it will never be wholly indifferent to public good, nor entirely unaffected with the tendency of characters and manners. And though this affection of humanity may not generally be esteemed so strong as vanity or ambition, yet, being common to all men, it can alone be the foundation of morals, or of any general system of blame or praise. One man's ambition is not another's ambition, nor will the same event or object satisfy both; but the humanity of one man is the humanity of every one, and the same object touches this passion in all human creatures.

But the sentiments, which arise from humanity, are not only the same in all human creatures, and produce the same approbation or censure; but they also comprehend all human creatures; nor is there any one whose conduct or character is not, by their means, an object to every one of censure or approbation. On the contrary, those other passions, commonly denominated selfish, both produce different sentiments in each individual, according to his particular situation; and also contemplate the greater part of mankind with the utmost indifference and unconcern. Whoever has a high regard and esteem for me flatters my vanity; whoever expresses contempt mortifies and displeases me; but as my name is known but to a small part of mankind, there are few who come within the sphere of this passion, or excite, on its account, either my affection or disgust. But if you represent a tyrannical, insolent, or barbarous behaviour, in any country or in any age of the world, I soon carry my eye to the pernicious tendency of such a conduct, and feel the sentiment of repugnance and displeasure towards it. No character can be so remote as to be, in this light, wholly indifferent to me. What is beneficial to society or to the person himself must still be preferred. And every quality or action, of every human being, must, by this means, be ranked under some class or denomination, expressive of general censure or applause.

What more, therefore, can we ask to distinguish the sentiments, dependent on humanity, from those connected with any other passion, or to satisfy us, why the former are the origin of morals, not the latter? Whatever conduct gains my approbation, by touching my humanity, procures also the applause of all mankind, by affecting the same principle in them; but what serves my avarice or ambition pleases these passions in me alone, and affects not the avarice and ambition of the rest of mankind. There is no circumstance of conduct in any man, provided it have a beneficial tendency, that is not agreeable to my humanity, however remote the person; but every man, so far removed as neither to cross nor serve my avarice and ambition, is regarded as wholly indifferent by those passions The distinction, therefore, between these species of sentiment being so great and evident, language must soon be moulded upon it, and must invent a peculiar set of terms, in order to express those universal sentiments of censure or approbation, which arise from humanity, or from views of general usefulness and its contrary. Virtue and Vice become then known; morals are recognized; certain general ideas are framed of human conduct and behaviour; such measures are expected from men in such situations. This action is determined to be conformable to our abstract rule; that other, contrary. And by such universal principles are the particular sentiments of self-love frequently controlled and limited.[5]

[5] It seems certain, both from reason and experience, that a rude, untaught savage regulates chiefly his love and hatred by the ideas of private utility and injury, and has but faint conceptions of a general rule or system of behaviour. The man who stands opposite to him in battle, he hates heartily, not only for the present moment, which is almost unavoidable, but for ever after; nor is he satisfied without the most extreme punishment and vengeance. But we, accustomed to society, and to more enlarged reflections, consider, that this man is serving his own country and community; that any man, in the same situation,

From instances of popular tumults, seditions, factions, panics, and of all passions, which are shared with a multitude, we may learn the influence of society in exciting and supporting any emotion; while the most ungovernable disorders are raised, we find, by that means, from the slightest and most frivolous occasions. Solon was not very cruel, though, perhaps, an unjust legislator, who punished neuters in civil wars; and few, I believe, would, in such cases, incur the penalty, were their affection and discourse allowed sufficient to absolve them. No selfishness, and scarce any philosophy, have there force sufficient to support a total coolness and indifference; and he must be more or less than man, who kindles not in the common blaze. What wonder then, that moral sentiments are found of such influence in life; though springing from principles, which may appear, at first sight, somewhat small and delicate? But these principles, we must remark, are social and universal; they form, in a manner, the *party* of humankind against vice or disorder, its common enemy. And as the benevolent concern for others is diffused, in a greater or less degree, over all men, and is the same in all, it occurs more frequently in discourse, is cherished by society and conversation, and the blame and approbation, consequent on it, are thereby roused from that lethargy into which they are probably lulled, in solitary and uncultivated nature. Other passions, though perhaps originally stronger, yet being selfish and private, are often overpowered by its force, and yield the dominion of our breast to those social and public principles.

---

would do the same; that we ourselves, in like circumstances, observe a like conduct; that, in general, human society is best supported on such maxims: and by these suppositions and views, we correct, in some measure, our ruder and narrower passions. And though much of our friendship and enmity be still regulated by private considerations of benefit and harm, we pay, at least, this homage to general rules, which we are accustomed to respect, that we commonly pervert our adversary's conduct, by imputing malice or injustice to him, in order to give vent to those passions, which arise from self-love and private interest. When the heart is full of rage, it never wants pretences of this nature; though sometimes as frivolous, as those from which Horace, being almost crushed by the fall of a tree, affects to accuse of parricide the first planter of it.

Another spring of our constitution, that brings a great addition of force to moral sentiments, is the love of fame; which rules, with such uncontrolled authority, in all generous minds, and is often the grand object of all their designs and undertakings. By our continual and earnest pursuit of a character, a name, a reputation in the world, we bring our own deportment and conduct frequently in review, and consider how they appear in the eyes of those who approach and regard us. This constant habit of surveying ourselves, as it were, in reflection, keeps alive all the sentiments of right and wrong, and begets, in noble natures, a certain reverence for themselves as well as others, which is the surest guardian of every virtue. The animal conveniencies and pleasures sink gradually in their value; while every inward beauty and moral grace is studiously acquired, and the mind is accomplished in every perfection, which can adorn or embellish a rational creature.

Here is the most perfect morality with which we are acquainted: here is displayed the force of many sympathies. Our moral sentiment is itself a feeling chiefly of that nature, and our regard to a character with others seems to arise only from a care of preserving a character with ourselves; and in order to attain this end, we find it necessary to prop our tottering judgement on the correspondent approbation of mankind.

But, that we may accommodate matters, and remove if possible every difficulty, let us allow all these reasonings to be false. Let us allow that, when we resolve the pleasure, which arises from views of utility, into the sentiments of humanity and sympathy, we have embraced a wrong hypothesis. Let us confess it necessary to find some other explication of that applause, which is paid to objects, whether inanimate, animate, or rational, if they have a tendency to promote the welfare and advantage of mankind. However difficult it be to conceive that an object is approved of on account of its tendency to a certain end, while the end itself is totally indifferent: let us swallow this absurdity, and consider what are the consequences. The preceding delineation or definition of Personal Merit must still retain its evidence and authority: it must still be allowed that every quality of the mind, which is *useful* or *agreeable* to the *person himself* or to *others*, communicates a pleasure to the spectator, engages his esteem, and is admitted under the honourable denomination of virtue or merit. Are not justice, fidelity, honour, veracity, allegiance, chastity, esteemed solely on account of their tendency to promote the good of society? Is not that tendency inseparable from humanity, benevolence, lenity, generosity, gratitude, moderation, tenderness, friendship, and all the other social virtues? Can it possibly be doubted that industry, discretion, frugality, secrecy, order, perseverance, forethought, judgement, and this whole class of virtues and accomplishments, of which many pages would not contain the catalogue; can it be doubted, I say, that the tendency of these qualities to promote the interest and happiness of their possessor, is the sole foundation of their merit? Who can dispute that a mind, which supports a perpetual serenity and cheerfulness, a noble dignity and undaunted spirit, a tender affection and good-will to all around; as it has more enjoyment within itself, is also a more animating and rejoicing spectacle, than if dejected with melancholy, tormented with anxiety, irritated with rage, or sunk into the most abject baseness and degeneracy? And as to the qualities, immediately *agreeable to others*, they speak sufficiently for themselves; and he must be unhappy, indeed, either in his own temper, or in his situation and company, who has never perceived the charms of a facetious wit or flowing affability, of a delicate modesty or decent genteelness of address and manner.

I am sensible, that nothing can be more unphilosophical than to be positive or dogmatical on any subject; and that, even if *excessive* scepticism could be maintained, it would not be more destructive to all just reasoning and inquiry. I am convinced that, where men are the most sure and arrogant, they are commonly the most mistaken, and have there given reins to passion, without that proper deliberation and suspense, which can alone secure them from the grossest absurdities. Yet, I must confess, that this enumeration puts the matter in so strong a light, that I cannot, *at present*, be more assured of any truth, which I learn from reasoning and argument, than that personal merit consists entirely in the usefulness or agreeableness of qualities to the person himself possessed of them, or to others, who have any intercourse with him. But when I reflect that, though the bulk and figure of the earth have been measured and delineated, though the motions of the tides have been accounted for, the order and economy of the heavenly bodies subjected to their proper laws, and Infinite itself reduced to calculation; yet men still dispute concerning the foundation of their moral duties. When I reflect on this, I say, I fall back into diffidence and scepticism, and suspect that an hypothesis, so obvious, had it been a true one, would, long ere now, have been received by the unanimous suffrage and consent of mankind.

## Part II

Having explained the moral *approbation* attending merit or virtue, there remains nothing but briefly to consider our interested *obligation* to it, and to inquire whether every man, who has any regard to his own happiness and welfare, will not best find his account in the practice of every moral duty. If this can be clearly ascertained from the foregoing theory, we shall have the satisfaction to reflect, that we have advanced principles, which not only, it is hoped, will stand the test of reasoning and inquiry, but may contribute to the amendment of men's lives, and their improvement in morality and social virtue. And though the philosophical truth of any proposition by no means depends on its tendency to promote the interests of society; yet a man has but a bad grace, who delivers a theory, however true, which, he must confess, leads to a practice dangerous and pernicious. Why rake into those corners of nature which spread a nuisance all around? Why dig up the pestilence from the pit in which it is buried? The ingenuity of your researches may be admired, but your systems will be detested; and mankind will agree, if they cannot refute them, to sink them, at least, in eternal silence and oblivion. Truths which are *pernicious* to society, if any such there be, will yield to errors which are salutary and *advantageous*.

But what philosophical truths can be more advantageous to society, than those here delivered, which represent virtue in all her genuine and most engaging charms, and make us approach her with ease, familiarity, and affection? The dismal dress falls off, with which many divines, and some philosophers, have covered her; and nothing appears but gentleness, humanity, beneficence, affability; nay, even at proper intervals, play, frolic, and gaiety. She talks not of useless austerities and rigours, suffering and self-denial. She declares that her sole purpose is to make her votaries and all mankind, during every instant of their existence, if possible, cheerful and happy; nor does she ever willingly part with any pleasure but in hopes of ample compensation in some other period of their lives. The sole trouble which she demands, is that of just calculation, and a steady preference of the greater happiness. And if any austere pretenders approach her, enemies to joy and pleasure, she either rejects them as hypocrites and deceivers; or, if she admit them in her train, they are ranked, however, among the least favoured of her votaries.

And, indeed, to drop all figurative expression, what hopes can we ever have of engaging mankind to a practice which we confess full of austerity and rigour? Or what theory of morals can ever serve any useful purpose, unless it can show, by a particular detail, that all the duties which it recommends, are also the true interest of each individual? The peculiar advantage of the foregoing system seems to be, that it furnishes proper mediums for that purpose.

That the virtues which are immediately *useful* or *agreeable* to the person possessed of them, are desirable in a view to self-interest, it would surely be superfluous to prove. Moralists, indeed, may spare themselves all the pains which they often take in recommending these duties. To what purpose collect arguments to evince that temperance is advantageous, and the excesses of pleasure hurtful, when it appears that these excesses are only denominated such, because they are hurtful; and that, if the unlimited use of strong liquors, for instance, no more impaired health or the faculties of mind and body than the use of air or water, it would not be a whit more vicious or blameable?

It seems equally superfluous to prove, that the *companionable* virtues of good manners and wit, decency and genteelness, are more desirable than the contrary qualities. Vanity alone, without any other consideration, is a sufficient motive to make us wish for the possession of these accomplishments. No man was ever willingly deficient in this particular. All our failures here proceed from bad education, want of capacity, or a perverse and unpliable disposition. Would you have your company coveted, admired, followed; rather than hated, despised, avoided? Can any one seriously deliberate in the case? As no enjoyment is sincere, without some reference to company and society; so no society can be agreeable, or even tolerable, where a man feels his presence unwelcome, and discovers all around him symptoms of disgust and aversion.

But why, in the greater society or confederacy of mankind, should not the case be the same as in particular clubs and companies? Why is it more doubtful, that the enlarged virtues of humanity, generosity, beneficence, are desirable with a view of happiness and self-interest, than the limited endowments of ingenuity and politeness? Are we apprehensive lest those social affections interfere, in a greater and more immediate degree than any other pursuits, with private utility, and cannot be gratified, without some important sacrifice of honour and advantage? If so, we are but ill-instructed in the nature of the human passions, and are more influenced by verbal distinctions than by real differences.

Whatever contradiction may vulgarly be supposed between the *selfish* and *social* sentiments or dispositions, they are really no more opposite than selfish and ambitious, selfish and revengeful, selfish and vain. It is requisite that there be an original propensity of some kind, in order to be a basis to self-love, by giving a relish to the objects of its pursuit; and none more fit for this purpose than benevolence or humanity. The goods of fortune are spent in one gratification or another: the miser who accumulates his annual income, and lends it out at interest, has really spent it in the gratification of his avarice. And it would be difficult to show why a man is more a loser by a generous action, than by any other method of expense; since the utmost which he can attain by the most elaborate selfishness, is the indulgence of some affection.

Now if life, without passion, must be altogether insipid and tiresome; let a man suppose that he has full power of modelling his own disposition, and let him deliberate what appetite or desire he would choose for the foundation of his happiness and enjoyment. Every affection, he would observe, when gratified by success, gives a satisfaction proportioned to its force and violence; but besides this advantage, common to all, the immediate feeling of benevolence and friendship, humanity and kindness, is sweet, smooth, tender, and agreeable, independent of all fortune and accidents. These virtues are besides attended with a pleasing consciousness or remembrance, and keep us in humour with ourselves as well as others; while we retain the agreeable reflection of having done our part towards mankind and society. And though all men show a jealousy of our success in the pursuits of avarice and ambition; yet are we almost sure of their good-will and good wishes, so long as we persevere in the paths of virtue, and employ ourselves in the execution of generous plans and purposes. What other passion is there where we shall find so many advantages united; an agreeable sentiment, a pleasing consciousness, a good reputation? But of these truths, we may observe, men are, of themselves, pretty much convinced; nor are they deficient in their duty to society, because they would not wish to be generous, friendly, and humane; but because they do not feel themselves such.

Treating vice with the greatest candour, and making it all possible concessions, we must acknowledge that there is not, in any instance, the smallest pretext for giving it the preference above virtue, with a view of self-interest; except, perhaps, in the case of justice, where a man, taking things in a certain light, may often seem to be a loser by his integrity. And though it is allowed that, without a regard to property, no society could subsist; yet according to the imperfect way in which human affairs are conducted, a sensible knave, in particular incidents, may think that an act of iniquity or infidelity will make a considerable addition to his fortune, without causing any considerable breach in the social union and confederacy. That *honesty is the best policy*, may be a good general rule, but is liable to many exceptions; and he, it may perhaps be thought, conducts himself with most wisdom, who observes the general rule, and takes advantage of all the exceptions.

I must confess that, if a man think that this reasoning much requires an answer, it would be a little difficult to find any which will to him appear satisfactory and convincing. If his heart rebel not against such pernicious maxims, if he feel no reluctance to the thoughts of villainy or baseness, he has indeed lost a considerable motive to virtue; and we may expect that this practice will be answerable to his speculation. But in all ingenuous natures, the antipathy to treachery and roguery is too strong to be counter-balanced by any views of profit or pecuniary advantage. Inward peace of mind, consciousness of integrity, a satisfactory review of our own conduct; these are circumstances, very requisite to happiness, and will be cherished and cultivated by every honest man, who feels the importance of them.

Such a one has, besides, the frequent satisfaction of seeing knaves, with all their pretended cunning and abilities, betrayed by their own maxims; and while they purpose to cheat with moderation and secrecy, a tempting incident occurs, nature is frail, and they give into the snare; whence they can never extricate themselves, without a total loss of reputation, and the forfeiture of all future trust and confidence with mankind.

But were they ever so secret and successful, the honest man, if he has any tincture of philosophy, or even common observation and reflection, will discover that they themselves are, in the end, the greatest dupes, and have sacrificed the invaluable enjoyment of a character, with themselves at least, for the acquisition of worthless toys and gewgaws. How little is requisite to supply the *necessities* of nature? And in a view to *pleasure*, what comparison between the unbought satisfaction of conversation, society, study, even health and the common beauties of nature, but above all the peaceful reflection on one's own conduct; what comparison, I say, between these and the feverish, empty amusements of luxury and expense? These natural pleasures, indeed, are really without price; both because they are below all price in their attainment, and above it in their enjoyment.

# Appendix I

## Concerning Moral Sentiment

If the foregoing hypothesis be received, it will now be easy for us to determine the question first started,[1] concerning the general principles of morals; and though we postponed the decision of that question, lest it should then involve us in intricate speculations, which are unfit for moral discourses, we may resume it at present, and examine how far either *reason* or *sentiment* enters into all decisions of praise or censure.

One principal foundation of moral praise being supposed to lie in the usefulness of any quality or action, it is evident that *reason* must enter for a considerable share in all decisions of this kind; since nothing but that faculty can instruct us in the tendency of qualities and actions, and point out their beneficial consequences to society and to their possessor. In many cases this is an affair liable to great controversy: doubts may arise; opposite interests may occur; and a preference must be given to one side, from very nice views; and a small overbalance of utility. This is particularly remarkable in questions with regard to justice; as is, indeed, natural to suppose, from that species of utility which attends this virtue.[2] Were every single instance of justice, like that of benevolence, useful to society; this would be a more simple state of the case, and seldom liable to great controversy. But as single instances of justice are often pernicious in their first and immediate tendency, and as the advantage to society results only from the observance of the general rule, and from the concurrence and combination of several persons in the same equitable conduct; the case here becomes more intricate and involved. The various circumstances of society; the various consequences of

[1] Sect. I.
[2] See App. III.

124

any practice; the various interests which may be proposed; these, on many occasions, are doubtful, and subject to great discussion and inquiry. The object of municipal laws is to fix all the questions with regard to justice: the debates of civilians; the reflections of politicians; the precedents of history and public records, are all directed to the same purpose. And a very accurate *reason* or *judgement* is often requisite, to give the true determination, amidst such intricate doubts arising from obscure or opposite utilities.

But though reason, when fully assisted and improved, be sufficient to instruct us in the pernicious or useful tendency of qualities and actions; it is not alone sufficient to produce any moral blame or approbation. Utility is only a tendency to a certain end; and were the end totally indifferent to us, we should feel the same indifference towards the means. It is requisite a *sentiment* should here display itself, in order to give a preference to the useful above the pernicious tendencies. This sentiment can be no other than a feeling for the happiness of mankind, and a resentment of their misery; since these are the different ends which virtue and vice have a tendency to promote. Here therefore *reason* instructs us in the several tendencies of actions, and *humanity* makes a distinction in favour of those which are useful and beneficial.

This partition between the faculties of understanding and sentiment, in all moral decisions, seems clear from the preceding hypothesis. But I shall suppose that hypothesis false: it will then be requisite to look out for some other theory that may be satisfactory; and I dare venture to affirm that none such will ever be found, so long as we suppose reason to be the sole source of morals. To prove this, it will be proper to weigh the five following considerations.

I. It is easy for a false hypothesis to maintain some appearance of truth, while it keeps wholly in generals, makes use of undefined terms, and employs comparisons, instead of instances. This is particularly remarkable in that philosophy, which ascribes the discernment of all moral distinctions to reason alone, without the concurrence of sentiment. It is impossible that, in any particular instance, this hypothesis can so much as be rendered intelligible, whatever specious figure it may make in general declamations and discourses. Examine the crime of *ingratitude*, for instance; which has place, wherever we observe good-will, expressed and known, together with good-offices performed, on the one side, and a return of ill-will or indifference, with ill-offices or neglect on the other: anatomize all these circumstances, and examine, by your reason alone, in what consists the demerit or blame. You never will come to any issue or conclusion.

Reason judges either of *matter of fact* or of *relations*. Enquire then, *first*, where is that matter of fact which we here call *crime*; point it out; determine the time of its existence; describe its essence or nature; explain the sense or faculty to which it discovers itself. It resides in the mind of the person who is ungrateful. He must, therefore, feel it, and be conscious of it. But nothing is there, except the passion of ill-will or absolute indifference. You cannot say that these, of themselves, always, and in all circumstances, are crimes. No, they are only crimes when direced towards persons who have before expressed and displayed good-will towards us. Consequently, we may infer, that the crime of ingratitude is not any particular individual *fact*; but arises from a complication of circumstances, which, being presented to the spectator, excites the *sentiment* of blame, by the particular structure and fabric of his mind.

This representation, you say, is false. Crime, indeed, consists not in a particular *fact*, of whose reality we are assured by *reason*; but it consists in certain *moral relations*, discovered by reason, in the same manner as we discover by reason the truths of geometry or algebra. But what are the relations, I ask, of which you here talk? In the case stated above, I see first good-will and good-offices in one person; then ill-will and ill-offices in the other. Between these, there is a relation of *contrariety*. Does the crime consist in that relation? But suppose a person bore me ill-will or did me ill-offices; and I, in return, were indifferent towards him, or did him good-offices. Here is the same relation of *contrariety*; and yet my conduct is often highly laudable. Twist and turn this matter as much as you will, you can never rest the morality on relation; but must have recourse to the decisions of sentiment.

When it is affirmed that two and three are equal to the half of ten, this relation of equality I understand perfectly. I conceive, that if ten be divided into two parts, of which one has as many units as the other; and if any of these parts be compared to two added to three, it will contain as many units as that compound number. But when you draw thence a comparison to moral relations, I own that I am altogether at a loss to understand you. A moral action, a crime, such as ingratitude, is a complicated object. Does the morality consist in the relation of its parts to each other? How? After what manner? Specify the relation: be more particular and explicit in your propositions, and you will easily see their falsehood.

No, say you, the morality consists in the relation of actions to the rule of right; and they are denominated good or ill, according as they agree or disagree with it. What then is this rule of right? In what does it consist? How is it determined? By reason, you say, which examines the moral relations of actions. So that moral relations are determined by the comparison of action to a rule. And that rule is determined by considering the moral relations of objects. Is not this fine reasoning?

All this is metaphysics, you cry. That is enough; there needs nothing more to give a strong presumption of falsehood. Yes, reply I, here are metaphysics surely; but they are all on your side, who advance an abstruse hypothesis, which can never be made intelligible, nor quadrate with any particular instance or illustration. The hypothesis which we embrace is plain. It maintains that morality is determined by sentiment. It defines virtue to be *whatever mental action or quality gives to a spectator the pleasing sentiment of approbation;* and vice the contrary. We then proceed to examine a plain matter of fact, to wit, what actions have this influence. We consider all the circumstances in which these actions agree, and thence endeavour to extract some general observations with regard to these sentiments. If you call this metaphysics, and find anything abstruse here, you need only conclude that your turn of mind is not suited to the moral sciences.

II. When a man, at any time, deliberates concerning his own conduct (as, whether he had better, in a particular emergence, assist a brother or a benefactor), he must consider these separate relations, with all the circumstances and situations of the persons, in order to determine the superior duty and obligation; and in order to determine the proportion of lines in any triangle, it is necessary to examine the nature of that figure, and the relation which its several parts bear to each other. But notwithstanding this appearing similarity in the two cases, there is, at bottom, an extreme difference between them. A speculative reasoner concerning triangles or circles considers the several known and given relations of the parts of these figures, and thence infers some unknown relation, which is dependent on the former. But in moral deliberations we must be acquainted beforehand with all the objects, and all their relations to each other; and from a comparison of the whole, fix our choice or approbation. No new fact to be ascertained; no new relation to be discovered. All the circumstances of the case are supposed to be laid before us, ere we can fix any sentence of blame or approbation. If any material circumstance be yet unknown or doubtful, we must first employ our inquiry or intellectual faculties to assure us of it; and must suspend for a time all moral decision or sentiment. While we are ignorant whether a man were aggressor or not, how can we determine whether the person who killed him be criminal or innocent? But after every circumstance, every relation is known, the understanding has no further room to operate, nor any object on which it could employ itself. The approbation or blame which then ensues, cannot be the work of the judgement, but of the heart; and is not a speculative proposition or affirmation, but an active feeling or sentiment. In the disquisitions of the understanding, from known circumstances and relations, we infer some new and unknown. In moral decisions, all the circumstances and relations must be previously known; and the mind, from the contemplation of the whole, feels some new impression of affection or disgust, esteem or contempt, approbation or blame.

Hence the great difference between a mistake of *fact* and one of *right*; and hence the reason why the one is commonly criminal and not the other. When Oedipus killed Laius, he was ignorant of the relation, and from circumstances, innocent and involuntary, formed erroneous opinions concerning the action which he committed. But when Nero killed Agrippina, all the relations between himself and the person, and all the circumstances of the fact, were previously known to him; but the motive of revenge, or fear, or interest, prevailed in his savage heart over the sentiments of duty and humanity. And when we express that detestation against him to which he himself, in a little time, became insensible, it is not that we see any relations, of which he was ignorant; but that, for the rectitude of our disposition, we feel sentiments against which he was hardened from flattery and a long perseverance in the most enormous crimes. In these sentiments then, not in a discovery of relations of any kind, do all moral determinations consist. Before we can pretend to form any decision of this kind, everything must be known and ascertained on the side of the object or action. Nothing remains but to feel, on our part, some sentiment of blame or approbation; whence we pronounce the action criminal or virtuous.

III. This doctrine will become still more evident, if we compare moral beauty with natural, to which in many particulars it bears so near a resemblance. It is on the proportion, relation, and position of parts, that all natural beauty depends; but it would be absurd thence to infer, that the perception of beauty, like that of truth in geometrical problems, consists wholly in the perception of relations, and was performed entirely by the understanding or intellectual faculties. In all the sciences, our mind from the known relations investigates the unknown. But in all decisions of taste or external beauty, all the relations are beforehand obvious to the eye; and we thence proceed to feel a sentiment of complacency or disgust, according to the nature of the object, and disposition of our organs.

Euclid has fully explained all the qualities of the circle; but has not in any proposition said a word of its beauty. The reason is evident. The beauty is not a quality of the circle. It lies not in any part of the line, whose parts are equally distant from a common centre. It is only the effect which that figure produces upon the mind, whose peculiar fabric of structure renders it susceptible of such sentiments. In vain would you look for it in the circle, or seek it, either by your senses or by mathematical reasoning, in all the properties of that figure.

Attend to Palladio and Perrault, while they explain all the parts and proportions of a pillar. They talk of the cornice, and frieze, and base, and entablature, and shaft and architrave; and give the description and position of each of these members. But should you ask the description and position of its beauty, they would readily reply, that the beauty is not in any of the parts or members of a pillar, but results from the whole, when that complicated figure is presented to an intelligent mind, susceptible to those finer sensations. Till such a spectator appear, there is nothing but a figure of such particular dimensions and proportions: from his sentiments alone arise its elegance and beauty.

Again; attend to Cicero, while he paints the crimes of a Verres or a Catiline. You must acknowledge that the moral turpitude results, in the same manner, from the contemplation of the whole, when presented to a being whose organs have such a particular structure and formation. The orator may paint rage, insolence, barbarity on the one side; meekness, suffering, sorrow, innocence on the other. But if you feel no indignation or compassion arise in you from this complication of circumstances, you would in vain ask him, in what consists the crime or villainy, which he so vehemently exclaims against? At what time, or on what subject it first began to exist? And what has a few months afterwards become of it, when every disposition and thought of all the actors is totally altered or annihilated? No satisfactory answer can be given to any of these questions, upon the abstract hypothesis of morals; and we must at last acknowledge, that the crime or immorality is no particular fact or relation, which can be the object of the understanding, but arises entirely from the sentiment of disapprobation, which, by the structure of human nature, we unavoidably feel on the apprehension of barbarity or treachery.

IV. Inanimate objects may bear to each other all the same relations which we observe in moral agents; though the former can never be the object of love or hatred, nor are consequently susceptible of merit or iniquity. A young tree, which over-tops and destroys its parent, stands in all the same relations with Nero, when he murdered Agrippina; and if morality consisted merely in relations, would no doubt be equally criminal.

V. It appears evident that the ultimate ends of human actions can never, in any case, be accounted for by *reason*, but recommend themselves entirely to the sentiments and affections of mankind, without any dependence on the intellectual faculties. Ask a man *why he uses exercise*; he will answer, *because he desires to keep his health*. If you then enquire, *why he desires health*, he will readily reply, *because sickness is painful*. If you push your enquiries farther, and desire a reason *why he hates pain*, it is impossible he can ever give any. This is an ultimate end, and is never referred to any other object.

Perhaps to your second question, *why he desires health*, he may also reply, that *it is necessary for the exercise of his calling*. If you ask, *why he is anxious on that head*, he will answer, *because he desires to get money*. If you demand *Why? It is the instrument of pleasure*, says he. And beyond this it is an absurdity to ask for a reason. It is impossible there can be a progress *in infinitum*; and that one thing can always be a reason why another is desired. Something must be desirable on its own account, and because of its immediate accord or agreement with human sentiment and affection.

Now as virtue is an end, and is desirable on its own account, without fee and reward, merely for the immediate satisfaction which it conveys; it is requisite that there should be some sentiment which it touches, some internal taste or feeling, or whatever you may please to call it, which distinguishes moral good and evil, and which embraces the one and rejects the other.

Thus the distinct boundaries and offices of *reason* and of *taste* are easily ascertained. The former conveys the knowledge of truth and falsehood: the latter gives the sentiment of beauty and deformity, vice and virtue. The one discovers objects as they really stand in nature, without addition or diminution: the other has a productive faculty, and gilding or staining all natural objects with the colours, borrowed from internal sentiment, raises in a manner a new creation. Reason being cool and disengaged, is no motive to action, and directs only the impulse received from appetite or inclination, by showing us the means of attaining happiness or avoiding misery: Taste, as it gives pleasure or pain, and thereby constitutes happiness or misery, becomes a motive to action, and is the first spring or impulse to desire and volition. From circumstances and relations, known or supposed, the former leads us to the discovery of the concealed and unknown: after all circumstances and relations are laid before us, the latter makes us feel from the whole a new sentiment of blame or approbation. The standard of the one, being founded on the nature of things, is eternal and inflexible, even by the will of the Supreme Being: the standard of the other, arising from the eternal frame and constitution of animals, is ultimately derived from that Supreme Will, which bestowed on each being its peculiar nature, and arranged the several classes and orders of existence.

# Appendix II

## Of Self-Love

There is a principle, supposed to prevail among many, which is utterly incompatible with all virtue or moral sentiment; and as it can proceed from nothing but the most depraved disposition, so in its turn it tends still further to encourage that depravity. This principle is, that all *benevolence* is mere hypocrisy, friendship a cheat, public spirit a farce, fidelity a snare to procure trust and confidence; and that while all of us, at bottom, pursue only our private interest, we wear these fair disguises, in order to put others off their guard, and expose them the more to our wiles and machinations. What heart one must be possessed of who possesses such principles, and who feels no internal sentiment that belies so pernicious a theory, it is easy to imagine: and also what degree of affection and benevolence he can bear to a species whom he represents under such odious colours, and supposes so little susceptible of gratitude or any return of affection. Or if we should not ascribe these principles wholly to a corrupted heart, we must at least account for them from the most careless and precipitate examination. Superficial reasoners, indeed, observing many false pretences among mankind, and feeling, perhaps, no very strong restraint in their own disposition, might draw a general and a hasty conclusion that all is equally corrupted, and that men, different from all other animals, and indeed from all other species of existence, admit of no degrees of good or bad, but are, in every instance, the same creatures under different disguises and appearances.

There is another principle, somewhat resembling the former; which has been much insisted on by philosophers, and has been the foundation of many a system; that, whatever affection one may feel, or imagine he feels for others, no passion is, or can be disinterested; that the most generous friendship, however sincere, is a modification of self-love; and that, even unknown to ourselves, we seek only our own gratification, while we appear the most deeply engaged in schemes for the liberty and happiness of mankind. By a turn of imagination, by a refinement of reflection, by an enthusiasm of passion, we seem to take part in the interests of others, and imagine ourselves divested of all selfish considerations: but, at bottom, the most generous patriot and most niggardly miser, the bravest hero and most abject coward, have, in every action, an equal regard to their own happiness and welfare.

Whoever concludes from the seeming tendency of this opinion, that those, who make profession of it, cannot possibly feel the true sentiments of benevolence, or have any regard for genuine virtue, will often find himself, in practice, very much mistaken. Probity and honour were no strangers to Epicurus and his sect. Atticus and Horace seem to have enjoyed from nature, and cultivated by reflection, as generous and friendly dispositions as any disciple of the austerer schools. And among the modern, Hobbes and Locke, who maintained the selfish system of morals, lived irreproachable lives; though the former lay not under any restraint of religion which might supply the defects of his philosophy.

An epicurean or a Hobbist readily allows, that there is such a thing as a friendship in the world, without hypocrisy or disguise; though he may attempt, by a philosophical chymistry, to resolve the elements of this passion, if I may so speak, into those of another, and explain every affection to be self-love, twisted and moulded, by a particular turn of imagination, into a variety of appearances. But as the same turn of imagination prevails not in every man, nor gives the same direction to the original passion; this is sufficient even according to the selfish system to make the widest difference in human characters, and denominate one man virtuous and humane, another vicious and meanly interested. I esteem the man whose self-love, by whatever means, is so directed as to give him a concern for others, and render him serviceable to society: as I hate or despise him, who has no regard to any thing beyond his own gratifications and enjoyments. In vain would you suggest that these characters, though seemingly opposite, are at bottom the same, and that a very inconsiderable turn of thought forms the whole difference between them. Each character, notwithstanding these inconsiderable differences, appears to me, in practice, pretty durable and untransmutable. And I find not in this more than in other subjects, that the natural sentiments arising from the general appearances of things are easily destroyed by subtile reflections concerning the minute origin of these appearances. Does not the lively, cheerful colour of a countenance inspire me with complacency and pleasure; even though I learn from philosophy that all difference of complexion arises from the most minute differences of thickness, in the most minute parts of the skin; by means of which a superficies is qualified to reflect one of the original colours of light, and absorb the others?

But though the question concerning the universal or partial selfishness of man be not so material as is usually imagined to morality and practice, it is certainly of consequence in the speculative science of human nature, and is a proper object of curiosity and enquiry. It may not, therefore, be unsuitable, in this place, to bestow a few reflections upon it.[1]

The most obvious objection to the selfish hypothesis is, that, as it is contrary to common feeling and our most unprejudiced notions, there is required the highest stretch of philosophy to establish so extraordinary a paradox. To the most careless observer there appear to be such dispositions as benevolence and generosity; such affections as love, friend-

---

[1] Benevolence naturally divides into two kinds, the *general* and the *particular*. The first is, where we have no friendship or connexion or esteem for the person, but feel only a general sympathy with him or a compassion for his pains, and a congratulation with his pleasures. The other species of benevolence is founded on an opinion of virtue, on services done us, or on some particular connexions. Both these sentiments must be allowed real in human nature: but whether they will resolve into some nice considerations of self-love, is a question more curious than important. The former sentiment, to wit, that of general benevolence, or humanity, or sympathy, we shall have occasion frequently to treat of in the course of this enquiry; and I assume it as real, from general experience, without any other proof.

ship, compassion, gratitude. These sentiments have their causes, effects, objects, and operations, marked by common language and observation, and plainly distinguished from those of the selfish passions. And as this is the obvious appearance of things, it must be admitted, till some hypothesis be discovered, which by penetrating deeper into human nature, may prove the former affections to be nothing but modifications of the latter. All attempts of this kind have hitherto proved fruitless, and seem to have proceeded entirely from that love of *simplicity* which has been the source of much false reasoning in philosophy. I shall not here enter into any detail on the present subject. Many able philosophers have shown the insufficiency of these systems. And I shall take for granted what, I believe, the smallest reflection will make evident to every impartial enquirer.

But the nature of the subject furnishes the strongest presumption, that no better system will ever, for the future, be invented, in order to account for the origin of the benevolent from the selfish affections, and reduce all the various emotions of the human mind to a perfect simplicity. The case is not the same in this species of philosophy as in physics. Many an hypothesis in nature, contrary to first appearances, has been found, on more accurate scrutiny, solid and satisfactory. Instances of this kind are so frequent that a judicious, as well as witty philosopher,[2] has ventured to affirm, if there be more than one way in which any phenomenon may be produced, that there is general presumption for its arising from the causes which are the least obvious and familiar. But the presumption always lies on the other side, in all enquiries concerning the origin of our passions, and of the internal operations of the human mind. The simplest and most obvious cause which can there be assigned for any phenomenon, is probably the true one. When a philosopher, in the explication of his system, is obliged to have recourse to some very intricate and refined reflections, and to suppose them essential to the production of any passion or emotion, we have reason to be extremely on our guard against so fallacious an hypothe-

[2] Mons. Fontenelle.

sis. The affections are not susceptible of any impression from the refinements of reason or imagination; and it is always found that a vigorous exertion of the latter faculties, necessarily, from the narrow capacity of the human mind, destroys all activity in the former. Our predominant motive or intention is, indeed, frequently concealed from ourselves when it is mingled and confounded with other motives which the mind, from vanity or self-conceit, is desirous of supposing more prevalent: but there is no instance that a concealment of this nature has ever arisen from the abstruseness and intricacy of the motive. A man that has lost a friend and patron may flatter himself that all his grief arises from generous sentiments, without any mixture of narrow or interested considerations: but a man that grieves for a valuable friend, who needed his patronage and protection; how can we suppose, that his passionate tenderness arises from some metaphysical regards to a self-interest, which has no foundation or reality? We may as well imagine that minute wheels and springs, like those of a watch, give motion to a loaded waggon, as account for the origin of passion from such abstruse reflections.

Animals are found susceptible of kindness, both to their own species and to ours; nor is there, in this case, the least suspicion of disguise or artifice. Shall we account for all *their* sentiments, too, from refined deductions of self-interest? Or if we admit a distinterested benevolence in the inferior species, by what rule of analogy can we refuse it in the superior?

Love between the sexes begets a complacency and good-will, very distinct from the gratification of an appetite. Tenderness to their offspring, in all sensible beings, is commonly able alone to counter-balance the strongest motives of self-love, and has no manner of dependance on that affection. What interest can a fond mother have in view, who loses her health by assiduous attendance on her sick child, and afterwards languishes and dies of grief, when freed, by its death, from the slavery of that attendance?

Is gratitude no affection of the human breast, or is that a word merely, without any meaning or reality? Have we no satisfaction in one man's company above another's, and no desire of the welfare of our friend, even though absence or death should prevent us from all participation in it? Or what is it commonly, that gives us any participation in it, even while alive and present, but our affection and regard to him?

These and a thousand other instances are marks of a general benevolence in human nature, where no *real* interest binds us to the object. And how an *imaginary* interest known and avowed for such, can be the origin of any passion or emotion, seems difficult to explain. No satisfactory hypothesis of this kind has yet been discovered; nor is there the smallest probability that the future industry of men will ever be attended with more favourable success.

But farther, if we consider rightly of the matter, we shall find that the hypothesis which allows of a disinterested benevolence, distinct from self-love, has really more *simplicity* in it, and is more comfortable to the analogy of nature than that which pretends to resolve all friendship and humanity into this latter principle. There are bodily wants or appetites acknowledged by every one, which necessarily precede all sensual enjoyment, and carry us directly to seek possession of the object. Thus, hunger and thirst have eating and drinking for their end; and from the gratification of these primary appetites arises a pleasure, which may become the object of another species of desire or inclination that is secondary and interested. In the same manner there are mental passions by which we are impelled immediately to seek particular objects, such as fame or power, or vengeance without any regard to interest; and when these objects are attained a pleasing enjoyment ensues, as the consequence of our indulged affections. Nature must, by the internal frame and constitution of the mind, give an original propensity to fame, ere we can reap any pleasure from that acquisition, or pursue it from motives of self-love, and desire of happiness. If I have no vanity, I take no delight in praise: if I be void of ambition, power gives me no enjoyment: if I be not angry, the punishment of an adversary is totally indifferent to me. In all these cases there is a passion which points immediately to the object, and constitutes it our good or happiness; as there are other secondary passions which afterwards arise and pursue it as a part of our happiness, when once it is constituted such by our original affections. Were there no appetite of any kind antecedent to self-love, that propensity could scarcely ever exert itself; because we should, in that case, have felt few and slender pains or pleasures, and have little misery or happiness to avoid or to pursue.

Now where is the difficulty in conceiving, that this may likewise be the case with benevolence and friendship, and that, from the original frame of our temper, we may feel a desire of another's happiness or good, which, by means of that affection, becomes our own good, and is afterwards pursued, from the combined motives of benevolence and self-enjoyments? Who sees not that vengeance, from the force alone of passion, may be so eagerly pursued, as to make us knowingly neglect every consideration of ease, interest, or safety; and, like some vindictive animals, infuse our very souls into the wounds we give an enemy;[3] and what a malignant philosophy must it be, that will not allow to humanity and friendship the same privileges which are undisputably granted to the darker passions of enmity and resentment; such a philosophy is more like a satyr than a true delineation or description of human nature; and may be a good foundation for paradoxical wit and raillery, but is a very bad one for any serious argument or reasoning.

[3] Animasque in vulnere ponunt. VIRG. Dum alteri noceat, sui negligens, says Seneca of Anger. De Ira, I. i.

## Appendix III

## Some Further Considerations
## with Regard to Justice

The intention of this Appendix is to give some more particular explication of the origin and nature of Justice, and to mark some differences between it and the other virtues.

The social virtues of humanity and benevolence exert their influence immediately by a direct tendency or instinct, which chiefly keeps in view the simple object, moving the affections, and comprehends not any scheme or system, nor the consequences resulting from the concurrence, imitation, or example of others. A parent flies to the relief of his child; transported by that natural sympathy which actuates him, and which affords no leisure to reflect on the sentiments or conduct of the rest of mankind in like circumstances. A generous man cheerfully embraces an opportunity of serving his friend; because he then feels himself under the dominion of the beneficent affections, nor is he concerned whether any other person in the universe were ever before actuated by such noble motives, or will ever afterwards prove their influence. In all these cases the social passions have in view a single individual object, and pursue the safety or happiness alone of the person loved and esteemed. With this they are satisfied: in this they acquiesce. And as the good, resulting from their benign influence, is in itself complete and entire, it also excites the moral sentiment of approbation, without any reflection on farther consequences, and without any more enlarged views of the concurrence or imitation of the other members of society. On the contrary, were the generous friend or disinterested patriot to stand alone in the practice of beneficence, this would rather inhance his value in our eyes, and join the praise of rarity and novelty to his other more exalted merits.

The case is not the same with the social virtues of justice and fidelity. They are highly useful, or indeed absolutely necessary to the well-being of mankind: but the benefit resulting from them is not the consequence of every individual single act; but arises from the whole scheme or system concurred in by the whole, or the greater part of the society. General peace and order are the attendants of justice or a general abstinence from the possessions of others; but a particular regard to the particular right of one individual citizen may frequently, considered in itself, be productive of pernicious consequences. The result of the individual acts is here, in many instances, directly opposite to that of the whole system of actions; and the former may be extremely hurtful, while the latter is, to the highest degree, advantageous. Riches, inherited from a parent, are, in a bad man's hand, the instrument of mischief. The right of succession may, in one instance, be hurtful. Its benefit arises only from the observance of the general rule; and it is sufficient, if compensation be thereby made for all the ills and inconveniences which flow from particular characters and situations.

Cyrus, young and unexperienced, considered only the individual case before him, and reflected on a limited fitness and convenience, when he assigned the long coat to the tall boy, and the short coat to the other of smaller size. His governor instructed him better, while he pointed out more enlarged views and consequences, and informed his pupil of the general, inflexible rules, necessary to support general peace and order in society.

The happiness and prosperity of mankind, arising from the social virtue of benevolence and its subdivisions, may be compared to a wall, built by many hands, which still rises by each stone that is heaped upon it, and receives increase proportional to the diligence and care of each workman. The same happiness, raised by the social virtue of justice and its subdivisions, may be compared to the building of a vault, where each individual stone would, of itself, fall to the ground; nor is the whole fabric supported but by the mutual assistance and combination of its corresponding parts.

All the laws of nature, which regulate property, as well as

all civil laws, are general, and regard alone some essential circumstances of the case, without taking into consideration the characters, situations, and connexions of the person concerned, or any particular consequences which may result from the determination of these laws in any particular case which offers. They deprive, without scruple, a beneficent man of all his possessions, if acquired by mistake, without a good title; in order to bestow them on a selfish miser, who has already heaped up immense stores of superfluous riches. Public utility requires that property should be regulated by general inflexible rules; and though such rules are adopted as best serve the same end of public utility, it is impossible for them to prevent all particular hardships, or make beneficial consequences result from every individual case. It is sufficient, if the whole plan or scheme be necessary to the support of civil society, and if the balance of good, in the main, do thereby preponderate much above that of evil. Even the general laws of the universe, though planned by infinite wisdom, cannot exclude all evil or inconvenience in every particular operation.

It has been asserted by some, that justice arises from Human Conventions, and proceeds from the voluntary choice, consent, or combination of mankind. If by *convention* be here meant a *promise* (which is the most usual sense of the word) nothing can be more absurd than this position. The observance of promises is itself one of the most considerable parts of justice, and we are not surely bound to keep our word because we have given our word to keep it. But if by convention be meant a sense of common interest; which sense each man feels in his own breast, which he remarks in his fellows, and which carries him, in concurrence with others, into a general plan or system of actions, which tends to public utility; it must be owned, that, in this sense, justice arises from human conventions. For if it be allowed (what is, indeed, evident) that the particular consequences of a particular act of justice may be hurtful to the public as well as. to individuals; it follows that every man, in embracing that virtue, must have an eye to the whole plan or system, and must expect the concurrence of his fellows in the same conduct and behaviour. Did all his views terminate in the consequences of each act of his own, his benevolence and humanity, as well as his self-love, might often prescribe to him measures of conduct very different from those which are agreeable to the strict rules of right and justice.

Thus, two men pull the oars of a boat by common convention for common interest, without any promise or contract: thus gold and silver are made the measures of exchange; thus speech and words and language are fixed by human convention and agreement. Whatever is advantageous to two or more persons, if all perform their part; but what loses all advantage if only one perform, can arise from no other principle. There would otherwise be no motive for any one of them to enter into that scheme of conduct.[1]

The word *natural* is commonly taken in so many senses and is of so loose a signification, that it seems vain to dispute whether justice be natural or not. If self-love, if benevolence be natural to man; if reason and forethought be also natural; then may the same epithet be applied to justice, order, fidelity, property, society. Men's inclination, their necessities, lead them to combine; their understanding and experience tell them that this combination is impossible where each governs himself by no rule, and pays no regard to the possessions of others: and from these passions and reflections conjoined, as soon as we observe like passions and reflections in others, the sentiment of justice, throughout all ages, has infallibly and certainly had place to some degree or other in every indi-

---

[1] This theory concerning the origin of property, and consequently of justice, is, in the main, the same with that hinted at and adopted by Grotius. "Hinc discimus, quae fuerit causa, ob quam a primaeva communione rerum primo mobilium, deinde et immobilium discessum est: nimirum quod cum non contenti homines vesci sponte natis, antra habitare, corpore aut nudo agere, aut corticibus arborum ferarumve pellibus vestito, vitae genus exquisitius delegissent, industria opus fuit, quam singuli rebus singulis adhiberent: Quo minus autem fructus in commune conferrentur, primum obstitit locorum, in quae homines discesserunt, distantia, deinde justitiae et amoris defectus, per quem fiebat, ut nec in labore, nec in consumtione fructuum, quae debebat, aequalitas servaretur. Simul discimus, quomodo res in proprietatem iverint; non animi actu solo, neque enim scire alii poterant, quid alii suum esse vellent, ut eo abstinerent, et idem velle plures poterant; sed pacto quodam aut expresso, ut per divisionem, aut tacito, ut per occupationem." *De jure belli et pacis.* Lib. ii. cap. 2. § 2. art. 4 and 5.

vidual of the human species. In so sagacious an animal, what necessarily arises from the exertion of his intellectual faculties may justly be esteemed natural.[2]

Among all civilized nations it has been the constant endeavour to remove everything arbitrary and partial from the decision of property, and to fix the sentence of judges by such general views and considerations as may be equal to every member of society. For besides, that nothing could be more dangerous than to accustom the bench, even in the smallest instance, to regard private friendship or enmity; it is certain, that men, where they imagine that there was no other reason for the preference of their adversary but personal favour, are apt to entertain the strongest ill-will against the magistrates and judges. When natural reason, therefore, points out no fixed view of public utility by which a controversy of property can be decided, positive laws are often framed to supply its place, and direct the procedure of all courts of judicature. Where these too fail, as often happens, precedents are called for; and a former decision, though given itself without any sufficient reason, justly becomes a sufficient reason for a new decision. If direct laws and precedents be wanting, imperfect and indirect ones are brought in aid; and the controverted case is ranged under them by analogical reasonings and comparisons, and similitudes, and correspondencies, which are often more fanciful than real. In general, it may safely be affirmed that jurisprudence is, in this respect, different from all the sciences; and that in many of its nicer questions, there cannot properly be said to be truth or falsehood on either side. If one pleader bring the case under any former law or precedent, by a refined analogy or comparison; the opposite pleader is not at a loss to find an opposite analogy

[2] Natural may be opposed, either to what is *unusual, miraculous,* or *artificial.* In the two former senses, justice and property are undoubtedly natural. But as they suppose reason, forethought, design, and a social union and confederacy among men, perhaps that epithet cannot strictly, in the last sense, be applied to them. Had men lived without society, property had never been known, and neither justice nor injustice had ever existed. But society among human creatures had been impossible without reason and forethought. Inferior animals, that unite, are guided by instinct, which supplies the place of reason. But all these disputes are merely verbal.

or comparison: and the preference given by the judge is often founded more on taste and imagination than on any solid argument. Public utility is the general object of all courts of judicature; and this utility too requires a stable rule in all controversies: but where several rules, nearly equal and indifferent, present themselves, it is a very slight turn of thought which fixes the decision in favour of either party.[3]

[3] That there be a separation or distinction of possessions, and that this separation be steady and constant; this is absolutely required by the interests of society, and hence the origin of justice and property. What possessions are assigned to particular persons; this is, generally speaking, pretty indifferent; and is often determined by very frivolous views and considerations. We shall mention a few particulars.

Were a society formed among several independent members, the most obvious rule, which could be agreed on, would be to annex property to *present* possession, and leave every one a right to what he at present enjoys. The relation of possession, which takes place between the person and the object, naturally draws on the relation of property.

For a like reason, occupation or first possession becomes the foundation of property.

Where a man bestows labour and industry upon any object, which before belonged to no body; as in cutting down and shaping a tree, in cultivating a field, &c., the alterations, which he produces, causes a relation between him and the object, and naturally engages us to annex it to him by the new relation of property. This cause here concurs with the public utility, which consists in the encouragement given to industry and labour.

Perhaps too, private humanity towards the possessor concurs, in this instance, with the other motives, and engages us to leave with him what he has acquired by his sweat and labour; and what he has flattered himself in the constant enjoyment of. For though private humanity can, by no means, be the origin of justice; since the latter virtue so often contradicts the former; yet when the rule of separate and constant possession is once formed by the indispensable necessities of society, private humanity, and an aversion to the doing a hardship to another, may, in a particular instance, give rise to a particular rule of property.

I am much inclined to think, that the right of succession or inheritance much depends on those connexions of the imagination, and that the relation to a former proprietor begetting a relation to the object, is the cause why the property is transferred to a man after the death of his kinsman. It is true; industry is more encouraged by the transference of possession to children or near relations: but this consideration will only have place in a cultivated society; whereas the right of succession is regarded even among the greatest Barbarians.

Acquisition of property by *accession* can be explained no way but by having recourse to the relations and connexions of the imagination.

The property of rivers, by the laws of most nations, and by the natural turn of our thoughts, is attributed to the proprietors of their banks, excepting such vast rivers as the Rhine or the Danube, which seem too large to follow as an accession to the property of the neigh-

We may just observe, before we conclude this subject, that after the laws of justice are fixed by views of general utility, the injury, the hardship, the harm, which result to any individual from a violation of them, enter very much into consideration, and are a great source of that universal blame which attends every wrong or iniquity. By the laws of society, this coat, this horse is mine, and *ought* to remain perpetually in my possession: I reckon on the secure enjoyment of it: by depriving me of it, you disappoint my expectations, and doubly displease me, and offend every bystander. It is a public wrong, so far as the rules of equity are violated: it is a private harm, so far as an individual is injured. And though the second consideration could have no place, were not the former previously established: for otherwise the distinction of *mine* and *thine* would be unknown in society: yet there is no question but the regard to general good is much enforced by the respect to particular. What injures the community, without hurting any individual, is often more lightly thought of. But where the greatest public wrong is also conjoined with a considerable private one, no wonder the highest disapprobation attends so iniquitous a behaviour.

---

bouring fields. Yet even these rivers are considered as the property of that nation, through whose dominions they run; the idea of a nation being of a suitable bulk to correspond with them, and bear them such a relation in the fancy.

The accessions, which are made to land, bordering upon rivers, follow the land, say the civilians, provided it be made by what they call *alluvion*, that is, insensibly and imperceptibly; which are circumstances, that assist the imagination in the conjunction.

Where there is any considerable portion torn at once from one bank and added to another, it becomes not *his* property, whose land it falls on, till it unite with the land, and till the trees and plants have spread their roots into both. Before that, the thought does not sufficiently join them.

In short, we must ever distinguish between the necessity of a separation and constancy in men's possession, and the rules, which assign particular objects to particular persons. The first necessity is obvious, strong, and invincible: the latter may depend on a public utility more light and frivolous, on the sentiment of private humanity and aversion to private hardship, on positive laws, on precedents, analogies, and very fine connexions and turns of the imagination.

# Appendix IV

## Of Some Verbal Disputes

Nothing is more usual than for philosophers to encroach upon the province of grammarians; and to engage in disputes of words, while they imagine that they are handling controversies of the deepest importance and concern. It was in order to avoid altercations, so frivolous and endless, that I endeavoured to state with the utmost caution the object of our present enquiry; and proposed simply to collect, on the one hand, a list of those mental qualities which are the object of love or esteem, and form a part of personal merit; and on the other hand, a catalogue of those qualities which are the object of censure or reproach, and which detract from the character of the person possessed of them; subjoining some reflections concerning the origin of these sentiments of praise or blame. On all occasions, where there might arise the least hesitation, I avoided the terms *virtue* and *vice*; because some of those qualities, which I classed among the objects of praise, receive, in the English language, the appellation of *talents*, rather than of virtues; as some of the blameable or censurable qualities are often called *defects*, rather than vices. It may now, perhaps, be expected that before we conclude this moral enquiry, we should exactly separate the one from the other; should mark the precise boundaries of virtues and talents, vices, and defects; and should explain the reason and origin of that distinction. But in order to excuse myself from this undertaking, which would, at last, prove only a grammatical enquiry, I shall subjoin the four following reflections, which shall contain all that I intend to say on the present subject.

*First*, I do not find that in the English, or any other modern tongue, the boundaries are exactly fixed between virtues and talents, vices and defects, or that a precise definition can be given of the one as contradistinguished from the

147

other. Were we to say, for instance, that the esteemable qualities alone, which are voluntary, are entitled to the appellation
of virtues; we should soon recollect the qualities of courage,
equanimity, patience, self-command; with many others, which
almost every language classes under this appellation, though
they depend little or not at all on our choice. Should we affirm
that the qualities alone, which prompt us to act our part in
society, are entitled to that honourable distinction; it must
immediately occur that these are indeed the most valuable
qualities, and are commonly denominated the *social* virtues;
but that this very epithet supposes that there are also virtues
of another species. Should we lay hold of the distinction between *intellectual* and *moral* endowments, and affirm the last
alone to be the real and genuine virtues, because they alone
lead to action; we should find that many of those qualities,
usually called intellectual virtues, such as prudence, penetration, discernment, discretion, had also a considerable influence on conduct. The distinction between the *heart* and the
*head* may also be adopted: the qualities of the first may be
defined such as in their immediate exertion are accompanied
with a feeling of sentiment; and these alone may be called
the genuine virtues: but industry, frugality, temperance, secrecy, perseverance, and many other laudable powers or habits,
generally stiled virtues, are exerted without any immediate
sentiment in the person possessed of them, and are only
known to him by their effects. It is fortunate, amidst all this
seeming perplexity, that the question, being merely verbal,
cannot possibly be of any importance. A moral, philosophical
discourse needs not enter into all these caprices of language,
which are so variable in different dialects, and in different
ages of the same dialect. But on the whole, it seems to me,
that though it is always allowed, that there are virtues of
many different kinds, yet, when a man is called *virtuous*, or
is denominated a man of virtue, we chiefly regard his social
qualities, which are, indeed, the most valuable. It is, at the
same time, certain, that any remarkable defect in courage,
temperance, economy, industry, understanding, dignity of
mind, would bereave even a very good-natured, honest man

of this honourable appellation. Who did ever say, except by way of irony, that such a one was a man of great virtue, but an egregious blockhead?

But, *secondly*, it is no wonder that languages should not be very precise in marking the boundaries between virtues and talents, vices and defects; since there is so little distinction made in our internal estimation of them. It seems indeed certain, that the *sentiment* of conscious worth, the self-satisfaction proceeding from a review of a man's own conduct and character; it seems certain, I say, that this sentiment, which, though the most common of all others, has no proper name in our language,[1] arises from the endowments of courage and capacity, industry and ingenuity, as well as from any other mental excellencies. Who, on the other hand, is not deeply mortified with reflecting on his own folly and dissoluteness, and feels not a secret sting or compunction whenever his memory presents any past occurrence, where he behaved with stupidity or ill-manners? No time can efface the cruel ideas of a man's own foolish conduct, or of affronts, which cowardice or impudence has brought upon him. They still haunt his solitary hours, damp his most aspiring thoughts, and show him, even to himself, in the most contemptible and most odious colours imaginable.

What is there too we are more anxious to conceal from others than such blunders, infirmities, and meannesses, or more dread to have exposed by raillery and satire? And is not the chief object of vanity, our bravery or learning, our wit or breeding, our eloquence or address, our taste or abilities? These we display with care, if not with ostentation; and we commonly show more ambition of excelling in them, than even in the social virtues themselves, which are, in reality, of such superior excellence. Good-nature and honesty, especially

---

[1] The term, pride, is commonly taken in a bad sense; but this sentiment seems indifferent, and may be either good or bad, according as it is well or ill founded, and according to the other circumstances which accompany it. The French express this sentiment by the term, *amour propre,* but as they also express self-love as well as vanity by the same term, there arises thence a great confusion in Rochefoucault, and many of their moral writers.

the latter, are so indispensably required, that, though the greatest censure attends any violation of these duties, no eminent praise follows such common instances of them, as seem essential to the support of human society. And hence the reason, in my opinion, why, though men often extol so liberally the qualities of their heart, they are shy in commending the endowments of their head: because the latter virtues, being supposed more rare and extraordinary, are observed to be the more usual objects of pride and self-conceit; and when boasted of, beget a strong suspicion of these sentiments.

It is hard to tell, whether you hurt a man's character most by calling him a knave or a coward, and whether a beastly glutton or drunkard be not as odious and contemptible, as a selfish, ungenerous miser. Give me my choice, and I would rather, for my own happiness and self-enjoyment, have a friendly, humane heart, than possess all the other virtues of Demosthenes and Philip united: but I would rather pass with the world for one endowed with extensive genius and intrepid courage, and should thence expect stronger instances of general applause and admiration. The figure which a man makes in life, the reception which he meets with in company, the esteem paid him by his acquaintance; all these advantages depend as much upon his good sense and judgement, as upon any other part of his character. Had a man the best intentions in the world, and were the farthest removed from all injustice and violence, he would never be able to make himself be much regarded, without a moderate share, at least, of parts and understanding.

What is it then we can here dispute about? If sense and courage, temperance and industry, wisdom and knowledge confessedly form a considerable part of *personal merit:* if a man, possessed of these qualities, is both better satisfied with himself, and better entitled to the good-will, esteem, and services of others, than one entirely destitute of them; if, in short, the *sentiments* are similar which arise from these endowments and from the social virtues; is there any reason for being so extremely scrupulous about a *word,* or disputing whether they be entitled to the denomination of virtues? It may, indeed, be pretended, that the sentiment of approbation, which those accomplishments produce, besides its being *inferior*, is also somewhat *different* from that which attends the virtues of justice and humanity. But this seems not a sufficient reason for ranking them entirely under different classes and appellations. The character of Caesar and that of Cato, as drawn by Sallust, are both of them virtuous, in the strictest and most limited sense of the word; but in a different way: nor are the sentiments entirely the same which arise from them. The one produces love, the other esteem: the one is amiable, the other awful: we should wish to meet the one character in a friend; the other we should be ambitious of in ourselves. In like manner the approbation, which attends temperance or industry or frugality, may be somewhat different from that which is paid to the social virtues, without making them entirely of a different species. And, indeed, we may observe, that these endowments, more than the other virtues, produce not, all of them, the same kind of approbation. Good sense and genius beget esteem and regard: wit and humour excite love and affection.[2]

[2] Love and esteem are nearly the same passion, and arise from similar causes. The qualities, which produce both, are such as communicate pleasure. But where this pleasure is severe and serious; or where its object is great, and makes a strong impression, or where it produces any degree of humility and awe: in all these cases, the passion, which arises from the pleasure, is more properly denominated esteem than love. Benevolence attends both: but is connected with love in a more eminent degree. There seems to be still a stronger mixture of pride in contempt than of humility in esteem; and the reason would not be difficult to one, who studied accurately the passions. All these various mixtures and compositions and appearances of sentiment form a very curious subject of speculation, but are wide of our present purpose. Throughout this enquiry, we always consider in general, what qualities are a subject of praise or of censure, without entering into all the minute differences of sentiment, which they excite. It is evident, that whatever is contemned, is also disliked, as well as what is hated; and we here endeavour to take objects, according to their most simple views and appearances. These sciences are but too apt to appear abstract to common readers, even with all the precautions which we can take to clear them from superfluous speculations, and bring them down to every capacity.

Most people, I believe, will naturally, without premedita-
tion, assent to the definition of the elegant and judicious
poet: —

> Virtue (for mere good-nature is a fool)
> Is sense and spirit with humanity.[3]

What pretensions has a man to our generous assistance or
good offices, who has dissipated his wealth in profuse ex-
penses, idle vanities, chimerical projects, dissolute pleasures
or extravagant gaming? These vices (for we scruple not to call
them such) bring misery unpitied, and contempt on every
one addicted to them.

Achaeus, a wise and prudent prince, fell into a fatal
snare, which cost him his crown and life, after having used
every reasonable precaution to guard himself against it. On
that account, says the historian, he is a just object of regard
and compassion: his betrayers alone of hatred and contempt.[4]

The precipitate flight and improvident negligence of
Pompey, at the beginning of the civil wars, appeared such
notorious blunders to Cicero, as quite palled his friendship
towards that great man. *In the same manner,* says he, *as want
of cleanliness, decency, or discretion in a mistress are found
to alienate our affections.* For so he expresses himself, where
he talks, not in the character of a philosopher, but in that of
a statesman and man of the world, to his friend Atticus.[5]

But the same Cicero, in imitation of all the ancient
moralists, when he reasons as a philosopher, enlarges very
much his ideas of virtue, and comprehends every laudable
quality or endowment of the mind, under that honourable
appellation. This leads to the *third* reflection, which we proposed to make, to wit, that the ancient moralists, the best
models, made no material distinction among the different
species of mental endowments and defects, but treated all alike
under the appellation of virtues and vices, and made them

[3] The Art of preserving Health. Book 4.
[4] Polybius, lib. viii. cap. 2.
[5] Lib. ix. epist. 10.

indiscriminately the object of their moral reasonings. The *prudence* explained in Cicero's *Offices*,[6] is that sagacity, which leads to the discovery of truth, and preserves us from error and mistake. *Magnanimity, temperance, decency,* are there also at large discoursed of. And as that eloquent moralist followed the common received division of the four cardinal virtues, our social duties form but one head, in the general distribution of his subject.[7]

We need only peruse the titles of chapters in Aristotle's Ethics to be convinced that he ranks courage, temperance, magnficence, magnanimity, modesty, prudence, and a manly openness, among the virtues, as well as justice and friendship.

To *sustain* and to *abstain*, that is, to be patient and continent, appeared to some of the ancients a summary comprehension of all morals.

Epictetus has scarcely ever mentioned the sentiment of humanity and compassion, but in order to put his disciples on their guard against it. The virtue of the *Stoics* seems to

---

[6] Lib. i. cap. 6.

[7] The following passage of Cicero is worth quoting, as being the most clear and express to our purpose, that any thing can be imagined, and, in a dispute, which is chiefly verbal, must, on account of the author, carry an authority, from which there can be no appeal.

"Virtus autem, quae est per se ipsa laudabilis, et sine qua nihil laudari potest, tamen habet plures partes, quarum alia est alia ad laudationem aptior. Sunt enim aliae virtutes, quae videntur in moribus hominum, et quadam comitate ac beneficentia positae: aliae quae in ingenii aliqua facultate, aut animi magnitudine ac robore. Nam clementia, justitia, benignitas, fides, fortitudo in periculis communibus, jucunda est auditu in laudationibus. Omnes enim hae virtutes non tam ipsis, qui eas in se habent, quam generi hominum fructuosae putantur. Sapientia et magnitudo animi, qua omnes res humanae tenues et pro nihilo putantur, et in cogitando vis quaedam ingenii, et ipsa eloquentia admirationis habet non minus, jucunditatis minus. Ipsos enim magis videntur, quos laudamus, quam illos, apud quos laudamus, ornare ac tueri: sed tamen in laudenda jungenda sunt etiam haec genera virtutum. Ferunt enim aures hominum, cum illa quae jucunda et grata, tum etiam illa, quae mirabilia sunt in virtute, laudari." *De orat.* lib. ii. cap. 84.

I suppose, if Cicero were now alive, it would be found difficult to fetter his moral sentiments by narrow systems; or persuade him, that no qualities were to be admitted as *virtues,* or acknowledged to be a part of *personal merit,* but what were recommended by *The Whole Duty of Man.*

consist chiefly in a firm temper and a sound understanding. With them, as with Solomon and the eastern moralists, folly and wisdom are equivalent to vice and virtue.

Men will praise thee, says David,[8] when thou dost well unto thyself. I hate a wise man, says the Greek poet, who is not wise to himself.[9]

Plutarch is no more cramped by systems in his philosophy than in his history. Where he compares the great men of Greece and Rome, he fairly sets in opposition all their blemishes and accomplishments of whatever kind, and omits nothing considerable, which can either depress or exalt their characters. His moral discourses contain the same free and natural censure of men and manners.

The character of Hannibal, as drawn by Livy,[10] is esteemed partial, but allows him many eminent virtues. Never was there a genius, says the historian, more equally fitted for those opposite offices of commanding and obeying; and it were, therefore, difficult to determine whether he rendered himself *dearer* to the general or to the army. To none would Hasdrubal entrust more willingly the conduct of any dangerous enterprize; under none did the soldiers discover more courage and confidence. Great boldness in facing danger; great prudence in the midst of it. No labour could fatigue his body or subdue his mind. Cold and heat were indifferent to him: meat and drink he sought as supplies to the necessities of nature, not as gratifications of his voluptuous appetites. Waking or rest he used indiscriminately, by night or by day.—These great Virtues were balanced by great Vices: inhuman cruelty; perfidy more than *punic*; no truth, no faith, no regard to oaths, promises, or religion.

The character of Alexander the Sixth, to be found in Guicciardin,[11] is pretty similar, but juster; and is a proof that even the moderns, where they speak naturally, hold the same language with the ancients. In this pope, says he, there

---

[8] Psalm 49th.
[9] Μισῶ σοφιστὴν ὅστις οὐκ αὐτῷ σοφός. EURIPIDES.
[10] Lib. xxi. cap. 4.
[11] Lib. i.

was a singular capacity and judgement: admirable prudence; a wonderful talent of persuasion; and in all momentous enterprizes a diligence and dexterity incredible. But these *virtues* were infinitely overbalanced by his *vices*; no faith, no religion, insatiable avarice, exorbitant ambition, and a more than barbarous cruelty.

Polybius,[12] reprehending Timaeus for his partiality against Agathocles, whom he himself allows to be the most cruel and impious of all tyrants, says: if he took refuge in Syracuse, as asserted by that historian, flying the dirt and smoke and toil of his former profession of a potter; and if proceeding from such slender beginnings, he became master, in a little time, of all Sicily; brought the Carthaginian state into the utmost danger; and at last died in old age, and in possession of sovereign dignity: must he not be allowed something prodigious and extraordinary, and to have possessed great talents and capacity for business and action? His historian, therefore, ought not to have alone related what tended to his reproach and infamy; but also what might redound to his Praise and Honour.

In general, we may observe, that the distinction of voluntary or involuntary was little regarded by the ancients in their moral reasonings; where they frequently treated the question as very doubtful, *whether virtue could be taught or not*?[13] They justly considered that cowardice, meanness, levity, anxiety, impatience, folly, and many other qualities of the mind, might appear ridiculous and deformed, contemptible and odious, though independent of the will. Nor could it be supposed, at all times, in every man's power to attain every kind of mental more than of exterior beauty.

And here there occurs the *fourth* reflection which I purposed to make, in suggesting the reason why modern philosophers have often followed a course in their moral enquiries so different from that of the ancients. In later times,

---

[12] Lib. xii.
[13] Vid. Plato in Menone, Seneca *de otio sap.* cap. 31. So also Horace, *Virtutem doctrina paret, naturane donet.* Epist. lib. i. ep. 18. Æschines Socraticus, Dial. 1.

philosophy of all kinds, especially ethics, have been more closely united with theology than ever they were observed to be among the heathens; and as this latter science admits of no terms of composition, but bends every branch of knowledge to its own purpose, without much regard to the phenomena of nature, or to the unbiassed sentiments of the mind, hence reasoning, and even language, have been warped from their natural course, and distinctions have been endeavoured to be established where the difference of the objects was, in a manner, imperceptible. Philosophers, or rather divines under that disguise, treating all morals as on a like footing with civil laws, guarded by the sanctions of reward and punishment, were necessarily led to render this circumstance, of *voluntary* or *involuntary*, the foundation of their whole theory. Every one may employ *terms* in what sense he pleases: but this, in the mean time, must be allowed, that *sentiments* are every day experienced of blame and praise, which have objects beyond the dominion of the will or choice, and of which it behoves us, if not as moralists, as speculative philosophers at least, to give some satisfactory theory and explication.

A blemish, a fault, a vice, a crime; these expressions seem to denote different degrees of censure and disapprobation; which are, however, all of them, at the bottom, pretty nearly all the same kind of species. The explication of one will easily lead us into a just conception of the others; and it is of greater consequence to attend to things than to verbal appellations. That we owe a duty to ourselves is confessed even in the most vulgar system of morals; and it must be of consequence to examine that duty, in order to see whether it bears any affinity to that which we owe to society. It is probable that the approbation attending the observance of both is of a similar nature, and arises from similar principles, whatever appellation we may give to either of these excellencies.

# A DIALOGUE

MY FRIEND, Palamedes, who is as great a rambler in his principles as in his person, who has run over, by study and travel, almost every region of the intellectual and material world, surprized me lately with an account of a nation, with whom, he told me, he had passed a considerable part of his life, and whom, he found, in the main, a people extremely civilized and intelligent.

There is a country, said he, in the world, called Fourli, no matter for its longitude or latitude, whose inhabitants have ways of thinking, in many things, particularly in morals, diametrically opposite to ours. When I came among them, I found that I must submit to double pains; first to learn the meaning of the terms in their language, and then to know the import of those terms, and the praise or blame attached to them. After a word had been explained to me, and the character, which it expressed, had been described, I concluded, that such an epithet must necessarily be the greatest reproach in the world; and was extremely surprized to find one in a public company, apply it to a person, with whom he lived in the strictest intimacy and friendship. *You fancy*, said I one day, to an acquaintance, *that* Changuis *is your mortal enemy: I love to extinguish quarrels; and I must, therefore, tell you, that I heard him talk of you in the most obliging manner.* But to my great astonishment, when I repeated Changuis's words, though I had both remembered and understood them perfectly, I found, that they were taken for the most mortal affront, and that I had very innocently rendered the breach between these persons altogether irreparable.

As it was my fortune to come among this people on a very advantageous footing, I was immediately introduced to the best company; and being desired by Alcheic to live with him, I readily accepted of his invitation; as I found him universally esteemed for his personal merit, and indeed regarded by every one in Fourli, as a perfect character.

**157**

One evening he invited me, as an amusement, to bear him company in a serenade, which he intended to give to Gulki, with whom, he told me, he was extremely enamoured; and I soon found that his taste was not singular: For we met many of his rivals, who had come on the same errand. I very naturally concluded, that this mistress of his must be one of the finest women in town; and I already felt a secret inclination to see her, and be acquainted with her. But as the moon began to rise, I was much surprized to find, that we were in the midst of the university, where Gulki studied: And I was somewhat ashamed for having attended my friend, on such an errand.

I was afterwards told, that Alcheic's choice of Gulki was very much approved of by all the good company in town; and that it was expected, while he gratified his own passion, he would perform to that young man the same good office, which he had himself owed to Elcouf. It seems Alcheic had been very handsome in his youth, had been courted by many lovers; but had bestowed his favours chiefly on the sage Elcouf; to whom he was supposed to owe, in great measure, the astonishing progress which he had made in philosophy and virtue.

It gave me some surprize, that Alcheic's wife (who by-the-bye happened also to be his sister) was no wise scandalized at this species of infidelity.

Much about the same time I discovered (for it was not attempted to be kept a secret from me or any body) that Alcheic was a murderer and a parricide, and had put to death an innocent person, the most nearly connected with him, and whom he was bound to protect and defend by all the ties of nature and humanity. When I asked, with all the caution and deference imaginable, what was his motive for this action; he replied coolly, that he was not then so much at ease in his circumstances as he is at present, and that he had acted, in that particular, by the advice of all his friends.

Having heard Alcheic's virtue so extremely celebrated, I pretended to join in the general voice of acclamation, and only asked, by way of curiosity, as a stranger, which of all his noble actions was most highly applauded; and I soon found, that all sentiments were united in giving the preference to the assassination of Usbek. This Usbek had been to the last moment Alcheic's intimate friend, had laid many high obligations upon him, had even saved his life on a certain occasion, and had, by his will, which was found after the murder, made him heir to a considerable part of his fortune. Alcheic, it seems, conspired with about twenty or thirty more, most of them also Usbek's friends; and falling all together on that unhappy man, when he was not aware, they had torne him with a hundred wounds; and given him that reward for his past favours and obligations. Usbek, said the general voice of the people, had many great and good qualities: His very vices were shining, magnificent, and generous: But this action of Alcheic's sets him far above Usbek in the eyes of all judges of merit; and is one of the noblest that ever perhaps the sun shone upon. Another part of Alcheic's conduct, which I also found highly applauded, was his behaviour towards Calish, with whom he was joined in a project or undertaking of some importance. Calish, being a passionate man, gave Alcheic, one day, a sound drubbing; which he took very patiently, waited the return of Calish's good-humour, kept still a fair correspondence with him; and by that means brought the affair, in which they were joined, to a happy issue, and gained to himself immortal honour by his remarkable temper and moderation.

I have lately received a letter from a correspondent in Fourli, by which I learn, that, since my departure, Alcheic, falling into a bad state of health, has fairly hanged himself; and has died universally regretted and applauded in that country. So virtuous and noble a life, says each Fourlian, could not be better crowned than by so noble an end; and Alcheic has proved by this, as well as by all his other actions, what he boasted of near his last moments, that a wise man is scarcely inferior to the great god, Vitzli. This is the name of the supreme deity among the Fourlians.

The notions of this people, continued Palamedes, are as extraordinary with regard to good-manners and sociableness, as with regard to morals. My friend Alcheic formed once a party for my entertainment, composed of all the prime wits and philosophers of Fourli; and each of us brought his mess along with him to the place where we assembled. I observed one of them to be worse provided than the rest, and offered him a share of my mess, which happened to be a roasted pullet: And I could not but remark, that he and all the rest of the company smiled at my simplicity. I was told, that Alcheic had once so much interest with this club as to prevail with them to eat in common, and that he had made use of an artifice for that purpose. He persuaded those, whom he observed to be *worst* provided, to offer their mess to the company; after which, the others, who had brought more delicate fare, were ashamed not to make the same offer. This is regarded as so extraordinary an event, that it has since, as I learn, been recorded in the history of Alcheic's life, composed by one of the greatest geniuses of Fourli.

Pray, said I, Palamedes, when you were at Fourli, did you also learn the art of turning your friends into ridicule, by telling them strange stories, and then laughing at them, if they believed you. I assure you, replied he, had I been disposed to learn such a lesson, there was no place in the world more proper. My friend, so often mentioned, did nothing, from morning to night, but sneer, and banter, and rally; and you could scarcely ever distinguish, whether he were in jest or earnest. But you think then, that my story is improbable; and that I have used, or rather abused the privilege of a traveller. To be sure, said I, you were but in jest. Such barbarous and savage manners are not only incompatible with a civilized, intelligent people, such as you said these were; but scarcely compatible with human nature. They exceed all we ever read of, among the Mingrelians, and Topinamboues.

Have a care, cried he, have a care! You are not aware that you are speaking blasphemy, and are abusing your favourites, the Greeks, especially the Athenians, whom I have couched, all along, under these bizarre names I employed. If you consider aright, there is not one stroke of the foregoing character, which might not be found in the man of highest merit at Athens, without diminishing in the least from the brightness of his character. The amours of the Greeks, their marriages,[1] and the exposing of their children cannot but strike you immediately. The death of Usbek is an exact counter-part to that of Caesar.

All to a trifle, said I, interrupting him: You did not mention that Usbek was an usurper.

I did not, replied he; lest you should discover the parallel I aimed at. But even adding this circumstance, we should make no scruple, according to our sentiments of morals, to denominate Brutus, and Cassius, ungrateful traitors and assassins: Though you know, that they are, perhaps, the highest characters of all antiquity; and the Athenians erected statues to them; which they placed near those of Harmodius and Aristogiton, their own deliverers. And if you think this circumstance, which you mention, so material to absolve these patriots, I shall compensate it by another, not mentioned, which will equally aggravate their crime. A few days before the execution of their fatal purpose, they all swore fealty to Caesar; and protesting to hold his person ever sacred, they touched the altar with those hands, which they had already armed for his destruction.[2]

I need not remind you of the famous and applauded story of Themistocles, and of his patience towards Eurybiades, the Spartan, his commanding officer, who, heated by debate, lifted his cane to him in a council of war (the same thing as if he had cudgelled him), *Strike!* cries the Athenian, *strike! but hear me.*

You are too good a scholar not to discover the ironical Socrates and his Athenian club in my last story; and you will certainly observe, that it is exactly copied from Xenophon, with a variation only of the names.[3] And I think I have fairly made it appear, that an Athenian man of merit might be such a one as with us would pass for incestuous, a parricide, an assassin, ungrateful, perjured traitor, and something else

---

[1] The laws of Athens allowed a man to marry his sister by the father. Solon's law forbid paederasty to slaves, as being an act of too great dignity for such mean persons.

[2] Appian, Bell. Civ. lib. iii. Suetonius in vita Caesaris.

[3] Mem. Soc. lib. iii. sub fine.

too abominable to be named; not to mention his rusticity and ill-manners. And having lived in this manner, his death might be entirely suitable: He might conclude the scene by a desperate act of self-murder, and die with the most absurd blasphemies in his mouth. And notwithstanding all this, he shall have statues, if not altars, erected to his memory; poems and orations shall be composed in his praise; great sects shall be proud of calling themselves by his name; and the most distant posterity shall blindly continue their admiration: Though were such a one to arise among themselves, they would justly regard him with horror and execration.

I might have been aware, replied I, of your artifice. You seem to take pleasure in this topic: and are indeed the only man I ever knew, who was well acquainted with the ancients, and did not extremely admire them. But instead of attacking their philosophy, their eloquence, or poetry, the usual subjects of controversy between us, you now seem to impeach their morals, and accuse them of ignorance in a science, which is the only one, in my opinion, in which they are not surpassed by the moderns. Geometry, physics, astronomy, anatomy, botany, geography, navigation; in these we justly claim the superiority: But what have we to oppose to their moralists? Your representation of things is fallacious. You have no indulgence for the manners and customs of different ages. Would you try a Greek or Roman by the common law of England? Hear him defend himself by his own maxims; and then pronounce.

There are no manners so innocent or reasonable, but may be rendered odious or ridiculous, if measured by a standard, unknown to the persons; especially, if you employ a little art or eloquence, in aggravating some circumstances, and extenuating others, as best suits the purpose of your discourse. All these artifices may easily be retorted on you. Could I inform the Athenians, for instance, that there was a nation, in which adultery, both active and passive, so to speak, was in the highest vogue and esteem: In which every man of education chose for his mistress a married woman, the wife, perhaps, of his friend and companion; and valued himself upon these infamous conquests, as much as if he had been several times a conqueror in boxing or wrestling at the *Olympic* games: In which every man also took a pride in his tameness and facility with regard to his own wife, and was glad to make friends or gain interest by allowing her to prostitute her charms; and even, without any such motive, gave her full liberty and indulgence: I ask, what sentiments the Athenians would entertain of such a people; they who never mentioned the crime of adultery but in conjunction with robbery and poisoning? Which would they admire most, the villany or the meanness of such a conduct?

Should I add, that the same people were as proud of their slavery and dependance as the Athenians of their liberty; and though a man among them were oppressed, disgraced, impoverished, insulted, or imprisoned by the tyrant, he would still regard it as the highest merit to love, serve, and obey him; and even to die for his smallest glory or satisfaction: These noble Greeks would probably ask me, whether I spoke of a human society, or of some inferior, servile species.

It was then I might inform my Athenian audience, that these people, however, wanted not spirit and bravery. If a man, say I, though their intimate friend, should throw out, in a private company, a raillery against them, nearly approaching any of those, with which your generals and demagogues every day regale each other, in the face of the whole city, they never can forgive him; but in order to revenge themselves, they oblige him immediately to run them through the body, or be himself murdered. And if a man, who is an absolute stranger to them, should desire them, at the peril of their own life, to cut the throat of their bosom-companion, they immediately obey, and think themselves highly obliged and honoured by the commission. These are their maxims of honour: This is their favourite morality.

But though so ready to draw their sword against their friends and countrymen; no disgrace, no infamy, no pain, no poverty will ever engage these people to turn the point of it against their own breast. A man of rank would row in the gallies, would beg his bread, would languish in prison, would suffer any tortures; and still preserve his wretched life. Rather than escape his enemies by a generous contempt of death, he would infamously receive the same death from his enemies, aggravated by their triumphant insults, and by the most exquisite sufferings.

It is very usual too, continue I, among this people to erect jails, where every art of plaguing and tormenting the unhappy prisoners is carefully studied and practised: And in these jails it is usual for a parent voluntarily to shut up several of his children; in order, that another child, whom he owns to have no greater or rather less merit than the rest, may enjoy his whole fortune, and wallow in every kind of voluptuousness and pleasure. Nothing so virtuous in their opinion as this barbarous partiality.

But what is more singular in this whimsical nation, say I to the Athenians, is, that a frolic of yours during the Saturnalia,[4] when the slaves are served by their masters, is seriously continued by them throughout the whole year, and throughout the whole course of their lives; accompanied too with some circumstances, which still farther augment the absurdity and ridicule. Your sport only elevates for a few days those whom fortune has thrown down, and whom she too, in sport, may really elevate for ever above you: But this nation gravely exalts those, whom nature has subjected to them, and whose inferiority and infirmities are absolutely incurable. The women, though without virtue, are their masters and sovereigns: These they reverence, praise, and magnify: To these, they pay the highest deference and respect: And in all places and all times, the superiority of the females is readily acknowledged and submitted to by every one, who has the least pretensions to education and politeness. Scarce any crime would be so universally detested as an infraction of this rule.

You need go no further, replied Palamedes; I can easily conjecture the people whom you aim at. The strokes, with which you have painted them, are pretty just; and yet you

4 The Greeks kept the feast of Saturn or Chronus, as well as the Romans. See Lucian, Epist. Saturn.

must acknowledge, that scarce any people are to be found, either in ancient or modern times, whose national character is, upon the whole, less liable to exception. But I give you thanks for helping me out with my argument. I had no intention of exalting the moderns at the expence of the ancients. I only meant to represent the uncertainty of all these judgments concerning characters; and to convince you, that fashion, vogue, custom, and law, were the chief foundation of all moral determinations. The Athenians surely, were a civilized, intelligent people, if ever there were one; and yet their man of merit might, in this age, be held in horror and execration. The French are also, without doubt, a very civilized, intelligent people; and yet their man of merit might, with the Athenians, be an object of the highest contempt and ridicule, and even hatred. And what renders the matter more extraordinary: These two people are supposed to be the most similar in their national character of any in ancient and modern times; and while the English flatter themselves that they resemble the Romans, their neighbours on the continent draw the parallel between themselves and those polite Greeks. What wide difference, therefore, in the sentiments of morals, must be found between civilized nations and Barbarians, or between nations whose characters have little in common? How shall we pretend to fix a standard for judgments of this nature?

By tracing matters, replied I, a little higher, and examining the first principles, which each nation establishes, of blame or censure. The Rhine flows north, the Rhone south; yet both spring from the *same* mountain, and are also actuated, in their opposite directions, by the *same* principle of gravity. The different inclinations of the ground, on which they run, cause all the difference of their courses.

In how many circumstances would an Athenian and a French man of merit certainly resemble each other? Good sense, knowledge, wit, eloquence, humanity, fidelity, truth, justice, courage, temperance, constancy, dignity of mind: These you have all omitted; in order to insist only on the points, in which they may, by accident, differ. Very well: I am willing to comply with you; and shall endeavour to account for these differences from the most universal, established principles of morals.

The Greek loves, I care not to examine more particularly. I shall only observe, that, however blameable, they arose from a very innocent cause, the frequency of the gymnastic exercises among that people; and were recommended, though absurdly, as the source of friendship, sympathy, mutual attachment, and fidelity;[5] qualities esteemed in all nations and all ages.

The marriage of half-brothers and sisters seems no great difficulty. Love between the nearer relations is contrary to reason and public utility; but the precise point, where we are to stop, can scarcely be determined by natural reason; and is therefore a very proper subject for municipal law or custom. If the Athenians went a little too far on the one side, the canon law has surely pushed matters a great way into the other extreme.[6]

Had you asked a parent at Athens, why he bereaved his child of that life, which he had so lately given it. It is because I love it, he would reply; and regard the poverty which it must inherit from me, as a greater evil than death, which it is not capable of dreading, feeling, or resenting.[7]

How is public liberty, the most valuable of all blessings, to be recovered from the hands of an usurper or tyrant, if his power shields him from public rebellion, and our scruples from private vengeance? That his crime is capital by law, you acknowledge: And must the highest aggravation of his crime, the putting of himself above law, form his full security? You can reply nothing, but by showing the great inconveniences of assassination; which could any one have proved clearly to the ancients, he had reformed their sentiments in this particular.

Again, to cast your eye on the picture which I have drawn of modern manners; there is almost as great difficulty, I ac-

---

[5] Plat. Symp. p. 182, ex edit. Ser.
[6] See Enquiry, Sect. IV.
[7] Plut. de amore prolis, sub fine.

knowledge, to justify French as Greek gallantry; except only, that the former is much more natural and agreeable than the latter. But our neighbours, it seems, have resolved to sacrifice some of the domestic to the sociable pleasures; and to prefer ease, freedom, and an open commerce, to a strict fidelity and constancy. These ends are both good, and are somewhat difficult to reconcile; nor need we be surprised, if the customs of nations incline too much, sometimes to the one side, sometimes to the other.

The most inviolable attachment to the laws of our country is every where acknowledged a capital virtue; and where the people are not so happy, as to have any legislature but a single person, the strictest loyalty is, in that case, the truest patriotism.

Nothing surely can be more absurd and barbarous than the practice of duelling; but those, who justify it, say, that it begets civility and good-manners. And a duellist, you may observe, always values himself upon his courage, his sense of honour, his fidelity and friendship; qualities, which are here indeed very oddly directed, but which have been esteemed universally, since the foundation of the world.

Have the gods forbid self-murder? An Athenian allows, that it ought to be forborn. Has the Deity permitted it? A Frenchman allows, that death is preferable to pain and infamy.

You see then, continued I, that the principles upon which men reason in morals are always the same; though the conclusions which they draw are often very different. That they all reason aright with regard to this subject, more than with regard to any other, it is not incumbent on any moralist to show. It is sufficient, that the original principles of censure or blame are uniform, and that erroneous conclusions can be corrected by sounder reasoning and larger experience. Though many ages have elapsed since the fall of Greece and Rome; though many changes have arrived in religion, language, laws, and customs; none of these revolutions has ever produced any considerable innovation in the primary sentiments of morals, more than in those of external beauty. Some minute differences, perhaps, may be observed in both. Horace[8] celebrates a low forehead, and Anacreon joined eye-brows:[9] But the Apollo and the Venus of antiquity are still our models for male and female beauty; in like manner as the character of Scipio continues our standard for the glory of heroes, and that of Cornelia for the honour of matrons.

It appears, that there never was any quality recommended by any one, as a virtue or moral excellence, but on account of its being *useful*, or *agreeable* to a man *himself*, or to *others*. For what other reason can ever be assigned for praise or approbation? Or where would be the sense of extolling a *good* character or action, which, at the same time, is allowed to be *good for nothing*? All the differences, therefore, in morals, may be reduced to this one general foundation, and may be accounted for by the different views, which people take of these circumstances.

Sometimes men differ in their judgment about the usefulness of any habit or action: Sometimes also the peculiar circumstances of things render one moral quality more useful than others, and give it a peculiar preference.

It is not surprising, that, during a period of war and disorder, the military virtues should be more celebrated than the pacific, and attract more the admiration and attention of mankind. "How usual is it," says Tully,[10] "to find Cimbrians, Celtiberians, and other Barbarians, who bear, with inflexible constancy, all the fatigues and dangers of the field; but are immediately dispirited under the pain and hazard of a languishing distemper: While, on the other hand, the Greeks patiently endure the slow approaches of death, when armed with sickness and disease; but timorously fly his presence, when he attacks them violently with swords and falchions!" So different is even the same virtue of courage among warlike or peaceful nations! And indeed, we may observe, that, as the difference between war and peace is the

---

[8] Epist. lib. i. epist. 7. Also lib. i. ode 3.
[9] Ode 28. Petronius (cap. 86) joins both these circumstances as beauties.
[10] Tusc. Quaest. lib. ii.

greatest that arises among nations and public societies, it produces also the greatest variations in moral sentiment, and diversifies the most our ideas of virtue and personal merit.

Sometimes too, magnanimity, greatness of mind, disdain of slavery, inflexible rigour and integrity, may better suit the circumstances of one age than those of another, and have a more kindly influence, both on public affairs, and on a man's own safety and advancement. Our idea of merit, therefore, will also vary a little with these variations; and Labeo, perhaps, be censured for the same qualities, which procured Cato the highest approbation.

A degree of luxury may be ruinous and pernicious in a native of Switzerland, which only fosters the arts, and encourages industry in a Frenchman or Englishman. We are not, therefore, to expect, either the same sentiments, or the same laws in Berne, which prevail in London or Paris.

Different customs have also some influence as well as different utilities; and by giving an early bias to the mind, may produce a superior propensity, either to the useful or the agreeable qualities; to those which regard self, or those which extend to society. These four sources of moral sentiment still subsist; but particular accidents may, at one time, make any one of them flow with greater abundance than at another.

The customs of some nations shut up the women from all social commerce: Those of others make them so essential a part of society and conversation, that, except where business is transacted, the male-sex alone are supposed almost wholly incapable of mutual discourse and entertainment. As this difference is the most material that can happen in private life, it must also produce the greatest variation in our moral sentiments.

Of all nations in the world, where polygamy was not allowed, the Greeks seem to have been the most reserved in their commerce with the fair sex, and to have imposed on them the strictest laws of modesty and decency. We have a strong instance of this in an oration of Lysias.[11] A widow injured, ruined, undone, calls a meeting of a few of her near-

[11] Orat. 33.

est friends and relations; and though never before accustomed, says the orator, to speak in the presence of men, the distress of her circumstances constrained her to lay the case before them. The very opening of her mouth in such company required, it seems, an apology.

When Demosthenes prosecuted his tutors, to make them refund his patrimony, it became necessary for him, in the course of the law-suit, to prove that the marriage of Aphobus's sister with Oneter was entirely fraudulent, and that, notwithstanding her sham marriage, she had lived with her brother at Athens for two years past, ever since her divorce from her former husband. And it is remarkable, that though these were people of the first fortune and distinction in the city, the orator could prove this fact no way, but by calling for her female slaves to be put to the question, and by the evidence of one physician, who had seen her in her brother's house during her illness.[12] So reserved were Greek manners.

We may be assured, that an extreme purity of manners was the consequence of this reserve. Accordingly we find, that, except the fabulous stories of an Helen and a Clytemnestra, there scarcely is an instance of any event in the Greek history, which proceeded from the intrigues of women. On the other hand, in modern times, particularly in a neighbouring nation, the females enter into all transactions and all management of church and state: And no man can expect success, who takes not care to obtain their good graces. Harry the third, by incurring the displeasure of the fair, endangered his crown, and lost his life, as much as by his indulgence to heresy.

It is needless to dissemble: The consequence of a very free commerce between the sexes, and of their living much together, will often terminate in intrigues and gallantry. We must sacrifice somewhat of the *useful*, if we be very anxious to obtain all the *agreeable* qualities; and cannot pretend to reach alike every kind of advantage. Instances of licence, daily multiplying, will weaken the scandal with the one sex, and teach the other by degrees, to adopt the famous maxim of La Fon-

[12] In Oneterem.

taine, with regard to female infidelity, *that if one knows it, it is but a small matter; if one knows it not, it is nothing.*[13]

Some people are inclined to think, that the best way of adjusting all differences, and of keeping the proper medium between the *agreeable* and the *useful* qualities of the sex, is to live with them after the manner of the Romans and the English (for the customs of these two nations seem similar in this respect);[14] that is, without gallantry,[15] and without jealousy. By a parity of reason, the customs of the Spaniards and of the Italians of an age ago (for the present are very different) must be the worst of any; because they favour both gallantry and jealousy.

Nor will these different customs of nations affect the one sex only: Their idea of personal merit in the males must also be somewhat different with regard, at least, to conversation, address, and humour. The one nation, where the men live much apart, will naturally more approve of prudence; the other of gaiety. With the one simplicity of manners will be in the highest esteem; with the other, politeness. The one will distinguish themselves by good-sense and judgment; the other, by taste and delicacy. The eloquence of the former will shine most in the senate; that of the other, on the theatre.

These, I say, are the *natural* effects of such customs. For it must be confessed, that chance has a great influence on national manners; and many events happen in society, which are not to be accounted for by general rules. Who could imagine, for instance, that the Romans, who lived freely with their women, should be very indifferent about music, and

[13] Quand on le sçait, c'est peu de chose:
Quand on l'ignore, ce n'est rien.
[14] During the times of the emperors, the Romans seem to have been more given to intrigues and gallantry than the English are at present: And the women of condition, in order to retain their lovers, endeavoured to fix a name of reproach on those who were addicted to wenching and low amours. They were called Ancillarioli. See Seneca de beneficiis, Lib. i. cap. 9. See also Martial, lib. xii. epig. 58.
[15] The gallantry here meant is that of amours and attachments, not that of complaisance, which is as much paid to the fair sex in England as in any other country.

esteem dancing infamous: While the Greeks, who never almost saw a woman but in their own houses, were continually piping, singing, and dancing?

The differences of moral sentiment, which naturally arise from a republican or monarchical government, are also very obvious; as well as those which proceed from general riches or poverty, union or faction, ignorance or learning. I shall conclude this long discourse with observing, that different customs and situations vary not the original ideas of merit (however they may, some consequences) in any very essential point, and prevail chiefly with regard to young men, who can aspire to the agreeable qualities, and may attempt to please. The Manner, the Ornaments, the Graces, which succeed in this shape, are more arbitrary and casual: But the merit of riper years is almost every where the same; and consists chiefly in integrity, humanity, ability, knowledge, and the other more solid and useful qualities of the human mind.

What you insist on, replied Palamedes, may have some foundation, when you adhere to the maxims of common life and ordinary conduct. Experience and the practice of the world readily correct any great extravagance on either side. But what say you to *artificial* lives and manners? How do you reconcile the maxims, on which, in different ages and nations, these are founded?

What do you understand by *artificial* lives and manners? said I. I explain myself, replied he. You know, that religion had, in ancient times, very little influence on common life, and that, after men had performed their duty in sacrifices and prayers at the temple, they thought, that the gods left the rest of their conduct to themselves, and were little pleased or offended with those virtues or vices, which only affected the peace and happiness of human society. In those ages, it was the business of philosophy alone to regulate men's ordinary behaviour and deportment; and accordingly, we may observe, that this being the sole principle, by which a man could elevate himself above his fellows, it acquired a mighty ascendant over many, and produced great singularities of maxims and of conduct. At present, when philosophy has lost the allurement of novelty, it has no such extensive influence; but seems to confine itself mostly to speculations in the closet; in the same manner, as the ancient religion was limited to sacrifices in the temple. Its place is now supplied by the modern religion, which inspects our whole conduct, and prescribes an universal rule to our actions, to our words, to our very thoughts and inclinations; a rule so much the more austere, as it is guarded by infinite, though distant, rewards and punishments; and no infraction of it can ever be concealed or disguised.

Diogenes is the most celebrated model of extravagant philosophy. Let us seek a parallel to him in modern times. We shall not disgrace any philosophic name by a comparison with the Dominics or Loyolas, or any canonized monk or friar. Let us compare him to Pascal, a man of parts and genius as well as Diogenes himself; and perhaps too, a man of virtue, had he allowed his virtuous inclinations to have exerted and displayed themselves.

The foundation of Diogenes's conduct was an endeavour to render himself an independent being as much as possible, and to confine all his wants and desires and pleasures within himself and his own mind: The aim of Pascal was to keep a perpetual sense of his dependence before his eyes, and never to forget his numberless wants and infirmities. The ancient supported himself by magnanimity, ostentation, pride, and the idea of his own superiority above his fellow-creatures. The modern made constant profession of humility and abasement, of the contempt and hatred of himself; and endeavoured to attain these supposed virtues, as far as they are attainable. The austerities of the Greek were in order to inure himself to hardships, and prevent his ever suffering: Those of the Frenchman were embraced merely for their own sake, and in order to suffer as much as possible. The philosopher indulged himself in the most beastly pleasures, even in public: The saint refused himself the most innocent, even in private. The former thought it his duty to love his friends, and to rail at them, and reprove them, and scold them: The latter endeavoured to be absolutely indifferent towards his nearest relations, and to love and speak well of his enemies. The great object of Diogenes's wit was every kind of superstition, that is every kind of religion known in his time. The mortality of the soul was his standard principle; and even his sentiments of a divine providence seem to have been licentious. The most ridiculous superstitions directed Pascal's faith and practice; and an extreme contempt of this life, in comparison of the future, was the chief foundation of his conduct.

In such a remarkable contrast do these two men stand: Yet both of them have met with general admiration in their different ages, and have been proposed as models of imitation. Where then is the universal standard of morals, which you talk of? And what rule shall we establish for the many different, nay contrary sentiments of mankind?

An experiment, said I, which succeeds in the air, will not always succeed in a vacuum. When men depart from the maxims of common reason, and affect these *artificial* lives, as you call them, no one can answer for what will please or displease them. They are in a different element from the rest of mankind; and the natural principles of their mind play not with the same regularity, as if left to themselves, free from the illusions of religious superstition or philosophical enthusiasm.

# A TREATISE OF HUMAN NATURE

# BOOK II. OF THE PASSIONS

## Part III

## Of the Will and Direct Passions

### Section III. Of the Influencing Motives of the Will

Nothing is more usual in philosophy, and even in common life, than to talk of the combat of passion and reason, to give the preference to reason, and to assert that men are only so far virtuous as they conform themselves to its dictates. Every rational creature, 'tis said, is oblig'd to regulate his actions by reason; and if any other motive or principle challenge the direction of his conduct, he ought to oppose it, 'till it be entirely subdu'd, or at least brought to a conformity with that superior principle. On this method of thinking the greatest part of moral philosophy, ancient and modern, seems to be founded; nor is there an ampler field, as well for metaphysical arguments, as popular declamations, than this suppos'd pre-eminence of reason above passion. The eternity, invariableness, and divine origin of the former have been display'd to the best advantage: The blindness, unconstancy and deceitfulness of the latter have been as strongly insisted on. In order to shew the fallacy of all this philosophy, I shall endeavour to prove *first*, that reason alone can never be a motive to any action of the will; and *secondly*, that it can never oppose passion in the direction of the will.

The understanding exerts itself after two different ways, as it judges from demonstration or probability; as it regards the abstract relations of our ideas, or those relations of objects, of which experience only gives us information. I believe it scarce will be asserted, that the first species of reasoning alone is ever the cause of any action. As its proper province is the

**177**

world of ideas, and as the will always places us in that of realities, demonstration and volition seem, upon that account, to be totally remov'd, from each other. Mathematics, indeed, are useful in all mechanical operations, and arithmetic in almost every art and profession: But 'tis not of themselves they have any influence. Mechanics are the art of regulating the motions of bodies *to some design'd end or purpose*; and the reason why we employ arithmetic in fixing the proportions of numbers, is only that we may discover the proportions of their influence and operation. A merchant is desirous of knowing the sum total of his accounts with any person: Why? but that he may learn what sum will have the same *effects* in paying his debt, and going to market, as all the particular articles taken together. Abstract or demonstrative reasoning, therefore, never influences any of our actions, but only as it directs our judgment concerning causes and effects; which leads us to the second operation of the understanding.

'Tis obvious, that when we have the prospect of pain or pleasure from any object, we feel a consequent emotion of aversion or propensity, and are carry'd to avoid or embrace what will give us this uneasiness or satisfaction. 'Tis also obvious, that this emotion rests not here, but making us cast our view on every side, comprehends whatever objects are connected with its original one by the relation of cause and effect. Here then reasoning takes place to discover this relation; and according as our reasoning varies, our actions receive a subsequent variation. But 'tis evident in this case, that the impulse arises not from reason, but is only directed by it. 'Tis from the prospect of pain or pleasure that the aversion or propensity arises towards any object: And these emotions extend themselves to the causes and effects of that object, as they are pointed out to us by reason and experience. It can never in the least concern us to know, that such objects are causes, and such others effects, if both the causes and effects be indifferent to us. Where the objects themselves do not affect us, their connexion can never give them any influence; and 'tis plain, that as reason is nothing but the discovery of this connexion, it cannot be by its means that the objects are able to affect us.

Since reason alone can never produce any action, or give rise to volition, I infer, that the same faculty is as incapable of preventing volition, or of disputing the preference with any passion or emotion. This consequence is necessary. 'Tis impossible reason cou'd have the latter effect of preventing volition, but by giving an impulse in a contrary direction to our passion; and that impulse, had it operated alone, wou'd have been able to produce volition. Nothing can oppose or retard the impulse of passion, but a contrary impulse; and if this contrary impulse ever arises from reason, that latter faculty must have an original influence on the will, and must be able to cause, as well as hinder any act of volition. But if reason has no original influence, 'tis impossible it can withstand any principle, which has such an efficacy, or ever keep the mind in suspense a moment. Thus it appears, that the principle, which opposes our passion, cannot be the same with reason, and is only call'd so in an improper sense. We speak not strictly and philosophically when we talk of the combat of passion and of reason. Reason is, and ought only to be the slave of the passions, and can never pretend to any other office than to serve and obey them. As this opinion may appear somewhat extraordinary, it may not be improper to confirm it by some other considerations.

A passion is an original existence, or, if you will, modification of existence, and contains not any representative quality, which renders it a copy of any other existence or modification. When I am angry, I am actually possest with the passion, and in that emotion have no more a reference to any other object, than when I am thirsty, or sick, or more than five foot high. 'Tis impossible, therefore, that this passion can be oppos'd by, or be contradictory to truth and reason; since this contradiction consists in the disagreement of ideas, consider'd as copies, with those objects, which they represent.

What may at first occur on this head, is, that as nothing can be contrary to truth or reason, except what has a reference to it, and as the judgments of our understanding only have this reference, it must follow, that passions can be contrary to reason only so far as they are *accompany'd* with some judgment or opinion. According to this principle, which is so obvious and natural, 'tis only in two senses, that any affection can be call'd unreasonable. First, When a passion, such as hope or fear, grief or joy, despair or security, is founded on the supposition of the existence of objects, which really do not exist. Secondly, When in exerting any passion in action, we chuse means insufficient for the design'd end, and deceive ourselves in our judgment of causes and effects. Where a passion is neither founded on false suppositions, nor chuses means insufficient for the end, the understanding can neither justify nor condemn it. 'Tis not contrary to reason to prefer the destruction of the whole world to the scratching of my finger. 'Tis not contrary to reason for me to chuse my total ruin, to prevent the least uneasiness of an *Indian* or person wholly unknown to me. 'Tis as little contrary to reason to prefer even my own acknowledg'd lesser good to my greater, and have a more ardent affection for the former than the latter. A trivial good may, from certain circumstances, produce a desire superior to what arises from the greatest and most valuable enjoyment; nor is there any thing more extraordinary in this, than in mechanics to see one pound weight raise up a hundred by the advantage of its situation. In short, a passion must be accompany'd with some false judgment, in order to its being unreasonable; and even then 'tis not the passion, properly speaking, which is unreasonable, but the judgment.

The consequences are evident. Since a passion can never, in any sense, be call'd unreasonable, but when founded on a false supposition, or when it chuses means insufficient for the design'd end, 'tis impossible, that reason and passion can ever oppose each other, or dispute for the government of the will and actions. The moment we perceive the falshood of any supposition, or the insufficiency of any means our passions yield to our reason without any opposition. I may desire any fruit as of an excellent relish; but whenever you convince me of my mistake, my longing ceases. I may will the performance of certain actions as means of obtaining any desir'd good; but as my willing of these actions is only secondary, and

founded on the supposition, that they are causes of the propos'd effect; as soon as I discover the falshood of that supposition, they must become indifferent to me.

'Tis natural for one, that does not examine objects with a
strict philosophic eye, to imagine, that those actions of the
mind are entirely the same, which produce not a different
sensation, and are not immediately distinguishable to the feeling and perception. Reason, for instance, exerts itself without
producing any sensible emotion; and except in the more
sublime disquisitions of philosophy, or in the frivolous subtilties of the schools, scarce ever conveys any pleasure or uneasiness. Hence it proceeds, that every action of the mind,
which operates with the same calmness and tranquillity, is
confounded with reason by all those, who judge of things from
the first view and appearance. Now 'tis certain, there are certain calm desires and tendencies, which, tho' they be real
passions, produce little emotion in the mind, and are more
known by their effects than by the immediate feeling or sensation. These desires are of two kinds; either certain instincts
originally implanted in our natures, such as benevolence and
resentment, the love of life, and kindness to children; or the
general appetite to good, and aversion to evil, consider'd
merely as such. When any of these passions are calm, and
cause no disorder in the soul, they are very readily taken for
the determinations of reason, and are suppos'd to proceed
from the same faculty, with that, which judges of truth and
falshood. Their nature and principles have been suppos'd the
same, because their sensations are not evidently different.

Beside these calm passions, which often determine the will,
there are certain violent emotions of the same kind, which
have likewise a great influence on that faculty. When I receive
any injury from another, I often feel a violent passion of
resentment, which makes me desire his evil and punishment,
independent of all considerations of pleasure and advantage
to myself. When I am immediately threaten'd with any grievous ill, my fears, apprehension, and aversions rise to a great
height, and produce a sensible emotion.

The common error of metaphysicians has lain in ascrib-ing the direction of the will entirely to one of these principles, and supposing the other to have no influence. Men often act knowingly against their interest: For which reason the view of the greatest possible good does not always influence them. Men often counter-act a violent passion in prosecution of their interests and designs: 'Tis not therefore the present uneasiness alone, which determines them. In general we may observe, that both these principles operate on the will; and where they are contrary, that either of them prevails, according to the *general* character or *present* disposition of the person. What we call strength of mind, implies the prevalence of the calm passions above the violent; tho' we may easily observe, there is no man so constantly possess'd of this virtue, as never on any occasion to yield to the sollicitations of passion and desire. From these variations of temper proceeds the great difficulty of deciding concerning the actions and resolutions of men, where there is any contrariety of motives and passions.

# BOOK III. OF MORALS

## Part I

## Of Virtue and Vice in General

### Section I. Moral Distinctions Not Deriv'd from Reason

There is an inconvenience which attends all abstruse reasoning, that it may silence, without convincing an antagonist, and requires the same intense study to make us sensible of its force, that was at first requisite for its invention. When we leave our closet, and engage in the common affairs of life, its conclusions seem to vanish, like the phantoms of the night on the appearance of the morning; and 'tis difficult for us to retain even that conviction, which we had attain'd with difficulty. This is still more conspicuous in a long chain of reasoning, where we must preserve to the end the evidence of the first propositions, and where we often lose sight of all the most receiv'd maxims, either of philosophy or common life. I am not, however, without hopes, that the present system of philosophy will acquire new force as it advances; and that our reasonings concerning *morals* will corroborate whatever has been said concerning the *understanding* and the *passions*. Morality is a subject that interests us above all others: We fancy the peace of society to be at stake in every decision concerning it; and 'tis evident, that this concern must make our speculations appear more real and solid, than where the subject is, in a great measure, indifferent to us. What affects us, we conclude can never be a chimera; and as our passion is engag'd on the one side or the other, we naturally think that the question lies within human comprehension; which, in other cases of this nature, we are apt to entertain some doubt of. Without this advantage I never should have ventur'd upon a third volume of such abstruse philosophy, in an age, wherein the greatest part of men seem agreed to convert reading into an amusement, and to reject every thing that requires any considerable degree of attention to be comprehended.

It has been observ'd, that nothing is ever present to the mind but its perceptions; and that all the actions of seeing, hearing, judging, loving, hating, and thinking, fall under this denomination. The mind can never exert itself in any action, which we may not comprehend under the term of *perception*; and consequently that term is no less applicable to those judgments, by which we distinguish moral good and evil, than to every other operation of the mind. To approve of one character, to condemn another, are only so many different perceptions.

Now as perceptions resolve themselves into two kinds, viz. *impressions* and *ideas*, this distinction gives rise to a question, with which we shall open up our present enquiry concerning morals, *Whether 'tis by means of our* ideas *or* impressions *we distinguish betwixt vice and virtue, and pronounce an action blameable or praise-worthy?* This will immediately cut off all loose discourses and declamations, and reduce us to something precise and exact on the present subject.

Those who affirm that virtue is nothing but a conformity to reason; that there are eternal fitnesses and unfitnesses of things, which are the same to every rational being that considers them; that the immutable measures of right and wrong impose an obligation, not only on human creatures, but also on the Deity himself: All these systems concur in the opinion, that morality, like truth, is discern'd merely by ideas, and by their juxta-position and comparison. In order, therefore, to judge of these systems, we need only consider, whether it be possible, from reason alone, to distinguish betwixt moral good and evil, or whether there must concur some other principles to enable us to make that distinction.

If morality had naturally no influence on human passions and actions, 'twere in vain to take such pains to inculcate it; and nothing wou'd be more fruitless than that multitude of rules and precepts, with which all moralists abound. Philosophy is commonly divided into *speculative* and *practical*; and as morality is always comprehended under the latter division, 'tis supposed to influence our passions and actions, and to go beyond the calm and indolent judgments of the understanding.

And this is confirm'd by common experience, which informs us, that men are often govern'd by their duties, and are deter'd from some actions by the opinion of injustice, and impell'd to others by that of obligation.

Since morals, therefore, have an influence on the actions and affections, it follows, that they cannot be deriv'd from reason; and that because reason alone, as we have already prov'd, can never have any such influence. Morals excite passions, and produce or prevent actions. Reason of itself is utterly impotent in this particular. The rules of morality, therefore, are not conclusions of our reason.

No one, I believe, will deny the justness of this inference; nor is there any other means of evading it, than by denying that principle, on which it is founded. As long as it is allow'd, that reason has no influence on our passions and actions, 'tis in vain to pretend, that morality is discover'd only by a deduction of reason. An active principle can never be founded on an inactive; and if reason be inactive in itself, it must remain so in all its shapes and appearances, whether it exerts itself in natural or moral subjects, whether it considers the powers of external bodies, or the actions of rational beings.

It would be tedious to repeat all the arguments, by which I have prov'd,[1] that reason is perfectly inert, and can never either prevent or produce any action or affection. 'Twill be easy to recollect what has been said upon that subject. I shall only recall on this occasion one of these arguments, which I shall endeavour to render still more conclusive, and more applicable to the present subject.

Reason is the discovery of truth or falshood. Truth or falshood consists in an agreement or disagreement either to the *real* relations of ideas, or to *real* existence and matter of fact. Whatever, therefore, is not susceptible of this agreement or disagreement, is incapable of being true or false, and can never be an object of our reason. Now 'tis evident our passions, volitions, and actions, are not susceptible of any such agreement or disagreement; being original facts and realities, compleat in themselves, and implying no reference to other

[1] Book II. Part III. sect. III.

passions, volitions, and actions. 'Tis impossible, therefore, they can be pronounced either true or false, and be either contrary or comformable to reason.

This argument is of double advantage to our present purpose. For it proves *directly*, that actions do not derive their merit from a conformity to reason, nor their blame from a contrariety to it; and it proves the same truth more *indirectly*, by shewing us, that as reason can never immediately prevent or produce any action by contradicting or approving of it, it cannot be the source of moral good and evil, which are found to have that influence. Actions may be laudable or blameable; but they cannot be reasonable or unreasonable: Laudable or blameable, therefore, are not the same with reasonable or unreasonable. The merit and demerit of actions frequently contradict, and sometimes control our natural propensities. But reason has no such influence. Moral distinctions, therefore, are not the offspring of reason. Reason is wholly inactive, and can never be the source of so active a principle as conscience, or a sense of morals.

But perhaps it may be said, that tho' no will or action can be immediately contradictory to reason, yet we may find such a contradiction in some of the attendants of the action, that is, in its causes or effects. The action may cause a judgment, or may be *obliquely* caus'd by one, when the judgment concurs with a passion; and by an abusive way of speaking, which philosophy will scarce allow of, the same contrariety may, upon that account, be ascrib'd to the action. How far this truth or falshood may be the source of morals, 'twill now be proper to consider.

It has been observ'd, that reason, in a strict and philosophical sense, can have an influence on our conduct only after two ways: Either when it excites a passion by informing us of the existence of something which is a proper object of it; or when it discovers the connexion of causes and effects, so as to afford us means of exerting any passion. These are the only kinds of judgment, which can accompany our actions, or can be said to produce them in any manner; and it must be allow'd, that these judgments may often be false and erroneous. A person may be affected with passion, by supposing a pain or pleasure to lie in an object, which has no tendency to produce either of these sensations, or which produces the contrary to what is imagin'd. A person may also take false measures for the attaining his end, and may retard, by his foolish conduct, instead of forwarding the execution of any project. These false judgments may be thought to affect the passions and actions, which are connected with them, and may be said to render them unreasonable, in a figurative and improper way of speaking. But tho' this be acknowledg'd, 'tis easy to observe, that these errors are so far from being the source of all immorality, that they are commonly very innocent, and draw no manner of guilt upon the person who is so unfortunate as to fall into them. They extend not beyond a mistake of *fact*, which moralists have not generally suppos'd criminal, as being perfectly involuntary. I am more to be lamented than blam'd, if I am mistaken with regard to the influence of objects in producing pain or pleasure, or if I know not the proper means of satisfying my desires. No one can ever regard such errors as a defect in my moral character. A fruit, for instance, that is really disagreeable, appears to me at a distance, and thro' mistake I fancy it to be pleasant and delicious. Here is one error. I chuse certain means of reaching this fruit, which are not proper for my end. Here is a second error; nor is there any third one, which can ever possibly enter into our reasonings concerning actions. I ask, therefore, if a man, in this situation, and guilty of these two errors, is to be regarded as vicious and criminal, however unavoidable they might have been? Or if it be possible to imagine, that such errors are the sources of all immorality?

And here it may be proper to observe, that if moral distinctions be deriv'd from the truth or falshood of those judgments, they must take place wherever we form the judgments; nor will there be any difference, whether the question be concerning an apple or a kingdom, or whether the error be avoidable or unavoidable. For as the very essence of morality is suppos'd to consist in an agreement or disagreement to reason, the other circumstances are entirely arbitrary, and can never either bestow on any action the character of virtuous or vicious, or deprive it of that character. To which we may add, that this agreement or disagreement, not admitting of degrees, all virtues and vices wou'd of course be equal.

Shou'd it be pretended, that tho' a mistake of *fact* be not criminal, yet a mistake of *right* often is; and that this may be the source of immorality: I would answer, that 'tis impossible such a mistake can ever be the original source of immorality, since it supposes a real right and wrong; that is, a real distinction in morals, independent of these judgments. A mistake, therefore, of right may become a species of immorality; but 'tis only a secondary one, and is founded on some other, antecedent to it.

As to those judgments which are the *effects* of our actions, and which, when false, give occasion to pronounce the actions contrary to truth and reason; we may observe, that our actions never cause any judgment, either true or false, in ourselves, and that 'tis only on others they have such an influence. 'Tis certain, that an action, on many occasions, may give rise to false conclusions in others; and that a person, who thro' a window sees any lewd behaviour of mine with my neighbour's wife, may be so simple as to imagine she is certainly my own. In this respect my action resembles somewhat a lye or falshood; only with this difference, which is material, that I perform not the action with any intention of giving rise to a false judgment in another, but merely to satisfy my lust and passion. It causes, however, a mistake and false judgment by accident; and the falshood of its effects may be ascribed, by some odd figurative way of speaking, to the action itself. But still I can see no pretext of reason for asserting, that the tendency to cause such an error is the first spring or original source of all immorality.[2]

[2] One might think it were entirely superfluous to prove this, if a late author, [Hume refers to William Wollaston's *Religion of Nature Delineated.*—Ed.] who has had the good fortune to obtain some reputation, had not seriously affirmed, that such a falshood is the foundation of all guilt and moral deformity. That we may discover the fallacy of his hypothesis, we need only consider, that a false conclusion is drawn from an action, only by means of an obscurity of natural principles, which makes a cause be secretly interrupted in its operation, by contrary causes, and renders the connexion betwixt two objects uncertain and variable. Now, as a like uncertainty and variety of causes take place, even in natural objects, and produce a like error in our judgment, if

Thus upon the whole, 'tis impossible, that the distinction betwixt moral good and evil, can be made by reason; since that distinction has an influence upon our actions, of which reason alone is incapable. Reason and judgment may, indeed, be the mediate cause of an action, by prompting, or by directing a passion: But it is not pretended, that a judgment of this kind, either in its truth or falshood, is attended with virtue or vice. And as to the judgments, which are caused by our judgments, they can still less bestow those moral qualities on the actions, which are their causes.

But to be more particular, and to shew, that those eternal immutable fitnesses and unfitnesses of things cannot be defended by sound philosophy, we may weigh the following considerations.

If the thought and understanding were alone capable of fixing the boundaries of right and wrong, the character of virtuous and vicious either must lie in some relations of objects, or must be a matter of fact, which is discovered by our

---

that tendency to produce error were the very essence of vice and immorality, it shou'd follow, that even inanimate objects might be vicious and immoral.

'Tis in vain to urge, that inanimate objects act without liberty and choice. For as liberty and choice are not necessary to make an action produce in us an erroneous conclusion, they can be, in no respect, essential to morality; and I do not readily perceive, upon this system, how they can ever come to be regarded by it. If the tendency to cause error be the origin of immorality, that tendency and immorality wou'd in every case be inseparable.

Add to this, that if I had used the precaution of shutting the windows, while I indulg'd myself in those liberties with my neighbour's wife, I should have been guilty of no immorality; and that because my action, being perfectly conceal'd, wou'd have had no tendency to produce any false conclusion.

For the same reason, a thief, who steals in by a ladder at a window, and takes all imaginable care to cause no disturbance, is in no respect criminal. For either he will not be perceiv'd, or if he be, 'tis impossible he can produce any error, nor will any one, from these circumstances, take him to be other than what he really is.

'Tis well known, that those who are squint-sighted, do very readily cause mistakes in others, and that we imagine they salute or are talking to one person, while they address themselves to another. Are they therefore, upon that account, immoral?

Besides, we may easily observe, that in all those arguments there is an evident reasoning in a circle. A person who takes possession of *another*'s goods, and uses them as his *own*, in a manner declares them

reasoning. This consequence is evident. As the operations of human understanding divide themselves into two kinds, the comparing of ideas, and the inferring of matter of fact; were virtue discover'd by the understanding; it must be an object of one of these operations, nor is there any third operation of the understanding, which can discover it. There has been an opinion very industriously propagated by certain philosophers, that morality is susceptible of demonstration; and tho' no one has ever been able to advance a single step in those demonstrations; yet 'tis taken for granted, that this science may be brought to an equal certainty with geometry or algebra. Upon this supposition, vice and virtue must consist in some relations; since 'tis allow'd on all hands, that no matter of fact is capable of being demonstrated. Let us, therefore, begin with examining this hypothesis, and endeavour, if possible, to fix those moral qualities, which have been so long the objects of our fruitless researches. Point out distinctly the relations, which constitute morality or obligation, that we may know wherein they consist, and after what manner we must judge of them.

---

to be his own; and this falshood is the source of the immorality of injustice. But is property, or right, or obligation, intelligible, without an antecedent morality?

A man that is ungrateful to his benefactor, in a manner affirms, that he never received any favours from him. But in what manner? Is it because 'tis his duty to be grateful? But this supposes, that there is some antecedent rule of duty and morals. Is it because human nature is generally grateful, and makes us conclude, that a man who does any harm never received any favour from the person he harm'd? But human nature is not so generally grateful, as to justify such a conclusion. Or if it were, is an exception to a general rule in every case criminal, for no other reason than because it is an exception?

But what may suffice entirely to destroy this whimsical system is, that it leaves us under the same difficulty to give a reason why truth is virtuous and falshood vicious, as to account for the merit or turpitude of any other action. I shall allow, if you please, that all immorality is derived from this supposed falshood in action, provided you can give me any plausible reason, why such a falshood is immoral. If you consider rightly of the matter, you will find yourself in the same difficulty as at the beginning.

This last argument is very conclusive; because, if there be not an evident merit or turpitude annex'd to this species of truth or falshood, it can never have any influence upon our actions. For, who ever thought of forbearing any action, because others might possibly draw false conclusions from it? Or, who ever perform'd any, that he might give rise to true conclusions?

If you assert, that vice and virtue consist in relations susceptible of certainty and demonstration, you must confine yourself to those *four* relations, which alone admit of that degree of evidence; and in that case you run into absurdities, from which you will never be able to extricate yourself. For as you make the very essence of morality to lie in the relations, and as there is no one of these relations but what *is* applicable, not only to an irrational, but also to an inanimate object; it follows, that even such objects must be susceptible of merit or demerit. *Resemblance, contrariety, degrees in quality,* and *proportions in quantity and number;* all these relations belong as properly to matter, as to our actions, passions, and volitions. 'Tis unquestionable, therefore, that morality lies not in any of these relations, nor the sense of it in their discovery.[3]

Shou'd it be asserted, that the sense of morality consists in the discovery of some relation, distinct from these, and that our enumeration was not compleat, when we comprehended all demonstrable relations under four general heads: To this I know not what to reply, till some one be so good as to point out to me this new relation. 'Tis impossible to refute a system, which has never yet been explain'd. In such a manner of fighting in the dark, a man loses his blows in the air, and often places them where the enemy is not present.

I must, therefore, on this occasion, rest contented with requiring the two following conditions of any one that wou'd undertake to clear up this system. *First,* As moral good and

---

[3] As a proof, how confus'd our way of thinking on this subject commonly is, we may observe, that those who assert, that morality is demonstrable, do not say, that morality lies in the relations, and that the relations are distinguishable by reason. They only say, that reason can discover such an action, in such relations, to be virtuous, and such another vicious. It seems they thought it sufficient, if they cou'd bring the word, Relation, into the proposition, without troubling themselves whether it was to the purpose or not. But here, I think, is plain argument. Demonstrative reason discovers only relations. But that reason, according to this hypothesis, discovers also vice and virtue. These moral qualities, therefore, must be relations. When we blame any action, in any situation, the whole complicated object, of action and situation, must form certain relations, wherein the essence of vice consists. This hypothesis is not otherwise intelligible. For what does reason discover, when it pronounces any action vicious? Does it discover a relation or a matter of fact? These questions are decisive, and must not be eluded.

evil belong only to the actions of the mind, and are deriv'd from our situation with regard to external objects, the relations, from which these moral distinctions arise, must lie only betwixt internal actions, and external objects, and must not be applicable either to internal actions, compared among themselves, or to external objects, when placed in opposition to other external objects. For as morality is supposed to attend certain relations, if these relations cou'd belong to internal actions consider'd singly, it wou'd follow, that we might be guilty of crimes in ourselves, and independent of our situation, with respect to the universe: And in like manner, if these moral relations cou'd be apply'd to external objects, it wou'd follow, that even inanimate beings wou'd be susceptible of moral beauty and deformity. Now it seems difficult to imagine, that any relation can be discover'd betwixt our passions, volitions and actions, compared to external objects, which relation might not belong either to these passions and volitions, or to these external objects, compar'd among *themselves.*

But it will be still more difficult to fulfil the *second* condition, requisite to justify this system. According to the principles of those who maintain an abstract rational difference betwixt moral good and evil, and a natural fitness and unfitness of things, 'tis not only suppos'd, that these relations, being eternal and immutable, are the same, when consider'd be very rational creature, but their *effects* are also suppos'd to be necessarily the same; and 'tis concluded they have no less, or rather a greater, influence in directing the will of the deity, than in governing the rational and virtuous of our own species. These two particulars are evidently distinct. 'Tis one thing to know virtue, and another to conform the will to it. In order, therefore, to prove, that the measures of right and wrong are eternal laws, *obligatory* on every rational mind, 'tis not sufficient to shew the relations upon which they are founded: We must also point out the connexion betwixt the relation and the will; and must prove that this connexion is so necessary, that in every well-disposed mind, it must take place and have its influence; tho' the difference betwixt these minds be in other respects immense and infinite. Now besides what I have already prov'd, that even in human nature no relation can ever alone produce any action; besides this, I say, it has been shewn, in treating of the understanding, that there is no connexion of cause and effect, such as this is suppos'd to be, which is discoverable otherwise than by experience, and of which we can pretend to have any security by the simple consideration of the objects. All beings in the universe, consider'd in themselves, appear entirely loose and independent of each other. 'Tis only by experience we learn their influence and connexion; and this influence we ought never to extend beyond experience.

Thus it will be impossible to fulfil the *first* condition required to the system of eternal rational measures of right and wrong; because it is impossible to shew those relations, upon which such a distinction may be founded: And 'tis as impossible to fulfil the *second* condition; because we cannot prove *a priori*, that these relations, if they really existed and were perceiv'd, wou'd be universally forcible and obligatory.

But to make these general reflexions more clear and convincing, we may illustrate them by some particular instances, wherein this character of moral good or evil is the most universally acknowledged. Of all crimes that human creatures are capable of committing, the most horrid and unnatural is ingratitude, especially when it is committed against parents, and appears in the more flagrant instances of wounds and death. This is acknowledg'd by all mankind, philosophers as well as the people; the question only arises among philosophers, whether the guilt or moral deformity of this action be discover'd by demonstrative reasoning, or be felt by an internal sense, and by means of some sentiment, which the reflecting on such an action naturally occasions. This question will soon be decided against the former opinion, if we can shew the same relations in other objects, without the notion of any guilt or iniquity attending them. Reason or science is nothing but the comparing of ideas, and the discovery of their relations; and if the same relations have different characters, it must evidently follow, that those characters are not discover'd merely by reason. To put the affair, therefore, to this trial, let us chuse any inanimate object, such as an oak or elm; and let us suppose, that by the dropping of its seed, it produces a sapling below it, which springing up by degrees, at last overtops and destroys the parent tree: I ask, if in this instance there be wanting any relation, which is discoverable in parricide or ingratitude? Is not the one tree the cause of the other's existence; and the latter the cause of the destruction of the former, in the same manner as when a child murders his parent? 'Tis not sufficient to reply, that a choice or will is wanting. For in the case of parricide, a will does not give rise to any *different* relations, but is only the cause from which the action is deriv'd; and consequently produces the *same* relations, that in the oak or elm arise from some other principles. 'Tis a will or choice, that determines a man to kill his parent; and they are the laws of matter and motion, that determine a sapling to destroy the oak, from which it sprung. Here then the same relations have different causes; but still the relations are the same: And as their discovery is not in both cases attended with a notion of immorality, it follows, that that notion does not arise from such a discovery.

But to chuse an instance, still more resembling; I would fain ask any one, why incest in the human species is criminal, and why the very same action, and the same relations in animals have not the smallest moral turpitude and deformity? If it be answer'd, that this action is innocent in animals, because they have not reason sufficient to discover its turpitude; but that man, being endow'd with that faculty, which *ought* to restrain him to his duty, the same action instantly becomes criminal to him; should this be said, I would reply, that this is evidently arguing in a circle. For before reason can perceive this turpitude, the turpitude must exist; and consequently is independent of the decisions of our reason, and is their object more properly than their effect. According to this system, then, every animal, that has sense, and appetite, and will; that is, every animal must be susceptible of all the same virtues and vices, for which we ascribe praise and blame to human creatures. All the difference is, that our superior reason may serve to discover the vice or virtue, and by that means may augment the blame or praise: But still this discovery supposes a separate being in these moral distinctions, and a being, which depends only on the will and appetite, and which, both in thought and reality, may be distinguish'd from the reason. Animals are susceptible of the same relations, with respect to each other, as the human species, and therefore wou'd also be susceptible of the same morality, if the essence of morality consisted in these relations. Their want of a sufficient degree of reason may hinder them from perceiving the duties and obligations of morality, but can never hinder these duties from existing; since they must antecedently exist, in order to their being perceiv'd. Reason must find them, and can never produce them. This argument deserves to be weigh'd, as being, in my opinion, entirely decisive.

Nor does this reasoning only prove, that morality consists not in any relations, that are the objects of science; but if examin'd, will prove with equal certainty, that it consists not in any *matter of fact*, which can be discover'd by the understanding. This is the *second* part of our argument; and if it can be made evident, we may conclude, that morality is not an object of reason. But can there be any difficulty in proving, that vice and virtue are not matters of fact, whose existence we can infer by reason? Take any action allow'd to be vicious: Wilful murder, for instance. Examine it in all lights, and see if you can find that matter of fact, or real existence, which you call *vice*. In which-ever way you take it, you find only certain passions, motives, volitions and thoughts. There is no other matter of fact in the case. The vice entirely escapes you, as long as you consider the object. You never can find it, till you turn your reflexion into your own breast, and find a sentiment of disapprobation, which arises in you, towards this action. Here is a matter of fact; but 'tis the object of feeling, not of reason. It lies in yourself, not in the object. So that when you pronounce any action or character to be vicious, you mean nothing, but that from the constitution of your nature you have a feeling or sentiment of blame from the contemplation of it. Vice and virtue, therefore, may be compar'd to sounds, colours, heat and cold, which, according to modern philosophy, are not qualities in objects, but perceptions in the mind: And this discovery in morals, like that other in physics, is to be regarded as a considerable advancement of the speculative sciences; tho', like that too, it has little or no influence on practice. Nothing can be more real, or concern us more, than our own sentiments of pleasure and uneasiness; and if these be favourable to virtue, and unfavourable to vice, no more can be requisite to the regulation of our conduct and behaviour.

I cannot forbear adding to these reasonings an observation, which may, perhaps, be found of some importance. In every system of morality, which I have hitherto met with, I have always remark'd, that the author proceeds for some time in the ordinary way of reasoning, and establishes the being of a God, or makes observations concerning human affairs; when of a sudden I am surpriz'd to find, that instead of the usual copulations of propositions, *is*, and *is not*, I meet with no proposition that is not connected with an *ought*, or an *ought not*. This change is imperceptible; but is, however, of the last consequence. For as this *ought*, or *ought not*, expresses some new relation or affirmation, 'tis necessary that it shou'd be observ'd and explain'd; and at the same time that a reason should be given, for what seems altogether inconceivable, how this new relation can be a deduction from others, which are entirely different from it. But as authors do not commonly use this precaution, I shall presume to recommend it to the readers; and am persuaded, that this small attention wou'd subvert all the vulgar systems of morality, and let us see, that the distinction of vice and virtue is not founded merely on the relations of objects, nor is perceiv'd by reason.

### Section II. Moral Distinctions Deriv'd from a Moral Sense

Thus the course of the argument leads us to conclude, that since vice and virtue are not discoverable merely by reason, or the comparison of ideas, it must be by means of some impression or sentiment they occasion, that we are able to mark the difference betwixt them. Our decisions concerning moral rectitude and depravity are evidently perceptions; and as all perceptions are either impressions or ideas, the exclusion of the one is a convincing argument for the other. Morality, therefore, is more properly felt than judg'd of; tho' this feeling or sentiment is commonly so soft and gentle, that we are apt to confound it with an idea, according to our common custom of taking all things for the same, which have any near resemblance to each other.

The next question is, Of what nature are these impressions, and after what manner do they operate upon us? Here we cannot remain long in suspense, but must pronounce the impression arising from virtue, to be agreeable, and that proceeding from vice to be uneasy. Every moment's experience must convince us of this. There is no spectacle so fair and beautiful as a noble and generous action; nor any which gives us more abhorrence than one that is cruel and treacherous. No enjoyment equals the satisfaction we receive from the company of those we love and esteem; as the greatest of all punishments is to be oblig'd to pass our lives with those we hate or contemn. A very play or romance may afford us instances of this pleasure, which virtue conveys to us; and pain, which arises from vice.

Now since the distinguishing impressions, by which moral good or evil is known, are nothing but *particular* pains or pleasures; it follows, that in all enquiries concerning these moral distinctions, it will be sufficient to shew the principles, which make us feel a satisfaction or uneasiness from the survey of any character, in order to satisfy us why the character is laudable or blameable. An action, or sentiment, or character is virtuous or vicious; why? because its view causes a pleasure or uneasiness of a particular kind. In giving a reason, therefore, for the pleasure or uneasiness, we sufficiently explain the vice or virtue. To have the sense of virtue, is nothing but to *feel* a satisfaction of a particular kind from the contemplation of a character. The very *feeling* constitutes our praise or admiration. We go no farther; nor do we enquire into the cause of the satisfaction. We do not infer a character to be virtuous, because it pleases: But in feeling that it pleases after such a particular manner, we in effect feel that it is virtuous. The case is the same as in our judgments concerning all kinds of beauty, and tastes, and sensations. Our approbation is imply'd in the immediate pleasure they convey to us.

I have objected to the system, which establishes eternal rational measures of right and wrong, that 'tis impossible to shew, in the actions of reasonable creatures, any relations, which are not found in external objects; and therefore, if morality always attended these relations, 'twere possible for inanimate matter to become virtuous or vicious. Now it may, in like manner, be objected to the present system, that if virtue and vice be determin'd by pleasure and pain, these qualities must, in every case, arise from the sensations; and consequently any object, whether animate or inanimate, rational or irrational, might become morally good or evil, provided it can excite a satisfaction or uneasiness. But tho' this objection seems to be the very same, it has by no means the same force, in the one case as in the other. For, *first*, 'tis evident, that under the term *pleasure*, we comprehend sensations, which are very different from each other, and which have only such a distant resemblance, as is requisite to make them be express'd by the same abstract term. A good composition of music and a bottle of good wine equally produce pleasure; and what is more, their goodness is determin'd merely by the pleasure. But shall we say upon that account, that the wine is harmonious, or the music of a good flavour? In like manner an inanimate object, and the character or sentiments of any person may, both of them, give satisfaction; but as the satisfaction is different, this keeps our sentiments concerning them from being confounded, and makes us ascribe virtue to the one, and not to the other. Nor is every sentiment of pleasure or pain, which arises from characters and actions, of that *peculiar* kind, which makes us praise or condemn. The good qualities of an enemy are hurtful to us; but may still command our esteem and respect. 'Tis only when a character is considered in general, without reference to our particular interest, that it causes such a feeling or sentiment, as denominates it morally good or evil. 'Tis true, those sentiments, from interest and morals, are apt to be confounded, and naturally run into one another. It seldom happens, that we do not think an enemy vicious, and can distinguish betwixt his opposition to our interest and real villainy or baseness. But this hinders not, but that the sentiments are, in themselves, distinct; and a man of temper and judgment may preserve himself from these illusions. In like manner, tho' 'tis certain a musical voice is nothing but one that naturally gives a *particular* kind of pleasure; yet 'tis difficult for a man to be sensible, that the voice of an enemy is agreeable, or to allow it to be musical. But a person of a fine ear, who has the command of himself, can separate these feelings, and give praise to what deserves it.

*Secondly,* We may call to remembrance the preceding system of the passions, in order to remark a still more considerable difference among our pains and pleasures. Pride and humility, love and hatred are excited, when there is any thing presented to us, that both bears a relation to the object of the passion, and produces a separate sensation related to the sensation of the passion. Now virtue and vice are attended with these circumstances. They must necessarily be plac'd either in ourselves or others, and excite either pleasure or uneasiness; and therefore must give rise to one of these four passions; which clearly distinguishes them from the pleasure and pain arising from inanimate objects, that often bear no relation to us: And this is, perhaps, the most considerable effect that virtue and vice have upon the human mind.

It may now be ask'd *in general,* concerning this pain or pleasure, that distinguishes moral good and evil, *From what principles is it derived, and whence does it arise in the human mind?* To this I reply, *first,* that 'tis absurd to imagine, that in every particular instance, these sentiments are produc'd by an *original* quality and *primary* constitution. For as the number of our duties is, in a manner, infinite, 'tis impossible that our original instincts should extend to each of them, and from our very first infancy impress on the human mind all that multitude of precepts, which are contain'd in the compleatest system of ethics. Such a method of proceeding is not conformable to the usual maxims, by which nature is conducted, where a few principles produce all that variety we observe in the universe, and every thing is carry'd on in the easiest and most simple manner. 'Tis necessary, therefore, to abridge these primary impulses, and find some more general principles, upon which all our notions of morals are founded.

But in the *second* place, should it be ask'd, Whether we ought to search for these principles in *nature*, or whether we must look for them in some other origin? I wou'd reply, that our answer to this question depends upon the definition of the word, Nature, than which there is none more ambiguous and equivocal. If *nature* be oppos'd to miracles, not only the distinction betwixt vice and virtue is natural, but also every event, which has ever happen'd in the world, *excepting those miracles, on which our religion is founded*. In saying, then, that the sentiments of vice and virtue are natural in this sense, we make no very extraordinary discovery.

But *nature* may also be opposed to rare and unusual; and in this sense of the word, which is the common one, there may often arise disputes concerning what is natural or unnatural; and one may in general affirm, that we are not possess'd of any very precise standard, by which these disputes can be decided. Frequent and rare depend upon the number of examples we have observ'd; and as this number may gradually encrease or diminish, 'twill be impossible to fix any exact boundaries betwixt them. We may only affirm on this head, that if ever there was any thing, which cou'd be call'd natural in this sense, the sentiments of morality certainly may; since there never was any nation of the world, nor any single person in any nation, who was utterly depriv'd of them, and who never, in any instance, shew'd the least approbation or dislike of manners. These sentiments are so rooted in our constitution and temper, that without entirely confounding the human mind by disease or madness, 'tis impossible to extirpate and destroy them.

But *nature* may also be opposed to artifice, as well as to what is rare and unusual; and in this sense it may be disputed, whether the notions of virtue be natural or not. We readily forget, that the designs, and projects, and views of men are principles as necessary in their operation as heat and cold, moist and dry: But taking them to be free and entirely our own, 'tis usual for us to set them in opposition to the other principles of nature. Shou'd it, therefore, be demanded, whether the sense of virtue be natural or artificial, I am of opinion, that 'tis impossible for me at present to give any precise answer to this question. Perhaps it will appear afterwards, that our sense of some virtues is artificial, and that of others natural. The discussion of this question will be more proper, when we enter upon an exact detail of each particular vice and virtue.[1]

Mean while it may not be amiss to observe from these definitions of *natural* and *unnatural*, that nothing can be more unphilosophical than those systems, which assert, that virtue is the same with what is natural, and vice with what is unnatural. For in the first sense of the word, Nature, as opposed to miracles, both vice and virtue are equally natural; and in the second sense, as oppos'd to what is unusual, perhaps virtue will be found to be the most unnatural. At least it must be own'd, that heroic virtue, being as unusual, is as little natural as the most brutal barbarity. As to the third sense of the word, 'tis certain, that both vice and virtue are equally artificial, and out of nature. For however it may be disputed, whether the notion of a merit or demerit in certain actions be natural or artificial, 'tis evident, that the actions themselves are artificial, and are perform'd with a certain design and intention; otherwise they cou'd never be rank'd under any of these denominations. 'Tis impossible, therefore, that the character of natural and unnatural can ever, in any sense, mark the boundaries of vice and virtue.

Thus we are still brought back to our first position, that virtue is distinguished by the pleasure, and vice by the pain, that any action, sentiment or character gives us by the mere view and contemplation. This decision is very commodious;

[1] In the following discourse *natural* is also opposed sometimes to *civil*, sometimes to *moral*. The opposition will always discover the sense, in which it is taken.

because it reduces us to this simple question, *Why any action or sentiment upon the general view or survey, gives a certain satisfaction or uneasiness,* in order to shew the origin of its moral rectitude or depravity, without looking for any incomprehensible relations and qualities, which never did exist in nature, nor even in our imagination, by any clear and distinct conception. I flatter myself I have executed a great part of my present design by a state of the question, which appears to me so free from ambiguity and obscurity.

## Part II

# Of Justice and Injustice

### Section I. Justice, Whether a Natural or Artificial Virtue?

I have already hinted, that our sense of every kind of virtue is not natural; but that there are some virtues, that produce pleasure and approbation by means of an artifice or contrivance, which arises from the circumstances and necessity of mankind. Of this kind I assert *justice* to be; and shall endeavour to defend this opinion by a short, and, I hope, convincing argument, before I examine the nature of the artifice, from which the sense of that virtue is derived.

'Tis evident, that when we praise any actions, we regard only the motives that produced them, and consider the actions as signs or indications of certain principles in the mind and temper. The external performance has no merit. We must look within to find the moral quality. This we cannot do directly; and therefore fix our attention on actions, as on external signs. But these actions are still considered as signs; and the ultimate object of our praise and approbation is the motive, that produc'd them.

After the same manner, when we require any action, or blame a person for not performing it, we always suppose, that one in that situation shou'd be influenc'd by the proper motive of that action, and we esteem it vicious in him to be regardless of it. If we find, upon enquiry, that the virtuous motive was still powerful over his breast, tho' check'd in its operation by some circumstances unknown to us, we retract our blame, and have the same esteem for him, as if he had actually perform'd the action, which we require of him.

It appears, therefore, that all virtuous actions derive their merit only from virtuous motives, and are consider'd merely as signs of those motives. From this principle I conclude, that the first virtuous motive, which bestows a merit on any action, can never be a regard to the virtue of that action, but must be some other natural motive or principle. To suppose, that the mere regard to the virtue of the action, may be the first motive, which produc'd the action, and render'd it virtuous, is to reason in a circle. Before we can have such a regard, the action must be really virtuous; and this virtue must be deriv'd from some virtuous motive: And consequently the virtuous motive must be different from the regard to the virtue of the action. A virtuous motive is requisite to render an action virtuous. An action must be virtuous, before we can have a regard to its virtue. Some virtuous motive, therefore, must be antecedent to that regard.

Nor is this merely a metaphysical subtilty; but enters into all our reasonings in common life, tho' perhaps we may not be able to place it in such distinct philosophical terms. We blame a father for neglecting his child. Why? because it shews a want of natural affection, which is the duty of every parent. Were not natural affection a duty, the care of children cou'd not be a duty; and 'twere impossible we cou'd have the duty in our eye in the attention we give to our offspring. In this case, therefore, all men suppose a motive to the action distinct from a sense of duty.

Here is a man, that does many benevolent actions; relieves the distress'd, comforts the afflicted, and extends his bounty even to the greatest strangers. No character can be more amiable and virtuous. We regard these actions as proofs of the greatest humanity. This humanity bestows a merit on the actions. A regard to this merit is, therefore, a secondary consideration, and deriv'd from the antecedent principle of humanity, which is meritorious and laudable.

In short, it may be establish'd as an undoubted maxim, *that no action can be virtuous, or morally good, unless there be in human nature some motive to produce it, distinct from the sense of its morality.*

But may not the sense of morality or duty produce an action, without any other motive? I answer, It may: But this is no objection to the present doctrine. When any virtuous motive or principle is common in human nature, a person, who feels his heart devoid of that motive, may hate himself upon that account, and may perform the action without the motive, from a certain sense of duty, in order to acquire by practice, that virtuous principle, or at least, to disguise to himself, as much as possible, his want of it. A man that really feels no gratitude in his temper, is still pleas'd to perform grateful actions, and thinks he has, by that means, fulfill'd his duty. Actions are at first only consider'd as signs of motives: But 'tis usual, in this case, as in all others, to fix our attention on the signs, and neglect, in some measure, the thing signify'd. But tho', on some occasions, a person may perform an action merely out of regard to its moral obligation, yet still this supposes in human nature some distinct principles, which are capable of producing the action, and whose moral beauty renders the action meritorious.

Now to apply all this to the present case; I suppose a person to have lent me a sum of money, on condition that it be restor'd in a few days; and also suppose, that after the expiration of the term agreed on, he demands the sum: I ask, *What reason or motive have I to restore the money?* It will, perhaps, be said, that my regard to justice, and abhorrence of villainy and knavery, are sufficient reasons for me, if I have the least grain of honesty, or sense of duty and obligation. And this answer, no doubt, is just and satisfactory to man in his civiliz'd state, and when train'd up according to a certain discipline and education. But in his rude and more *natural* condition, if you are pleas'd to call such a condition natural, this answer wou'd be rejected as perfectly unintelligible and sophistical. For one in that situation wou'd immediately ask you, *Wherein consists this honesty and justice, which you find in restoring a loan, and abstaining from the property of others?* It does not surely lie in the external action. It must, therefore, be plac'd in the motive, from which the external action is deriv'd. This motive can never be a regard to the honesty of the action. For 'tis a plain fallacy to say, that a virtuous motive is requisite to render an action honest, and at the same time that a regard to the honesty is the motive of the action. We can never have a regard to the virtue of an action, unless the action be antecedently virtuous. No action can be virtuous, but so far as it proceeds from a virtuous motive. A virtuous motive, therefore, must precede the regard to the virtue; and 'tis impossible, that the virtuous motive and the regard to the virtue can be the same.

'Tis requisite, then, to find some motive to acts of justice and honesty, distinct from our regard to the honesty; and in this lies the great difficulty. For shou'd we say, that a concern for our private interest or reputation is the legitimate motive to all honest actions; it wou'd follow, that wherever that concern ceases, honesty can no longer have place. But 'tis certain, that self-love, when it acts at its liberty, instead of engaging us to honest actions, is the source of all injustice and violence; nor can a man ever correct those vices, without correcting and restraining the *natural* movements of that appetite.

But shou'd it be affirm'd, that the reason or motive of such actions is the *regard to publick interest*, to which nothing is more contrary than examples of injustice and dishonesty; shou'd this be said, I wou'd propose the three following considerations, as worthy of our attention. *First*, public interest is not naturally attach'd to the observation of the rules of justice; but is only connected with it, after an artificial convention for the establishment of these rules, as shall be shewn more at large hereafter. *Secondly*, if we suppose, that the loan was secret, and that it is necessary for the interest of the person, that the money be restor'd in the same manner (as when the lender wou'd conceal his riches) in that case the example ceases, and the public is no longer interested in the actions of the borrower; tho' I suppose there is no moralist, who will affirm, that the duty and obligation ceases. *Thirdly*, experience sufficiently proves, that men, in the ordinary conduct of life, look not so far as the public interest, when they pay their creditors, perform their promises, and abstain from theft, and robbery, and injustice of every kind. That is a motive too remote and too sublime to affect the generality of mankind, and operate with any force in actions so contrary to private interest as are frequently those of justice and common honesty.

In general, it may be affirm'd, that there is no such passion in human minds, as the love of mankind, merely as such, independent of personal qualities, of services, or of relation to ourself. 'Tis true, there is no human, and indeed no sensible, creature, whose happiness or misery does not, in some measure, affect us, when brought near to us, and represented in lively colours: But this proceeds merely from sympathy, and is no proof of such an universal affection to mankind, since this concern extends itself beyond our own species. An affection betwixt the sexes is a passion evidently implanted in human nature; and this passion not only appears in its peculiar symptoms, but also in inflaming every other principle of affection, and raising a stronger love from beauty, wit, kindness, than what wou'd otherwise flow from them. Were there an universal love among all human creatures, it wou'd appear after the same manner. Any degree of a good quality wou'd cause a stronger affection than the same degree of a bad quality wou'd cause hatred; contrary to what we find by experience. Men's tempers are different, and some have a propensity to the tender, and others to the rougher, affections: But in the main, we may affirm, that man in general, or human nature, is nothing but the object of love and hatred, and requires some other cause, which by a double relation of impressions and ideas, may excite these passions. In vain wou'd we endeavour to elude this hypothesis. There are no phænomena that point out any such kind affection to men, independent of their merit, and every other circumstance. We love company in general; but 'tis as we love any other amusement. An *Englishman* in *Italy* is a friend: A *European* in *China*; and perhaps a man wou'd be belov'd as such, were we to meet him in the moon. But this proceeds only from the relation to ourselves; which in these cases gathers force by being confined to a few persons.

If publick benevolence, therefore, or a regard to the interests of mankind, cannot be the original motive to justice, much less can *private benevolence*, or a *regard to the interests of the party concern'd*, be this motive. For what if he be my enemy, and has given me just cause to hate him? What if he be a vicious man, and deserves the hatred of all mankind? What if he be a miser, and can make no use of what I wou'd deprive him of? What if he be a profligate debauchee, and wou'd rather receive harm than benefit from large possessions? What if I be in necessity, and have urgent motives to acquire something to my family? In all these cases, the original motive to justice wou'd fail; and consequently the justice itself, and along with it all property, right, and obligation.

A rich man lies under a moral obligation to communicate to those in necessity a share of his superfluities. Were private benevolence the original motive to justice, a man wou'd not be oblig'd to leave others in the possession of more than he is oblig'd to give them. At least the difference wou'd be very inconsiderable. Men generally fix their affections more on what they are possess'd of, than on what they never enjoy'd: For this reason, it wou'd be greater cruelty to dispossess a man of any thing, than not to give it him. But who will assert, that this is the only foundation of justice?

Besides, we must consider, that the chief reason, why men attach themselves so much to their possessions is, that they consider them as their property, and as secur'd to them inviolably by the laws of society. But this is a secondary consideration, and dependent on the preceding notions of justice and property.

A man's property is suppos'd to be fenc'd against every mortal, in every possible case. But private benevolence is, and ought to be, weaker in some persons, than in others: And in many, or indeed in most persons, must absolutely fail. Private benevolence, therefore, is not the original motive of justice.

From all this it follows, that we have no real or universal motive for observing the laws of equity, but the very equity and merit of that observance; and as no action can be equitable or meritorious, where it cannot arise from some separate motive, there is here an evident sophistry and reasoning in a circle. Unless, therefore, we will allow, that nature has establish'd a sophistry, and render'd it necessary and unavoidable, we must allow, that the sense of justice and injustice is not deriv'd from nature, but arises artificially, tho' necessarily from education, and human conventions.

I shall add, as a corollary to this reasoning, that since no action can be laudable or blameable, without some motives or impelling passions, distinct from the sense of morals, these distinct passions must have a great influence on that sense. 'Tis according to their general force in human nature, that we blame or praise. In judging of the beauty of animal bodies, we always carry in our eye the œconomy of a certain species; and where the limbs and features observe that proportion, which is common to the species, we pronounce them handsome and beautiful. In like manner we always consider the *natural* and *usual* force of the passions, when we determine concerning vice and virtue; and if the passions depart very much from the common measures on either side, they are always disapprov'd as vicious. A man naturally loves his children better than his nephews, his nephews better than his cousins, his cousins better than strangers, where every thing else is equal. Hence arise our common measures of duty, in preferring the one to the other. Our sense of duty always follows the common and natural course of our passions.

To avoid giving offence, I must here observe, that when I deny justice to be a natural virtue, I make use of the word, *natural*, only as oppos'd to *artificial*. In another sense of the word; as no principle of the human mind is more natural than a sense of virtue; so no virtue is more natural than justice. Mankind is an inventive species; and where an invention is obvious and absolutely necessary, it may as properly be said to be natural as any thing that proceeds immediately from original principles, without the intervention of thought or reflexion. Tho' the rules of justice be *artificial*, they are not *arbitrary*. Nor is the expression improper to call them *Laws of Nature*; if by natural we understand what is common to any species, or even if we confine it to mean what is inseparable from the species.

## Section II. Of the Origin of Justice and Property

We now proceed to examine two questions, viz. *concerning the manner, in which the rules of justice are establish'd by the artifice of men;* and *concerning the reasons, which determine us to attribute to the observance or neglect of these rules a moral beauty and deformity.* These questions will appear afterwards to be distinct. We shall begin with the former.

Of all the animals, with which this globe is peopled, there is none towards whom nature seems, at first sight, to have exercis'd more cruelty than towards man, in the numberless wants and necessities, with which she has loaded him, and in the slender means, which she affords to the relieving these necessities. In other creatures these two particulars generally compensate each other. If we consider the lion as a voracious and carnivorous animal, we shall easily discover him to be very necessitous; but if we turn our eye to his make and temper, his agility, his courage, his arms, and his force, we shall find, that his advantages hold proportion with his wants. The sheep and ox are depriv'd of all these advantages; but their appetites are moderate, and their food is of easy purchase. In man alone, this unnatural conjunction of infirmity, and of necessity, may be observ'd in its greatest perfection. Not only the food, which is requir'd for his sustenance, flies his search and approach, or at least requires his labour to be produc'd, but he must be possess'd of cloaths and lodging, to defend him against the injuries of the weather; tho' to consider him only in himself, he is provided neither with arms, nor force, nor other natural abilities, which are in any degree answerable to so many necessities.

'Tis by society alone he is able to supply his defects, and raise himself up to an equality with his fellow-creatures, and even acquire a superiority above them. By society all his infirmities are compensated; and tho' in that situation his wants multiply every moment upon him, yet his abilities are still more augmented, and leave him in every respect more satisfied and happy, than 'tis possible for him, in his savage and solitary condition, ever to become. When every individual person labours a-part, and only for himself, his force is too small to execute any considerable work; his labour being employ'd in supplying all his different necessities, he never attains a perfection in any particular art; and as his force and success are not at all times equal, the least failure in either of these particulars must be attended with inevitable ruin and misery. Society provides a remedy for these *three* inconveniences. By the conjunction of forces, our power is augmented: By the partition of employments, our ability encreases: And by mutual succour we are less expos'd to fortune and accidents. 'Tis by this additional *force, ability*, and *security*, that society becomes advantageous.

But in order to form society, 'tis requisite not only that it be advantageous, but also that men be sensible of these advantages; and 'tis impossible, in their wild uncultivated state, that by study and reflexion alone, they should ever be able to attain this knowledge. Most fortunately, therefore, there is conjoin'd to those necessities, whose remedies are remote and obscure, another necessity, which having a present and more obvious remedy, may justly be regarded as the first and original principle of human society. This necessity is no other than that natural appetite betwixt the sexes, which unites them together, and preserves their union, till a new tye takes place in their concern for their common offspring. This new concern becomes also a principle of union betwixt the parents and offspring, and forms a more numerous society; where the parents govern by the advantage of their superior strength and wisdom, and at the same time are restrain'd in the exercise of their authority by that natural affection, which they bear their children. In a little time, custom and habit operating on the tender minds of the children, makes them sensible of the advantages, which they may reap from society, as well as fashions them by degrees for it, by rubbing off those rough corners and untoward affections, which prevent their coalition.

For it must be confest, that however the circumstances of human nature may render an union necessary, and however those passions of lust and natural affection may seem to render it unavoidable; yet there are other particulars in our *natural temper*, and in our *outward circumstances*, which are very incommodious, and are even contrary to the requisite conjunction. Among the former, we may justly esteem our *selfishness* to be the most considerable. I am sensible, that, generally speaking, the representations of this quality have been carried much too far; and that the descriptions, which certain philosophers delight so much to form of mankind in this particular, are as wide of nature as any accounts of monsters, which we meet with in fables and romances. So far from thinking, that men have no affection for any thing beyond themselves, I am of opinion, that tho' it be rare to meet with one, who loves any single person better than himself; yet 'tis as rare to meet with one, in whom all the kind affections, taken together, do not over-balance all the selfish. Consult common experience: Do you not see, that tho' the whole expence of the family be generally under the direction of the master of it, yet there are few that do not bestow the largest part of their fortunes on the pleasures of their wives, and the education of their children, reserving the smallest portion for their own proper use and entertainment. This is what we may observe concerning such as have those endearing ties; and may presume, that the case would be the same with others, were they plac'd in a like situation.

But tho' this generosity must be acknowledg'd to the honour of human nature, we may at the same time remark, that so noble an affection, instead of fitting men for large societies, is almost as contrary to them, as the most narrow selfishness. For while each person loves himself better than any other single person, and in his love to others bears the greatest affection to his relations and acquaintance, this must necessarily produce an opposition of passions, and a consequent opposition of actions; which cannot but be dangerous to the new-establish'd union.

'Tis however worth while to remark, that this contrariety of passions wou'd be attended with but small danger, did it not concur with a peculiarity in our *outward circumstances*, which affords it an opportunity of exerting itself. There are three different species of goods, which we are possess'd of; the internal satisfaction of our minds, the external advantages of our body, and the enjoyment of such possessions as we have acquir'd by our industry and good fortune. We are perfectly secure in the enjoyment of the first. The second may be ravish'd from us, but can be of no advantage to him who deprives us of them. The last only are both expos'd to the violence of others, and may be transferr'd without suffering any loss or alteration; while at the same time, there is not a sufficient quantity of them to supply every one's desires and necessities. As the improvement, therefore, of these goods is the chief advantage of society, so the *instability* of their possession, along with their *scarcity*, is the chief impediment.

In vain shou'd we expect to find, in *uncultivated nature*, a remedy to this inconvenience; or hope for any inartificial principle of the human mind, which might controul those partial affections, and make us overcome the temptations arising from our circumstances. The idea of justice can never serve to this purpose, or be taken for a natural principle, capable of inspiring men with an equitable conduct towards each other. That virtue, as it is now understood, wou'd never have been dream'd of among rude and savage men. For the notion of injury or injustice implies an immorality or vice committed against some other person: And as every immorality is deriv'd from some defect or unsoundness of the passions, and as this defect must be judg'd of, in a great measure, from the ordinary course of nature in the constitution of the mind; 'twill be easy to know, whether we be guilty of any immorality, with regard to others, by considering the natural, and usual force of those several affections, which are directed towards them. Now it appers, that in the original frame of our mind, our strongest attention is confin'd to ourselves; our next is extended to our relations and acquaintance; and 'tis only the weakest which reaches to strangers and indifferent persons. This partiality, then, and unequal affection, must not only have an influence on our behaviour and conduct in society, but even on our ideas of vice and virtue; so as to make us regard any remarkable transgression of such a degree of partiality, either by too great an enlargement, or contraction of the affections, as vicious and immoral. This we may observe in our common judgments concerning actions, where we blame a person, who either centers all his affections in his family, or is so regardless of them, as, in any opposition of interest, to give the preference to a stranger, or mere chance acquaintance. From all which it follows, that our natural uncultivated ideas of morality, instead of providing a remedy for the partiality of our affections, do rather conform themselves to that partiality, and give it an additional force and influence.

The remedy, then, is not deriv'd from nature, but from *artifice*; or more properly speaking, nature provides a remedy in the judgment and understanding, for what is irregular and incommodious in the affections. For when men, from their early education in society, have become sensible of the infinite advantages that result from it, and have besides acquir'd a new affection to company and conversation; and when they have observ'd, that the principal disturbance in society arises from those goods, which we call external, and from their looseness and easy transition from one person to another; they must seek for a remedy, by putting these goods, as far as possible, on the same footing with the fix'd and constant advantages of the mind and body. This can be done after no other manner, than by a convention enter'd into by all the members of the society to bestow stability on the possession of those external goods, and leave every one in the peaceable enjoyment of what he may acquire by his fortune and industry. By this means, every one knows what he may safely possess; and the passions are restrain'd in their partial and contradictory motions. Nor is such a restraint contrary to these passions; for if so, it cou'd never be enter'd into, nor maintain'd; but it is only contrary to their heedless and impetuous movement. Instead of departing from our own interest, or from that of our nearest friends, by abstaining from the possessions of others, we cannot better consult both these interests, than by such a convention;

because it is by that means we maintain society, which is so necessary to their well-being and subsistence, as well as to our own.

This convention is not of the nature of a *promise*: For even promises themselves, as we shall see afterwards, arise from human conventions. It is only a general sense of common interest; which sense all the members of the society express to one another, and which induces them to regulate their conduct by certain rules. I observe, that it will be for my interest to leave another in the possession of his goods, *provided* he will act in the same manner with regard to me. He is sensible of a like interest in the regulation of his conduct. When this common sense of interest is mutually express'd, and is known to both, it produces a suitable resolution and behaviour. And this may properly enough be call'd a convention or agreement betwixt us, tho' without the interposition of a promise; since the actions of each of us have a reference to those of the other, and are perform'd upon the supposition, that something is to be perform'd on the other part. Two men, who pull the oars of a boat, do it by an agreement or convention, tho' they have never given promises to each other. Nor is the rule concerning the stability of possession the less deriv'd from human conventions, that it arises gradually, and acquires force by a slow progression, and by our repeated experience of the inconveniences of transgressing it. On the contrary, this experience assures us still more, that the sense of interest has become common to all our fellows, and gives us a confidence of the future regularity of their conduct: And 'tis only on the expectation of this, that our moderation and abstinence are founded. In like manner are languages gradually establish'd by human conventions without any promise. In like manner do gold and silver become the common measures of exchange, and are esteem'd sufficient payment for what is of a hundred times their value.

After this convention, concerning abstinence from the possessions of others, is enter'd into, and every one has acquir'd a stability in his possessions, there immediately arise the ideas of justice and injustice; as also those of *property,* *right,* and *obligation.* The latter are altogether unintelligible without first understanding the former. Our property is nothing but those goods, whose constant possession is establish'd by the laws of society; that is, by the laws of justice. Those, therefore, who make use of the words *property,* or *obligation,* before they have explain'd the origin of justice, or even make use of them in that explication, are guilty of a very gross fallacy, and can never reason upon any solid foundation. A man's property is some object related to him. This relation is not natural, but moral, and founded on justice. 'Tis very preposterous, therefore, to imagine, that we can have any idea of property, without fully comprehending the nature of justice, and shewing its origin in the artifice and contrivance of men. The origin of justice explains that of property. The same artifice gives rise to both. As our first and most natural sentiment of morals is founded on the nature of our passions, and gives the preference to ourselves and friends, above strangers; 'tis impossible there can be naturally any such thing as a fix'd right or property, while the opposite passions of men impel them in contrary directions, and are not restrain'd by any convention or agreement.

No one can doubt, that the convention for the distinction of property, and for the stability of possession, is of all circumstances the most necessary to the establishment of human society, and that after the agreement for the fixing and observing of this rule, there remains little or nothing to be done towards settling a perfect harmony and concord. All the other passions, beside this of interest, are either easily restrain'd, or are not of such pernicious consequence, when indulg'd. *Vanity* is rather to be esteem'd a social passion, and a bond of union among men. *Pity* and *love* are to be consider'd in the same light. And as to *envy* and *revenge,* tho' pernicious, they operate only by intervals, and are directed against particular persons, whom we consider as our superiors or enemies. This avidity alone, of acquiring goods and possessions for ourselves and our nearest friends, is insatiable, perpetual, universal, and directly destructive of society. There scarce is any one, who is not actuated by it; and there is no one, who has not reason to fear from it, when it acts without any restraint, and gives way to its first and most natural movements. So that upon the whole, we are to esteem the difficulties in the establishment of society, to be greater or less, according to those we encounter in regulating and restraining this passion.

'Tis certain, that no affection of the human mind has both a sufficient force, and a proper direction to counter-balance the love of gain, and render men fit members of society, by making them abstain from the possessions of others. Benevolence to strangers is too weak for this purpose; and as to the other passions, they rather inflame this avidity, when we observe, that the larger our possessions are, the more ability we have of gratifying all our appetites. There is no passion, therefore, capable of controlling the interested affection, but the very affection itself, by an alteration of its direction. Now this alteration must necessarily take place upon the least reflection; since 'tis evident, that the passion is much better satisfy'd by its restraint, than by its liberty, and that in preserving society, we make much greater advances in the acquiring possessions, than in the solitary and forlorn condition, which must follow upon violence and an universal licence. The question, therefore, concerning the wickedness or goodness of human nature, enters not in the least into that other question concerning the origin of society; nor is there any thing to be consider'd but the degrees of men's sagacity or folly. For whether the passion of self-interest be esteemed vicious or virtuous, 'tis all a case; since itself alone restrains it: So that if it be virtuous, men become social by their virtue; if vicious, their vice has the same effect.

Now as 'tis by establishing the rule for the stability of possession, that this passion restrains itself: if that rule be very abstruse, and of difficult invention; society must be esteem'd, in a manner, accidental, and the effect of many ages. But if it be found, that nothing can be more simple and obvious than that rule; that every parent, in order to preserve peace among his children, must establish it; and that these first rudiments of justice must every day be improv'd, as the society enlarges: If all this appear evident, as it certainly must, we may conclude, that 'tis utterly impossible for men to remain any considerable time in that savage condition, which precedes society; but that his very first state and situation may justly be esteem'd social. This, however, hinders not, but that philosophers may, if they please, extend their reasoning to the suppos'd *state of nature*; provided they allow it to be a mere philosophical fiction, which never had, and never cou'd have any reality. Human nature being compos'd of two principal parts, which are requisite in all its actions, the affections and understanding; 'tis certain, that the blind motions of the former, without the direction of the latter, incapacitate men for society: And it may be allow'd us to consider separately the effects, that result from the separate operations of these two component parts of the mind. The same liberty may be permitted to moral, which is allow'd to natural philosophers; and 'tis very usual with the latter to consider any motion as compounded and consisting of two parts separate from each other, tho' at the same time they acknowledge it to be in itself uncompounded and inseparable.

This *state of nature*, therefore, is to be regarded as a mere fiction, not unlike that of the *golden age*, which poets have invented; only with this difference, that the former is describ'd as full of war, violence and injustice; whereas the latter is painted out to us, as the most charming and most peaceable condition, that can possibly be imagin'd. The seasons, in that first age of nature, were so temperate, if we may believe the poets, that there was no necessity for men to provide themselves with cloaths and houses as a security against the violence of heat and cold. The rivers flow'd with wine and milk: The oaks yielded honey; and nature spontaneously produc'd her greatest delicacies. Nor were these the chief advantages of that happy age. The storms and tempests were not alone remov'd from nature; but those more furious tempests were unknown to human breasts, which now cause such uproar, and engender such confusion. Avarice, ambition, cruelty, selfishness, were never heard of: Cordial affection, compassion, sympathy, were the only movements, with which the human mind was yet acquainted. Even the distinction of *mine* and *thine* was banish'd from that happy race of mortals, and carry'd with them the very notions of property and obligation, justice and injustice.

This, no doubt, is to be regarded as an idle fiction; but yet deserves our attention, because nothing can more evidently shew the origin of those virtues, which are the subjects of our present enquiry. I have already observ'd, that justice takes its rise from human conventions; and that these are intended as a remedy to some inconveniences, which proceed from the concurrence of certain *qualities* of the human mind with the *situation* of external objects. The qualities of the mind are *selfishness* and *limited generosity*: And the situation of external objects is their *easy change,* join'd to their *scarcity* in comparison of the wants and desires of men. But however philosophers may have been bewilder'd in those speculations, poets have been guided more infallibly, by a certain taste or common instinct, which in most kinds of reasoning goes farther than any of that art and philosophy, with which we have been yet acquainted. They easily perceiv'd, if every man had a tender regard for another, or if nature supplied abundantly all our wants and desires, that the jealousy of interest, which justice supposes, could no longer have place; nor would there be any occasion for those distinctions and limits of property and possession, which at present are in use among mankind. Encrease to a sufficient degree the benevolence of men, or the bounty of nature, and you render justice useless, by supplying its place with much nobler virtues, and more valuable blessings. The selfishness of men is animated by the few possessions we have, in proportion to our wants; and 'tis to restrain this selfishness, that men have been oblig'd to separate themselves from the community, and to distinguish betwixt their own goods and those of others.

Nor need we have recourse to the fictions of poets to learn

this; but beside the reason of the thing, may discover the same truth by common experience and observation. 'Tis easy to remark, that a cordial affection renders all things common among friends; and that married people in particular mutually lose their property, and are unacquainted with the *mine* and *thine*, which are so necessary, and yet cause such disturbance in human society. The same effect arises from any alteration in the circumstances of mankind; as when there is such a plenty of any thing as satisfies all the desires of men: In which case the distinction of property is entirely lost, and every thing remains in common. This we may observe with regard to air and water, tho' the most valuable of all external objects; and may easily conclude, that if men were supplied with every thing in the same abundance, or if *every one* had the same affection and tender regard for *every one* as for himself; justice and injustice would be equally unknown among mankind.

Here then is a proposition, which, I think, may be regarded as certain, *that 'tis only from the selfishness and confin'd generosity of men, along with the scanty provision nature has made for his wants, that justice derives its origin.* If we look backward we shall find, that this proposition bestows an additional force on some of those observations, which we have already made on this subject.

*First,* we may conclude from it, that a regard to publick interest, or a strong extensive benevolence, is not our first and original motive for the observation of the rules of justice; since 'tis allow'd, that if men were endow'd with such a benevolence, these rules would never have been dreamt of.

*Secondly,* we may conclude from the same principle, that the sense of justice is not founded on reason, or on the discovery of certain connexions and relations of ideas, which are eternal, immutable, and universally obligatory. For since it is confest, that such an alteration as that above-mention'd, in the temper and circumstances of mankind, wou'd entirely alter our duties and obligations, 'tis necessary upon the common system, *that the sense of virtue is deriv'd from reason,* to shew the change which this must produce in the relations and ideas. But 'tis evident, that the only cause, why the extensive generosity of man, and the perfect abundance of every thing, wou'd destroy the very idea of justice, is because they render it useless; and that, on the other hand, his confin'd benevolence, and his necessitous condition, give rise to that virtue, only by making it requisite to the publick interest, and to that of every individual. 'Twas therefore a concern for our own, and the publick interest, which made us establish the laws of justice; and nothing can be more certain, than that it is not any relation of ideas, which gives us this concern, but our impressions and sentiments, without which every thing in nature is perfectly indifferent to us, and can never in the least affect us. The sense of justice, therefore, is not founded on our ideas, but on our impressions.

*Thirdly,* we may farther confirm the foregoing proposition, *that those impressions, which give rise to this sense of justice, are not natural to the mind of man, but arise from artifice and human conventions.* For since any considerable alteration of temper and circumstances destroys equally justice and injustice; and since such an alteration has an effect only by changing our own and the publick interest; it follows, that the first establishment of the rules of justice depends on these different interests. But if men pursu'd the publick interest naturally, and with a hearty affection, they wou'd never have dream'd of restraining each other by these rules; and if they pursu'd their own interest, without any precaution, they wou'd run head-long into every kind of injustice and violence. These rules, therefore, are artificial, and seek their end in an oblique and indirect manner; nor is the interest, which gives rise to them, of a kind that cou'd be pursu'd by the natural and inartificial passions of men.

To make this more evident, consider, that tho' the rules of justice are establish'd merely by interest, their connexion with interest is somewhat singular, and is different from what may be observ'd on other occasions. A single act of justice is frequently contrary to *public interest*; and were it to stand alone, without being follow'd by other acts, may, in itself, be very prejudicial to society. When a man of merit, of a beneficent disposition, restores a great fortune to a miser, or a seditious bigot, he has acted justly and laudably, but the public is a real sufferer. Nor is every single act of justice, consider'd apart, more conducive to private interest, than to public; and 'tis easily conceiv'd how a man may impoverish himself by a signal instance of integrity, and have reason to wish, that with regard to that single act, the laws of justice were for a moment suspended in the universe. But however single acts of justice may be contrary, either to public or private interest, 'tis certain, that the whole plan or scheme is highly conducive, or indeed absolutely requisite, both to the support of society, and the well-being of every individual. 'Tis impossible to separate the good from the ill. Property must be stable, and must be fix'd by general rules. Tho' in one instance the public be a sufferer, this momentary ill is amply compensated by the steady prosecution of the rule, and by the peace and order, which it establishes in society. And even every individual person must find himself a gainer, on balancing the account; since, without justice, society must immediately dissolve, and every one must fall into that savage and solitary condition, which is infinitely worse than the worst situation that can possibly be suppos'd in society. When therefore men have had experience enough to observe, that whatever may be the consequence of any single act of justice, perform'd by a single person, yet the whole system of actions, concurr'd in by the whole society, is infinitely advantageous to the whole, and to every part; it is not long before justice and property take place. Every member of society is sensible of this interest: Every one expresses this sense to his fellows, along with the resolution he has taken of squaring his actions by it, on condition that others will do the same. No more is requisite to induce any one of them to perform an act of justice, who has the first opportunity. This becomes an example to others. And thus justice establishes itself by a kind of convention or agreement; that is, by a sense of interest, suppos'd to be common to all, and where every single act is perform'd in expectation that others are to perform the like. Without such a convention, no one wou'd ever have dream'd, that there was such a virtue as justice, or have been induc'd to conform his actions to it. Taking any single act, my justice may be pernicious in every respect; and 'tis only upon the supposition, that others are to imitate my example, that I can be induc'd to embrace that virtue; since nothing but this combination can render justice advantageous, or afford me any motives to conform my self to its rules.

We come now to the *second* question we propos'd, *viz. Why we annex the idea of virtue to justice, and of vice to injustice.* This question will not detain us long after the principles, which we have already establish'd. All we can say of it at present will be dispatch'd in a few words: And for farther satisfaction, the reader must wait till we come to the *third* part of this book. The *natural* obligation to justice, *viz.* interest, has been fully explain'd; but as to the *moral* obligation, or the sentiment of right and wrong, 'twill first be requisite to examine the natural virtues, before we can give a full and satisfactory account of it.

After men have found by experience, that their selfishness and confin'd generosity, acting at their liberty, totally incapacitate them for society; and at the same time have observ'd, that society is necessary to the satisfaction of those very passions, they are naturally induc'd to lay themselves under the restraint of such rules, as may render their commerce more safe and commodious. To the imposition then, and observance of these rules, both in general, and in every particular instance, they are at first induc'd only by a regard to interest; and this motive, on the first formation of society, is sufficiently strong and forcible. But when society has become numerous, and has encreas'd to a tribe or nation, this interest is more remote; nor do men so readily perceive, that disorder and confusion follow upon every breach of these rules, as in a more narrow and contracted society. But tho' in our own actions we may frequently lose sight of that interest, which we have in maintaining order, and may follow a lesser and more present interest, we never fail to observe the prejudice we receive, either mediately or immediately, from the injustice of others; as not being in that case either blinded by passion, or byass'd by any contrary temptation. Nay when the injustice is so distant from us, as no way to affect our interest, it still displeases us; because we consider it as prejudicial to human society, and pernicious to every one that approaches the person guilty of it. We partake of their uneasiness by *sympathy*; and as every thing, which gives uneasiness in human actions, upon the general survey, is call'd Vice, and whatever produces satisfaction, in the same manner, is denominated Virtue; this is the reason why the sense of moral good and evil follows upon justice and injustice. And tho' this sense, in the present case, be deriv'd only from contemplating the actions of others, yet we fail not to extend it even to our own actions. The *general rule* reaches beyond those instances, from which it arose; while at the same time we naturally *sympathize* with others in the sentiments they entertain of us. *Thus self-interest is the original motive to the* establishment *of justice: but a* sympathy *with public interest is the source of the* moral approbation, *which attends that virtue.*

Tho' this progress of the sentiments be *natural*, and even necessary, 'tis certain, that it is here forwarded by the artifice of politicians, who, in order to govern men more easily, and preserve peace in human society, have endeavour'd to produce an esteem for justice, and an abhorrence of injustice. This, no doubt, must have its effect; but nothing can be more evident, than that the matter has been carry'd too far by certain writers on morals, who seem to have employ'd their utmost efforts to extirpate all sense of virtue from among mankind. Any artifice of politicians may assist nature in the producing of those sentiments, which she suggests to us, and may even on some occasions, produce alone an approbation or esteem for any particular action; but 'tis impossible it should be the sole cause of the distinction we make betwixt vice and virtue. For if nature did not aid us in this particular, 'twou'd be in vain for politicians to talk of *honourable* or *dishonourable*, *praiseworthy* or *blameable*. These words wou'd be perfectly unintelligible, and wou'd no more have any idea annex'd to them, than if they were of a tongue perfectly unknown to us. The utmost politicians can perform, is, to extend the natural sentiments beyond their original bounds; but still nature must furnish the materials, and give us some notion of moral distinctions.

As publick praise and blame encrease our esteem for justice; so private education and instruction contribute to the same effect. For as parents easily observe, that a man is the more useful, both to himself and others, the greater degree of probity and honour he is endow'd with; and that those principles have greater force, when custom and education assist interest and reflexion: For these reasons they are induc'd to inculcate on their children, from their earliest infancy, the principles of probity, and teach them to regard the observance of those rules, by which society is maintain'd, as worthy and honourable, and their violation as base and infamous. By this means the sentiments of honour may take root in their tender minds, and acquire such firmness and solidity, that they may fall little short of those principles, which are the most essential to our natures, and the most deeply radicated in our internal constitution.

What farther contributes to encrease their solidity, is the interest of our reputation, after the opinion, *that a merit or demerit attends justice or injustice,* is once firmly establish'd among mankind. There is nothing, which touches us more nearly than our reputation, and nothing on which our reputation more depends than our conduct, with relation to the property of others. For this reason, every one, who has any regard to his character, or who intends to live on good terms with mankind, must fix an inviolable law to himself, never, by any temptation, to be induc'd to violate those principles, which are essential to a man of probity and honour.

I shall make only one observation before I leave this subject, *viz.* that tho' I assert, that in the *state of nature,* or that imaginary state, which preceded society, there be neither justice nor injustice, yet I assert not, that it was allowable, in such a state, to violate the property of others. I only maintain, that there was no such thing as property; and consequently cou'd be no such thing as justice or injustice. I shall have occasion to make a similar reflexion with regard to *promises*, when I come to treat of them; and I hope this reflexion, when duly weigh'd, will suffice to remove all odium from the foregoing opinions, with regard to justice and injustice.

### Section V. Of the Obligation of Promises

That the rule of morality, which enjoins the performance of promises, is not *natural*, will sufficiently appear from these two propositions, which I proceed to prove, viz. *that a promise wou'd not be intelligible, before human conventions had establish'd it; and that even if it were intelligible, it wou'd not be attended with any moral obligation.*

I say, *first*, that a promise is not intelligible naturally, nor antecedent to human conventions; and that a man, unacquainted with society, could never enter into any engagements with another, even tho' they could perceive each other's thoughts by intuition. If promises be natural and intelligible, there must be some act of the mind attending these words, *I promise*; and on this act of the mind must the obligation depend. Let us, therefore, run over all the faculties of the soul, and see which of them is exerted in our promises.

The act of the mind, exprest by a promise, is not a *resolution* to perform any thing: For that alone never imposes any obligation. Nor is it a *desire* of such a performance: For we may bind ourselves without such a desire, or even with an aversion, declar'd and avow'd. Neither is it the *willing* of that action, which we promise to perform: For a promise always regards some future time, and the will has an influence only on present actions. It follows, therefore, that since the act of the mind, which enters into a promise, and produces its obligation, is neither the resolving, desiring, nor willing of any particular performance, it must necessarily be the *willing* of that *obligation*, which arises from the promise. Nor is this only a conclusion of philosophy; but is entirely conformable to our common ways of thinking and of expressing ourselves, when we say that we are bound by our own consent, and that the obligation arises from our mere will and pleasure. The only question, then, is, whether there be not a manifest absurdity in supposing this act of the mind, and such an absurdity as no man cou'd fall into, whose ideas are not confounded with prejudice and the fallacious use of language.

All morality depends upon our sentiments; and when any action, or quality of the mind, pleases us *after a certain manner*, we say it is virtuous; and when the neglect, or nonperformance of it, displeases us *after a like manner*, we say that we lie under an obligation to perform it. A change of the obligation supposes a change of the sentiment; and a creation of a new obligation supposes some new sentiment to arise. But 'tis certain we can naturally no more change our own sentiments, than the motions of the heavens; nor by a single act of our will, that is, by a promise, render any action agreeable or disagreeable, moral or immoral; which, without that act, wou'd have produc'd contrary impressions, or have been endow'd with different qualities. It wou'd be absurd, therefore, to will any new obligation, that is, any new sentiment of pain or pleasure; nor is it possible, that men cou'd naturally fall into so gross an absurdity. A promise, therefore, is *naturally* something altogether unintelligible, nor is there any act of the mind belonging to it.[1]

[1] Were morality discoverable by reason, and not by sentiment, 'twou'd be still more evident, that promises cou'd make no alteration upon it. Morality is suppos'd to consist in relation. Every new imposition of morality, therefore, must arise from some new relation of objects; and consequently the will cou'd not produce *immediately* any change in morals, but cou'd have that effect only by producing a change upon the objects. But as the moral obligation of a promise is the pure effect of the will, without the least change in any part of the universe; it follows, that promises have no *natural* obligation.

Shou'd it be said, that this act of the will being in effect a new object, produces new relations and new duties; I wou'd answer, that this is a pure sophism, which may be detected by a very moderate share of accuracy and exactness. To will a new obligation, is to will a new relation of objects; and therefore, if this new relation of objects were form'd by the volition itself, we shou'd in effect will the volition; which is plainly absurd and impossible. The will has here no object to which it cou'd tend; but must return upon itself *in infinitum*. The new obligation depends upon new relations. The new relations depend upon a new volition. The new volition has for object a new obligation, and consequently new relations, and consequently a new volition; which volition again has in view a new obligation, relation and volition, without any termination. 'Tis impossible, therefore, we cou'd ever will a new obligation; and consequently 'tis impossible the will cou'd ever accompany a promise, or produce a new obligation of morality.

But, *secondly*, if there was any act of the mind belonging to it, it could not *naturally* produce any obligation. This appears evidently from the foregoing reasoning. A promise creates a new obligation. A new obligation supposes new sentiments to arise. The will never creates new sentiments. There could not naturally, therefore, arise any obligation from a promise, even supposing the mind could fall into the absurdity of willing that obligation.

The same truth may be prov'd still more evidently by that reasoning, which prov'd justice in general to be an artificial virtue. No action can be requir'd of us as our duty, unless there be implanted in human nature some actuating passion or motive, capable of producing the action. This motive cannot be the sense of duty. A sense of duty supposes an antecedent obligation: And where an action is not requir'd by any natural passion, it cannot be requir'd by any natural obligation; since it may be omitted without proving any defect or imperfection in the mind and temper, and consequently without any vice. Now 'tis evident we have no motive leading us to the performance of promises, distinct from a sense of duty. If we thought, that promises had no moral obligation, we never shou'd feel any inclination to observe them. This is not the case with the natural virtues. Tho' there was no obligation to relieve the miserable, our humanity wou'd lead us to it; and when we omit that duty, the immorality of the omission arises from its being a proof, that we want the natural sentiments of humanity. A father knows it to be his duty to take care of his children: But he has also a natural inclination to it. And if no human creature had that inclination, no one cou'd lie under any such obligation. But as there is naturally no inclination to observe promises, distinct from a sense of their obligation; it follows, that fidelity is no natural virtue, and that promises have no force, antecedent to human conventions.

If any one dissent from this, he must give a regular proof of these two propositions, viz. *that there is a peculiar act of the mind, annext to promises;* and *that consequent to this act of the mind, there arises an inclination to perform, distinct from a sense of duty.* I presume, that it is impossible to prove either of these two points; and therefore I venture to conclude, that promises are human inventions, founded on the necessities and interests of society.

In order to discover these necessities and interests, we must consider the same qualities of human nature, which we have already found to give rise to the preceding laws of society. Men being naturally selfish, or endow'd only with a confin'd generosity, they are not easily induc'd to perform any action for the interest of strangers, except with a view to some reciprocal advantage, which they had no hope of obtaining but by such a performance. Now as it frequently happens, that these mutual performances cannot be finish'd at the same instant, 'tis necessary, that one party be contented to remain in uncertainty, and depend upon the gratitude of the other for a return of kindness. But so much corruption is there among men, that, generally speaking, this becomes but a slender security; and as the benefactor is here suppos'd to bestow his favours with a view to self-interest, this both takes off from the obligation, and sets an example of selfishness, which is the true mother of ingratitude. Were we, therefore, to follow the natural course of our passions and inclinations, we shou'd perform but few actions for the advantage of others, from disinterested views; because we are naturally very limited in our kindness and affection: And we shou'd perform as few of that kind, out of a regard to interest; because we cannot depend upon their gratitude. Here then is the mutual commerce of good offices in a manner lost among mankind, and every one reduc'd to his own skill and industry for his well-being and subsistence. The invention of the law of nature, concerning the *stability* of possession, has already render'd men tolerable to each other; that of the *transference* of property and possession by consent has begun to render them mutually advantageous: But still these laws of nature, however strictly observ'd, are not sufficient to render them so serviceable to each other, as by nature they are fitted to become. Tho' possession be *stable*, men may often reap but small advantage from it, while they are possess'd of a greater quantity of any species of goods than they have occasion for, and at the same time suffer by the want of others. The *transference* of property, which is the proper remedy for this inconvenience, cannot remedy it entirely; because it can only take place with regard to such objects as are *present* and *individual*, but not to such as are *absent* or *general*. One cannot transfer the property of a particular house, twenty leagues distant; because the consent cannot be attended with delivery, which is a requisite circumstance. Neither can one transfer the property of ten bushels of corn, or five hogsheads of wine, by the mere expression and consent; because these are only general terms, and have no direct relation to any particular heap of corn, or barrels of wine. Besides, the commerce of mankind is not confin'd to the barter of commodities, but may extend to services and actions, which we may exchange to our mutual interest and advantage. Your corn is ripe today; mine will be so to-morrow. 'Tis profitable for us both, that I shou'd labour with you to-day, and that you shou'd aid me to-morrow. I have no kindness for you, and know you have as little for me. I will not, therefore, take any pains upon your account; and should I labour with you upon my own account, in expectation of a return, I know I shou'd be disappointed, and that I shou'd in vain depend upon your gratitude. Here then I leave you to labour alone: You treat me in the same manner. The seasons change; and both of us lose our harvests for want of mutual confidence and security.

All this is the effect of the natural and inherent principles and passions of human nature; and as these passions and principles are inalterable, it may be thought, that our conduct, which depends on them, must be so too, and that 'twou'd be in vain, either for moralists or politicians, to tamper with us, or attempt to change the usual course of our actions, with a view to public interest. And indeed, did the success of their designs depend upon their success in correcting the selfishness and ingratitude of men, they wou'd never make any progress, unless aided by omnipotence, which is alone able to new-mould the human mind, and change its character in such fundamental articles. All they can pretend to, is, to give a new direction to those natural passions, and teach us that we can better satisfy our appetites in an oblique and artificial manner, than by their headlong and impetuous motion. Hence I learn to do a service to another, without bearing him any real kindness; because I foresee, that he will return my service, in expectation of another of the same kind, and in order to maintain the same correspondence of good offices with me or with others. And accordingly, after I have serv'd him, and he is in possession of the advantage arising from my action, he is induc'd to perform his part, as foreseeing the consequences of his refusal.

But tho' this self-interested commerce of men begins to take place, and to predominate in society, it does not entirely abolish the more generous and noble intercourse of friendship and good offices. I may still do services to such persons as I love, and am more particularly acquainted with, without any prospect of advantage; and they may make me a return in the same manner, without any view but that of recompensing my past services. In order, therefore, to distinguish those two different sorts of commerce, the interested and the disinterested, there is a *certain form of words* invented for the former, by which we bind ourselves to the performance of any action. This form of words constitutes what we call a *promise*, which is the sanction of the interested commerce of mankind. When a man says *he promises any thing*, he in effect expresses a *resolution* of performing it; and along with that, by making use of this *form of words*, subjects himself to the penalty of never being trusted again in case of failure. A resolution is the natural act of the mind, which promises express: But were there no more than a resolution in the case, promises wou'd only declare our former motives, and wou'd not create any new motive or obligation. They are the conventions of men, which create a new motive, when experience has taught us, that human affairs wou'd be conducted much more for mutual advantage, were there certain *symbols* or *signs* instituted, by which we might give each other security of our conduct in any particular incident. After these signs are instituted, whoever uses them is immediately bound by his interest to execute his engagements, and must never expect to be trusted any more, if he refuse to perform what he promis'd.

Nor is that knowledge, which is requisite to make mankind sensible of this interest in the *institution* and *observance* of promises, to be esteem'd superior to the capacity of human nature, however savage and uncultivated. There needs but a very little practice of the world, to make us perceive all these consequences and advantages. The shortest experience of society discovers them to every mortal; and when each individual perceives the same sense of interest in all his fellows, he immediately performs his part of any contract, as being assur'd, that they will not be wanting in theirs. All of them, by concert, enter into a scheme of actions, calculated for common benefit, and agree to be true to their word; nor is there any thing requisite to form this concert or convention, but that every one have a sense of interest in the faithful fulfilling of engagements, and express that sense to other members of the society. This immediately causes that interest to operate upon them; and interest is the *first* obligation to the performance of promises.

Afterwards a sentiment of morals concurs with interest, and becomes a new obligation upon mankind. This sentiment of morality, in the performance of promises, arises from the same principles as that in the abstinence from the property of others. *Public interest, education,* and the *artifices of politicians,* have the same effect in both cases. The difficulties, that occur to us, in supposing a moral obligation to attend promises, we either surmount or elude. For instance; the expression of a resolution is not commonly suppos'd to be obligatory; and we cannot readily conceive how the making use of a certain form of words shou'd be able to cause any material difference. Here, therefore, we *feign* a new act of the mind, which we call the *willing* an obligation; and on this we suppose the morality to depend. But we have prov'd already, that there is no such act of the mind, and consequently that promises impose no natural obligation.

To confirm this, we may subjoin some other reflexions

concerning that will, which is suppos'd to enter into a promise, and to cause its obligation. 'Tis evident, that the will alone is never suppos'd to cause the obligation, but must be express'd by words or signs, in order to impose a tye upon any man. The expression being once brought in as subservient to the will, soon becomes the principal part of the promise; nor will a man be less bound by his word, tho' he secretly give a different direction to his intention, and with-hold himself both from a resolution, and from willing an obligation. But tho' the expression makes on most occasions the whole of the promise, yet it does not always so; and one, who shou'd make use of any expression, of which he knows not the meaning, and which he uses without any intention of binding himself, wou'd not certainly be bound by it. Nay, tho' he knows its meaning, yet if he uses it in jest only, and with such signs as shew evidently he has no serious intention of binding himself, he wou'd not lie under any obligation of performance; but 'tis necessary, that the words be a perfect expression of the will, without any contrary signs. Nay, even this we must not carry so far as to imagine, that one, whom, by our quickness of understanding, we conjecture, from certain signs, to have an intention of deceiving us, is not bound by his expression or verbal promise, if we accept of it; but must limit this conclusion to those cases, where the signs are of a different kind from those of deceit. All these contradictions are easily accounted for, if the obligation of promises be merely a human invention for the convenience of society; but will never be explain'd, if it be something *real* and *natural*, arising from any action of the mind or body.

I shall farther observe, that since every new promise imposes a new obligation of morality on the person who promises, and since this new obligation arises from his will; 'tis one of the most mysterious and incomprehensible operations that can possibly be imagin'd, and may even be compar'd to *transubstantiation*, or *holy orders*,[2] where a certain form of words, along with a certain intention, changes entirely the nature of

[2] I mean so far, as holy orders are suppos'd to produce the *indelible character*. In other respects they are only a legal qualification.

an external object, and even of a human creature. But tho' these mysteries be so far alike, 'tis very remarkable, that they differ widely in other particulars, and that this difference may be regarded as a strong proof of the difference of their origins. As the obligation of promises is an invention for the interest of society, 'tis warp'd into as many different forms as that interest requires, and even runs into direct contradictions, rather than lose sight of its object. But as those other monstrous doctrines are merely priestly inventions, and have no public interest in view, they are less disturb'd in their progress by new obstacles; and it must be own'd, that, after the first absurdity, they follow more directly the current of reason and good sense. Theologians clearly perceiv'd, that the external form of words, being mere sound, require an intention to make them have any efficacy; and that this intention being once consider'd as a requisite circumstance, its absence must equally prevent the effect, whether avow'd or conceal'd, whether sincere or deceitful. Accordingly they have commonly determin'd, that the intention of the priest makes the sacrament, and that when he secretly withdraws his intention, he is highly criminal in himself; but still destroys the baptism, or communion, or holy orders. The terrible consequences of this doctrine were not able to hinder its taking place; as the inconvenience of a similar doctrine, with regard to promises, have prevented that doctrine from establishing itself. Men are always more concern'd about the present life than the future; and are apt to think the smallest evil, which regards the former, more important than the greatest, which regards the latter.

We may draw the same conclusion, concerning the origin of promises, from the *force*, which is suppos'd to invalidate all contracts, and to free us from their obligation. Such a principle is a proof, that promises have no natural obligation, and are mere artificial contrivances for the convenience and advantage of society. If we consider aright of the matter, force is not essentially different from any other motive of hope or fear, which may induce us to engage our word and lay ourselves under any obligation. A man, dangerously wounded, who promises a competent sum to a surgeon to cure him, wou'd certainly be bound to performance; tho' the case be not so much different from that of one, who promises a sum to a robber, as to produce so great a difference in our sentiments of morality, if these sentiments were not built entirely on public interest and convenience.

## Part III

# Of the Other Virtues and Vices

### Section I. Of the Origin of the Natural Virtues and Vices

We come now to the examination of such virtues and vices as are entirely natural, and have no dependance on the artifice and contrivance of men. The examination of these will conclude this system of morals.

The chief spring or actuating principle of the human mind is pleasure or pain; and when these sensations are remov'd, both from our thought and feeling, we are, in a great measure, incapable of passion or action, of desire or volition. The most immediate effects of pleasure and pain are the propense and averse motions of the mind; which are diversified into volition, into desire and aversion, grief and joy, hope and fear, according as the pleasure or pain changes its situation, and becomes probable or improbable, certain or uncertain, or is consider'd as out of our power for the present moment. But when along with this, the objects, that cause pleasure or pain, acquire a relation to ourselves or others; they still continue to excite desire and aversion, grief and joy: But cause, at the same time, the indirect passions of pride or humility, love or hatred, which in this case have a double relation of impressions and ideas to the pain or pleasure.

We have already observ'd, that moral distinctions depend entirely on certain peculiar sentiments of pain and pleasure, and that whatever mental quality in ourselves or others gives us a satisfaction, by the survey or reflexion, is of course virtuous; as every thing of this nature, that gives uneasiness, is vicious. Now since every quality in ourselves or others, which gives pleasure, always causes pride or love; as every one, that produces uneasiness, excites humility or hatred: It follows, that these two particulars are to be consider'd as equivalent, with regard to our mental qualities, *virtue* and the power of producing love or pride, *vice* and the power of producing humility or hatred. In every case, therefore, we must judge of the one by the other; and may pronounce any *quality* of the mind virtuous, which causes love or pride; and any one vicious, which causes hatred or humility.

If any *action* be either virtuous or vicious, 'tis only as a sign of some quality or character. It must depend upon durable principles of the mind, which extend over the whole conduct, and enter into the personal character. Actions themselves, not proceeding from any constant principle, have no influence on love or hatred, pride or humility; and consequently are never consider'd in morality.

This reflexion is self-evident, and deserves to be attended to, as being of the utmost importance in the present subject. We are never to consider any single action in our enquiries concerning the origin of morals; but only the quality or character from which the action proceeded. These alone are *durable* enough to affect our sentiments concerning the person. Actions are, indeed, better indications of a character than words, or even wishes and sentiments; but 'tis only so far as they are such indications, that they are attended with love or hatred, praise or blame.

To discover the true origin of morals, and of that love or hatred, which arises from mental qualities, we must take the matter pretty deep, and compare some principles, which have been already examin'd and explain'd.

We may begin with considering a-new the nature and force of *sympathy*. The minds of all men are similar in their feelings and operations, nor can any one be actuated by any affection, of which all others are not, in some degree, susceptible. As in strings equally wound up, the motion of one communicates itself to the rest; so all the affections readily pass from one person to another, and beget correspondent movements in every human creature. When I see the *effects* of passion in the voice and gesture of any person, my mind immediately passes from these effects to their causes, and forms such a lively idea of the passion, as is presently converted into the passion itself. In like manner, when I perceive the *causes* of any emotion, my mind is convey'd to the effects, and is actuated with a like emotion. Were I present at any of the more terrible operations of surgery, 'tis certain, that even before it begun, the preparation of the instruments, the laying of the bandages in order, the heating of the irons, with all the signs of anxiety and concern in the patients and assistants, wou'd have a great effect upon my mind, and excite the strongest sentiments of pity and terror. No passion of another discovers itself immediately to the mind. We are only sensible of its causes or effects. From *these* we infer the passion: And consequently *these* give rise to our sympathy.

Our sense of beauty depends very much on this principle; and where any object has a tendency to produce pleasure in its possessor, it is always regarded as beautiful; as every object, that has a tendency to produce pain, is disagreeable and deform'd. Thus the conveniency of a house, the fertility of a field, the strength of a horse, the capacity, security, and swift-sailing of a vessel, form the principal beauty of these several objects. Here the object, which is denominated beautiful, pleases only by its tendency to produce a certain effect. That effect is the pleasure or advantage of some other person. Now the pleasure of a stranger, for whom we have no friendship, pleases us only by sympathy. To this principle, therefore, is owing the beauty, which we find in every thing that is useful. How considerable a part this is of beauty will easily appear upon reflexion. Wherever an object has a tendency to produce pleasure in the possessor, or in other words, is the proper *cause* of pleasure, it is sure to please the spectator, by a delicate sympathy with the possessor. Most of the works of art are esteem'd beautiful, in proportion to their fitness for the use of man, and even many of the productions of nature derive their beauty from that source. Handsome and beautiful, on most occasions, is not an absolute but a relative quality, and pleases us by nothing but its tendency to produce an end that is agreeable.[1]

---

[1] Decentior equus cujus astricta sunt ilia; sed idem velocior. Pulcher aspectu sit athleta, cujus lacertos exercitatio expressit; idem certamini paratior. Nunquam vero *species* ab *utilitate* dividitur. Sed hoc quidem discernere, modici judicii est. *Quinct.* lib. 8.

The same principle produces, in many instances, our sentiments of morals, as well as those of beauty. No virtue is more esteem'd than justice, and no vice more detested than injustice; nor are there any qualities, which go farther to the fixing the character, either as amiable or odious. Now justice is a moral virtue, merely because it has that tendency to the good of mankind; and, indeed, is nothing but an artificial invention to that purpose. The same may be said of allegiance, of the laws of nations, of modesty, and of good-manners. All these are mere human contrivances for the interest of society. And since there is a very strong sentiment of morals, which in all nations, and all ages, has attended them, we must allow, that the reflecting on the tendency of characters and mental qualities, is sufficient to give us the sentiments of approbation and blame. Now as the means to an end can only be agreeable, where the end is agreeable; and as the good of society, where our own interest is not concern'd, or that of our friends, pleases only by sympathy: It follows, that sympathy is the source of the esteem, which we pay to all the artificial virtues.

Thus it appears, *that* sympathy is a very powerful principle in human nature, *that* it has a great influence on our taste of beauty, and *that* it produces our sentiment of morals in all the artificial virtues. From thence we may presume, that it also gives rise to many of the other virtues; and that qualities acquire our approbation, because of their tendency to the good of mankind. This presumption must become a certainty, when we find that most of those qualities, which we *naturally* approve of, have actually that tendency, and render a man a proper member of society: While the qualities, which we *naturally* disapprove of, have a contrary tendency, and render any intercourse with the person dangerous or disagreeable. For having found, that such tendencies have force enough to produce the strongest sentiment of morals, we can never reasonably, in these cases, look for any other cause of approbation or blame; it being an inviolable maxim in philosophy, that where any particular cause is sufficient for an effect, we ought to rest satisfied with it, and ought not to multiply causes without necessity. We have happily attain'd experiments in the artificial virtues, where the tendency of qualities to the good of society, is the *sole* cause of our approbation, without any suspicion of the concurrence of another principle. From thence we learn the force of that principle. And where that principle may take place, and the quality approv'd of is really beneficial to society, a true philosopher will never require any other principle to account for the strongest approbation and esteem.

That many of the natural virtues have this tendency to the good of society, no one can doubt of. Meekness, beneficence, charity, generosity, clemency, moderation, equity, bear the greatest figure among the moral qualities, and are commonly denominated the *social* virtues, to mark their tendency to the good of society. This goes so far, that some philosophers have represented all moral distinctions as the effect of artifice and education, when skilful politicians endeavour'd to restrain the turbulent passions of men, and make them operate to the public good, by the notions of honour and shame. This system, however, is not consistent with experience. For, *first*, there are other virtues and vices beside those which have this tendency to the public advantage and loss. *Secondly*, had not men a natural sentiment of approbation and blame, it cou'd never be excited by politicians; nor wou'd the words *laudable* and *praise-worthy*, *blameable* and *odious*, be any more intelligible, than if they were a language perfectly unknown to us, as we have already observ'd. But tho' this system be erroneous, it may teach us, that moral distinctions arise, in a great measure, from the tendency of qualities and characters to the interests of society, and that 'tis our concern for that interest, which makes us approve or disapprove of them. Now we have no such extensive concern for society but from sympathy; and consequently 'tis that principle, which takes us so far out of ourselves, as to give us the same pleasure or uneasiness in the characters of others, as if they had a tendency to our own advantage or loss.

The only difference betwixt the natural virtues and justice lies in this, that the good, which results from the former, arises from every single act, and is the object of some natural passion: Whereas a single act of justice, consider'd in itself, may often be contrary to the public good; and 'tis only the concurrence of mankind, in a general scheme or system of action, which is advantageous. When I relieve persons in distress, my natural humanity is my motive; and so far as my succour extends, so far have I promoted the happiness of my fellow-creatures. But if we examine all the questions, that come before any tribunal of justice, we shall find, that, considering each case apart, it wou'd as often be an instance of humanity to decide contrary to the laws of justice as conformable to them. Judges take from a poor man to give to a rich; they bestow on the dissolute the labour of the industrious; and put into the hands of the vicious the means of harming both themselves and others. The whole scheme, however, of law and justice is advantageous to the society; and 'twas with a view to this advantage, that men, by their voluntary conventions, establish'd it. After it is once establish'd by these conventions, it is *naturally* attended with a strong sentiment of morals; which can proceed from nothing but our sympathy with the interests of society. We need no other explication of that esteem, which attends such of the natural virtues, as have a tendency to the public good.

I must farther add, that there are several circumstances, which render this hypothesis much more probable with regard to the natural than the artificial virtues. 'Tis certain, that the imagination is more affected by what is particular, than by what is general; and that the sentiments are always mov'd with difficulty, where their objects are, in any degree, loose and undetermin'd: Now every particular act of justice is not beneficial to society, but the whole scheme or system: And it may not, perhaps, be any individual person, for whom we are concern'd, who receives benefit from justice, but the whole society alike. On the contrary, every particular act of generosity, or relief of the industrious and indigent, is beneficial; and is beneficial to a particular person, who is not undeserving of it. 'Tis more natural, therefore, to think, that the tendencies of the latter virtue will affect our sentiments, and command our approbation, than those of the former; and therefore, since we find, that the approbation of the former arises from their tendencies, we may ascribe, with better reason, the same cause to the approbation of the latter. In any number of similar effects, if a cause can be discover'd for one, we ought to extend that cause to all the other effects, which can be accounted for by it: But much more, if these other effects be attended with peculiar circumstances, which facilitate the operation of that cause.

Before I proceed farther, I must observe two remarkable circumstances in this affair, which may seem objections to the present system. The first may be thus explain'd. When any quality, or character, has a tendency to the good of mankind, we are pleas'd with it, and approve of it; because it presents the lively idea of pleasure; which idea affects us by sympathy, and is itself a kind of pleasure. But as this sympathy is very variable, it may be thought, that our sentiments of morals must admit of all the same variations. We sympathize more with persons contiguous to us, than with persons remote from us: With our acquaintance, than with strangers: With our countrymen, than with foreigners. But notwithstanding this variation of our sympathy, we give the same approbation to the same moral qualities in *China* as in *England*. They appear equally virtuous, and recommend themselves equally to the esteem of a judicious spectator. The sympathy varies without a variation in our esteem. Our esteem, therefore, proceeds not from sympathy.

To this I answer: The approbation of moral qualities most certainly is not deriv'd from reason, or any comparison of ideas; but proceeds entirely from a moral taste, and from certain sentiments of pleasure or disgust, which arise upon the contemplation and view of particular qualities or characters. Now 'tis evident, that those sentiments, whence-ever they are deriv'd, must vary according to the distance or contiguity of the objects; nor can I feel the same lively pleasure from the virtues of a person, who liv'd in *Greece* two thousand years ago, that I feel from the virtues of a familiar friend and acquaintance. Yet I do not say, that I esteem the one more than the other: And therefore, if the variation of the sentiment, without a variation of the esteem, be an objection, it must have equal force against every other system, as against that of sympathy. But to consider the matter a-right, it has no force at all; and 'tis the easiest matter in the world to account for it. Our situation, with regard both to persons and things, is in continual fluctuation; and a man, that lies at a distance from us, may, in a little time, become a familiar acquaintance. Besides, every particular man has a peculiar position with regard to others; and 'tis impossible we cou'd ever converse together on any reasonable terms, were each of us to consider characters and persons, only as they appear from his peculiar point of view. In order, therefore, to prevent those continual *contradictions*, and arrive at a more *stable* judgment of things, we fix on some *steady* and *general* points of view; and always, in our thoughts, place ourselves in them, whatever may be our present situation. In like manner, external beauty is determin'd merely by pleasure; and 'tis evident, a beautiful countenance cannot give so much pleasure, when seen at the distance of twenty paces, as when it is brought nearer us. We say not, however, that it appears to us less beautiful: Because we know what effect it will have in such a position, and by that reflexion we correct its momentary appearance.

In general, all sentiments of blame or praise are variable, according to our situation of nearness or remoteness, with regard the person blam'd or prais'd, and according to the present disposition of our mind. But these variations we regard not in our general decisions, but still apply the terms expressive of our liking or dislike, in the same manner, as if we remain'd in one point of view. Experience soon teaches us this method of correcting our sentiments, or at least, of correcting our language, where the sentiments are more stubborn and inalterable. Our servant, if diligent and faithful, may excite stronger sentiments of love and kindness than *Marcus Brutus*, as represented in history; but we say not upon that account, that the former character is more laudable than the latter. We know, that were we to approach equally near to that renown'd patriot, he wou'd command a much higher degree of affection and admiration. Such corrections are common with regard to all the senses; and indeed 'twere impossible we cou'd ever make use of language, or communicate our sentiments to one another, did we not correct the momentary appearances of things, and overlook our present situation.

'Tis therefore from the influence of characters and qualities, upon those who have an intercourse with any person, that we blame or praise him. We consider not whether the persons, affected by the qualities, be our acquaintance or strangers, countrymen or foreigners. Nay, we over-look our own interest in those general judgments; and blame not a man for opposing us in any of our pretensions, when his own interest is particularly concern'd. We make allowance for a certain degree of selfishness in men; because we know it to be inseparable from human nature, and inherent in our frame and constitution. By this reflexion we correct those sentiments of blame, which so naturally arise upon any opposition.

But however the general principle of our blame or praise may be corrected by those other principles, 'tis certain, they are not altogether efficacious, nor do our passions often correspond entirely to the present theory. 'Tis seldom men heartily love what lies at a distance from them, and what no way redounds to their particular benefit; as 'tis no less rare to meet with persons, who can pardon another any opposition he makes to their interest, however justifiable that opposition may be by the general rules of morality. Here we are contented with saying, that reason requires such an impartial conduct, but that 'tis seldom we can bring ourselves to it, and that our passions do not readily follow the determination of our judgment. This language will be easily understood, if we consider what we formerly said concerning that *reason*, which is able to oppose our passion; and which we have found to be nothing but a general calm determination of the passions, founded on some distant view or reflexion. When we form our judgments of persons, merely from the tendency of their characters to our own benefit, or to that of our friends, we find so many contradictions to our sentiments in society and conversation, and such an uncertainty from the incessant changes of our situation, that we seek some other standard of merit and demerit, which may not admit of so great variation. Being thus loosen'd from our first station, we cannot afterwards fix ourselves so commodiously by any means as by a sympathy with those, who have any commerce with the person we consider. This is far from being as lively as when our own interest is concern'd, or that of our particular friends; nor has it such an influence on our love and hatred: But being equally conformable to our calm and general principles, 'tis said to have an equal authority over our reason, and to command our judgment and opinion. We blame equally a bad action, which we read of in history, with one perform'd in our neighbourhood t'other day: The meaning of which is, that we know from reflexion, that the former action wou'd excite as strong sentiments of disapprobation as the latter, were it plac'd in the same position.

I now proceed to the *second* remarkable circumstance, which I propos'd to take notice of. Where a person is possess'd of a character, that in its natural tendency is beneficial to society, we esteem him virtuous, and are delighted with the view of his character, even tho' particular accidents prevent its operation, and incapacitate him from being serviceable to his friends and country. Virtue in rags is still virtue; and the love, which it procures, attends a man into a dungeon or desart, where the virtue can no longer be exerted in action, and is lost to all the world. Now this may be esteem'd an objection to the present system. Sympathy interests us in the good of mankind; and if sympathy were the source of our esteem for virtue, that sentiment of approbation cou'd only take place, where the virtue actually attain'd its end, and was beneficial to mankind. Where it fails of its end, 'tis only an imperfect means; and therefore can never acquire any merit from that end. The goodness of an end can bestow a merit on such means alone as are compleat, and actually produce the end.

To this we may reply, that where any object, in all its parts, is fitted to attain any agreeable end, it naturally gives us pleasure, and is esteem'd beautiful, even tho' some external circumstances be wanting to render it altogether effectual. 'Tis sufficient if every thing be compleat in the object itself. A house, that is contriv'd with great judgment for all the commodities of life, pleases us upon that account; tho' perhaps we are sensible, that no-one will ever dwell in it. A fertile soil, and a happy climate, delight us by a reflexion on the happiness which they wou'd afford the inhabitants, tho' at present the country be desart and uninhabited. A man, whose limbs and shape promise strength and activity, is esteem'd handsome, tho' condemn'd to perpetual imprisonment. The imagination has a set of passions belonging to it, upon which our sentiments of beauty much depend. These passions are mov'd by degrees of liveliness and strength, which are inferior to *belief*, and independent of the real existence of their objects. Where a character is, in every respect, fitted to be beneficial to society, the imagination passes easily from the cause to the effect, without considering that there are still some circumstances wanting to render the cause a compleat one. *General rules* create a species of probability, which sometimes influences the judgment, and always the imagination.

'Tis true, when the cause is compleat, and a good disposition is attended with good fortune, which renders it really beneficial to society, it gives a stronger pleasure to the spectator, and is attended with a more lively sympathy. We are more affected by it; and yet we do not say that it is more virtuous, or that we esteem it more. We know, that an alteration of fortune may render the benevolent disposition entirely impotent; and therefore we separate, as much as possible, the fortune from the disposition. The case is the same, as when we correct the different sentiments of virtue, which proceed from its different distances from ourselves. The passions do not always follow our corrections; but these corrections serve sufficiently to regulate our abstract notions, and are alone regarded, when we pronounce in general concerning the degrees of vice and virtue.

'Tis observ'd by critics, that all words or sentences, which are difficult to the pronunciation, are disagreeable to the ear.

There is no difference, whether a man hear them pronounc'd, or read them silently to himself. When I run over a book with my eye, I imagine I hear it all; and also, by the force of imagination, enter into the uneasiness, which the delivery of it wou'd give the speaker. The uneasiness is not real; but as such a composition of words has a natural tendency to produce it, this is sufficient to affect the mind with a painful sentiment, and render the discourse harsh and disagreeable. 'Tis a similar case, where any real quality is, by accidental circumstances, render'd impotent, and is depriv'd of its natural influence on society.

Upon these principles we may easily remove any contradiction, which may appear to be betwixt the *extensive sympathy*, on which our sentiments of virtue depend, and that *limited generosity* which I have frequently observ'd to be natural to men, and which justice and property suppose, according to the precedent reasoning. My sympathy with another may give me the sentiment of pain and disapprobation, when any object is presented, that has a tendency to give him uneasiness; tho' I may not be willing to sacrifice any thing of my own interest, or cross any of my passions, for his satisfaction. A house may displease me by being ill-contriv'd for the convenience of the owner; and yet I may refuse to give a shilling towards the rebuilding of it. Sentiments must touch the heart, to make them controul our passions: But they need not extend beyond the imagination, to make them influence our taste. When a building seems clumsy and tottering to the eye, it is ugly and disagreeable; tho' we be fully assur'd of the solidity of the workmanship. 'Tis a kind of fear, which causes this sentiment of disapprobation; but the passion is not the same with that which we feel, when oblig'd to stand under a wall, that we really think tottering and insecure. The *seeming tendencies* of objects affect the mind: And the emotions they excite are of a like species with those, which proceed from the *real consequences* of objects, but their feeling is different. Nay, these emotions are so different in their feeling, that they may often be contrary, without destroying each other; as when the fortifications of a city belonging to an enemy are esteem'd beautiful upon account of their strength, tho' we cou'd wish that they were entirely destroy'd. The imagination adheres to the *general* views of things, and distinguishes the feelings they produce, from those which arise from our particular and momentary situation.

If we examine the panegyrics that are commonly made of great men, we shall find, that most of the qualities, which are attributed to them, may be divided into two kinds, *viz.* such as make them perform their part in society; and such as render them serviceable to themselves, and enable them to promote their own interest. Their *prudence, temperance, frugality, industry, assiduity, enterprize, dexterity,* are celebrated, as well as their *generosity* and *humanity.* If we ever give an indulgence to any quality, that disables a man from making a figure in life, 'tis to that of *indolence,* which is not suppos'd to deprive one of his parts and capacity, but only suspends their exercise; and that without any inconvenience to the person himself, since 'tis, in some measure, from his own choice. Yet indolence is always allow'd to be a fault, and a very great one, if extreme: Nor do a man's friends ever acknowledge him to be subject to it, but in order to save his character in more material articles. He cou'd make a figure, say they, if he pleas'd to give application: His understanding is sound, his conception quick, and his memory tenacious; but he hates business, and is indifferent about his fortune. And this a man sometimes may make even a subject of vanity; tho' with the air of confessing a fault: Because he may think, that this incapacity for business implies much more noble qualities; such as a philosophical spirit, a fine taste, a delicate wit, or a relish for pleasure and society. But take any other case: Suppose a quality, that without being an indication of any other good qualities, incapacitates a man *always* for business, and is destructive to his interest; such as a blundering understanding, and a wrong judgment of every thing in life; inconstancy and irresolution; or a want of address in the management of men and business: These are all allow'd to be imperfections in a character; and many men wou'd rather acknowledge the greatest crimes, than have it suspected, that they are, in any degree, subject to them.

'Tis very happy, in our philosophical researches, when we find the same phænomenon diversified by a variety of circumstances; and by discovering what is common among them, can the better assure ourselves of the truth of any hypothesis we may make use of to explain it. Were nothing esteem'd virtue but what were beneficial to society, I am persuaded, that the foregoing explication of the moral sense ought still to be receiv'd, and that upon sufficient evidence: But this evidence must grow upon us, when we find other kinds of virtue, which will not admit of any explication except from that hypothesis. Here is a man, who is not remarkably defective in his social qualities; but what principally recommends him is his dexterity in business, by which he has extricated himself from the greatest difficulties, and conducted the most delicate affairs with a singular address and prudence. I find an esteem for him immediately to arise in me: His company is a satisfaction to me; and before I have any farther acquaintance with him, I wou'd rather do him a service than another, whose character is in every other respect equal, but is deficient in that particular. In this case, the qualities that please me are all consider'd as useful to the person, and as having a tendency to promote his interest and satisfaction. They are only regarded as means to an end, and please me in proportion to their fitness for that end. The end, therefore, must be agreeable to me. But what makes the end agreeable? The person is a stranger: I am no way interested in him, nor lie under any obligation to him: His happiness concerns not me, farther than the happiness of every human, and indeed of every sensible creature: That is, it affects me only by sympathy. From that principle, whenever I discover his happiness and good, whether in its causes or effects, I enter so deeply into it, that it gives me a sensible emotion. The appearance of qualities, that have a *tendency* to promote it, have an agreeable effect upon my imagination, and command my love and esteem.

This theory may serve to explain, why the same qualities,

in all cases, produce both pride and love, humility and hatred; and the same man is always virtuous or vicious, accomplish'd or despicable to others, who is so to himself. A person, in whom we discover any passion or habit, which originally is only incommodious to himself, becomes always disagreeable to us, merely on its account; as on the other hand, one whose character is only dangerous and disagreeable to others, can never be satisfied with himself, as long as he is sensible of that disadvantage. Nor is this observable only with regard to characters and manners, but may be remark'd even in the most minute circumstances. A violent cough in another gives us uneasiness; tho' in itself it does not in the least affect us. A man will be mortified, if you tell him he has a stinking breath; tho' 'tis evidently no annoyance to himself. Our fancy easily changes its situation; and either surveying ourselves as we appear to others, or considering others as they feel themselves, we enter, by that means, into sentiments, which no way belong to us, and in which nothing but sympathy is able to interest us. And this sympathy we sometimes carry so far, as even to be displeas'd with a quality commodious to us, merely because it displeases others, and makes us disagreeable in their eyes; tho' perhaps we never can have any interest in rendering ourselves agreeable to them.

There have been many systems of morality advanc'd by philosophers in all ages; but if they are strictly examin'd, they may be reduc'd to two, which alone merit our attention. Moral good and evil are certainly distinguish'd by our *sentiments*, not by *reason*: But these sentiments may arise either from the mere species or appearance of characters and passions, or from reflexions on their tendency to the happiness of mankind, and of particular persons. My opinion is, that both these causes are intermix'd in our judgments of morals; after the same manner as they are in our decisions concerning most kinds of external beauty: Tho' I am also of opinion, that reflexions on the tendencies of actions have by far the greatest influence, and determine all the great lines of our duty. There are, however, instances, in cases of less moment, wherein this immediate taste or sentiment produces our approbation. Wit, and a certain easy and disengag'd behaviour, are qualities *immediately agreeable* to others, and command their love and esteem. Some of these qualities produce satisfaction in others by particular *original* principles of human nature, which cannot be accounted for: Others may be resolv'd into principles, which are more general. This will best appear upon a particular enquiry.

As some qualities acquire their merit from their being *immediately agreeable* to others, without any tendency to public interest; so some are denominated virtuous from their being *immediately agreeable* to the person himself, who possesses them. Each of the passions and operations of the mind has a particular feeling, which must be either agreeable or disagreeable. The first is virtuous, the second vicious. This particular feeling constitutes the very nature of the passion; and therefore needs not be accounted for.

But however directly the distinction of vice and virtue may seem to flow from the immediate pleasure or uneasiness, which particular qualities cause to ourselves or others; 'tis easy to observe, that it has also a considerable dependence on the principle of *sympathy* so often insisted on. We approve of a person, who is possess'd of qualities *immediately agreeable* to those, with whom he has any commerce; tho' perhaps we ourselves never reap'd any pleasure from them. We also approve of one, who is possess'd of qualities, that are *immediately agreeable* to himself; tho' they be of no service to any mortal. To account for this we must have recourse to the foregoing principles.

Thus, to take a general review of the present hypothesis: Every quality of the mind is denominated virtuous, which gives pleasure by the mere survey; as every quality, which produces pain, is call'd vicious. This pleasure and this pain may arise from four different sources. For we reap a pleasure from the view of a character, which is naturally fitted to be useful to others, or to the person himself, or which is agreeable to others, or to the person himself. One may, perhaps, be surpriz'd, that amidst all these interests and pleasures, we shou'd forget our own, which touch us so nearly on every other occasion. But we shall easily satisfy ourselves on this head, when we consider, that every particular person's pleasure and interest being different, 'tis impossible men cou'd ever agree in their sentiments and judgments, unless they chose some common point of view, from which they might survey their object, and which might cause it to appear the same to all of them. Now, in judging of characters, the only interest or pleasure, which appears the same to every spectator, is that of the person himself, whose character is examin'd; or that of persons, who have a connexion with him. And tho' such interests and pleasures touch us more faintly than our own, yet being more constant and universal, they counter-ballance the latter even in practice, and are alone admitted in speculation as the standard of virtue and morality. They alone produce that particular feeling or sentiment, on which moral distinctions depend.

As to the good or ill desert of virtue or vice, 'tis an evident consequence of the sentiments of pleasure or uneasiness. These sentiments produce love or hatred; and love or hatred, by the original constitution of human passion, is attended with benevolence or anger; that is, with a desire of making happy the person we love, and miserable the person we hate. We have treated of this more fully on another occasion.

ESSAYS

# OF THE ORIGINAL CONTRACT

As NO PARTY, in the present age, can well support itself, without a philosophical or speculative system of principles, annexed to its political or practical one; we accordingly find, that each of the factions, into which this nation is divided, has reared up a fabric of the former kind, in order to protect and cover that scheme of actions, which it pursues. The people being commonly very rude builders, especially in this speculative way, and more especially still, when actuated by party-zeal; it is natural to imagine, that their workmanship must be a little unshapely, and discover evident marks of that violence and hurry, in which it was raised. The one party, by tracing up Government to the DEITY, endeavour to render it so sacred and inviolate, that it must be little less than sacrilege, however tyrannical it may become, to touch or invade it, in the smallest article. The other party, by founding government altogether on the consent of the PEOPLE, suppose that there is a kind of *original contract*, by which the subjects have tacitly reserved the power of resisting their sovereign, whenever they find themselves aggrieved by that authority, with which they have, for certain purposes, voluntarily entrusted him. These are the speculative principles of the two parties; and these too are the practical consequences deduced from them.

I shall venture to affirm, *That both these* systems *of speculative principles are just; though not in the sense, intended by the parties:* And, *That both the* schemes *of practical consequences are prudent; though not in the extremes, to which each party, in opposition to the other, has commonly endeavoured to carry them.*

That the DEITY is the ultimate author of all government, will never be denied by any, who admit a general providence, and allow, that all events in the universe are conducted by an uniform plan, and directed to wise purposes. As it is impossible for the human race to subsist, at least in any comfortable or secure state, without the protection of government;

this institution must certainly have been intended by that beneficent Being, who means the good of all his creatures: And as it has universally, in fact, taken place, in all countries, and all ages; we may conclude, with still greater certainty, that it was intended by that omniscient Being, who can never be deceived by any event or operation. But since he gave rise to it, not by any particular or miraculous interposition, but by his concealed and universal efficacy; a sovereign cannot, properly speaking, be called his vice-gerent, in any other sense than every power or force, being derived from him, may be said to act by his commission. Whatever actually happens is comprehended in the general plan or intention of providence; nor has the greatest and most lawful prince any more reason, upon that account, to plead a peculiar sacredness or inviolable authority, than an inferior magistrate, or even an usurper, or even a robber and a pyrate. The same divine superintendant, who, for wise purposes, invested[1] a TITUS or a TRAJAN with authority, did also, for purposes, no doubt, equally wise, though unknown, bestow power on a BORGIA or an ANGRIA. The same causes, which gave rise to the sovereign power in every state, established likewise every petty jurisdiction in it, and every limited authority. A constable, therefore, no less than a king, acts by a divine commission, and possesses an indefeasible right.

When we consider how nearly equal all men are in their bodily force, and even in their mental powers and faculties, till cultivated by education; we must necessarily allow, that nothing but their own consent could, at first, associate them together, and subject them to any authority. The people, if we trace government to its first origin in the woods and desarts, are the source of all power and jurisdiction, and voluntarily, for the sake of peace and order, abandoned their native liberty, and received laws from their equal and companion. The conditions, upon which they were willing to submit, were either expressed, or were so clear and obvious, that it might well be esteemed superfluous to express them. If this, then, be meant by the *original contract*, it cannot be denied, that

[1] An Elizabeth or a Henry the IVth of France: in editions before 1770.

all government is, at first, founded on a contract, and that the most ancient rude combinations of mankind were formed chiefly by that principle. In vain, are we asked in what records this charter of our liberties is registered. It was not written on parchment, nor yet on leaves or barks of trees. It preceded the use of writing and all the other civilized arts of life. But we trace it plainly in the nature of man, and in the equality, or something approaching equality, which we find in all the individuals of that species. The force, which now prevails, and which is founded on fleets and armies, is plainly political, and derived from authority, the effect of established government. A man's natural force consists only in the vigour of his limbs, and the firmness of his courage; which could never subject multitudes to the command of one. Nothing but their own consent, and their sense of the advantages resulting from peace and order, could have had that influence.

Yet even this consent was long very imperfect, and could not be the basis of a regular administration. The chieftain, who had probably acquired his influence during the continuance of war, ruled more by persuasion than command; and till he could employ force to reduce the refractory and disobedient, the society could scarcely be said to have attained a state of civil government. No compact or agreement, it is evident, was expressly formed for general submission; an idea far beyond the comprehension of savages: Each exertion of authority in the chieftain must have been particular, and called forth by the present exigencies of the case: The sensible utility, resulting from his interposition, made these exertions become daily more frequent; and their frequency gradually produced an habitual, and, if you please to call it so, a voluntary, and therefore precarious, acquiescence in the people.

But philosophers, who have embraced a party (if that be not a contradiction in terms) are not contented with these concessions. They assert, not only that government in its earliest infancy arose from consent or rather the voluntary acquiescence of the people; but also, that, even at present, when it has attained its full maturity, it rests on no other foundation. They affirm, that all men are still born equal, and owe allegiance to no prince or government, unless bound by the obligation and sanction of a *promise*. And as no man, without some equivalent, would forego the advantages of his native liberty, and subject himself to the will of another; this promise is always understood to be conditional, and imposes on him no obligation, unless he meet with justice and protection from his sovereign. These advantages the sovereign promises him in return; and if he fail in the execution, he has broken, on his part, the articles of engagement, and has thereby freed his subject from all obligations to allegiance. Such, according to these philosophers, is the foundation of authority in every government; and such the right of resistance, possessed by every subject.

But would these reasoners look abroad into the world, they would meet with nothing that, in the least, corresponds to their ideas, or can warrant so refined and philosophical a system. On the contrary, we find, every where, princes, who claim their subjects as their property, and assert their independent right of sovereignty, from conquest or succession. We find also, every where, subjects, who acknowledge this right in their prince, and suppose themselves born under obligations of obedience to a certain sovereign, as much as under the ties of reverence and duty to certain parents. These connexions are always conceived to be equally independent of our consent, in PERSIA and CHINA; in FRANCE and SPAIN; and even in HOLLAND and ENGLAND, wherever the doctrines abovementioned have not been carefully inculcated. Obedience or subjection becomes so familiar, that most men never make any enquiry about its origin or cause, more than about the principle of gravity, resistance, or the most universal laws of nature. Or if curiosity ever move them; as soon as they learn, that they themselves and their ancestors have, for several ages, or from time immemorial, been subject to such a form of government or such a family; they immediately acquiesce, and acknowledge their obligation to allegiance. Were you to preach, in most parts of the world, that political connexions are founded altogether on voluntary consent or a mutual promise, the magistrate would soon imprison you, as seditious, for loosening the ties of obedience; if your friends did not before shut you up as delirious, for advancing such absurdities. It is strange, that an act of the mind, which every individual is supposed to have formed, and after he came to the use of reason too, otherwise it could have no authority; that this act, I say, should be so much unknown to all of them, that, over the face of the whole earth, there scarcely remain any traces or memory of it.

But the contract, on which government is founded, is said to be the *original contract*; and consequently may be supposed too old to fall under the knowledge of the present generation. If the agreement, by which savage men first associated and conjoined their force, be here meant, this is acknowledged to be real; but being so ancient, and being obliterated by a thousand changes of government and princes, it cannot now be supposed to retain any authority. If we would say any thing to the purpose, we must assert, that every particular government, which is lawful, and which imposes any duty of allegiance on the subject, was, at first, founded on consent and a voluntary compact. But besides that this supposes the consent of the fathers to bind the children, even to the most remote generations, (which republican writers will never allow) besides this, I say, it is not justified by history or experience, in any age or country of the world.

Almost all the governments, which exist at present, or of which there remains any record in story, have been founded originally, either on usurpation or conquest, or both, without any pretence of a fair consent, or voluntary subjection of the people. When an artful and bold man is placed at the head of an army or faction, it is often easy for him, by employing, sometimes violence, sometimes false pretences, to establish his dominion over a people a hundred times more numerous than his partizans. He allows no such open communication, that his enemies can know, with certainty, their number or force. He gives them no leisure to assemble together in a body to oppose him. Even all those, who are the instruments of his usurpation, may wish his fall; but their ignorance of each other's intention keeps them in awe, and is the sole cause of his security. By such arts as these, many governments have been established; and this is all the *original contract*, which they have to boast of.

The face of the earth is continually changing, by the encrease of small kingdoms into great empires, by the dissolution of great empires into smaller kingdoms, by the planting of colonies, by the migration of tribes. Is there any thing discoverable in all these events, but force and violence? Where is the mutual agreement or voluntary association so much talked of?

Even the smoothest way, by which a nation may receive a foreign master, by marriage or a will, is not extremely honourable for the people; but supposes them to be disposed of, like a dowry or a legacy, according to the pleasure or interest of their rulers.

But where no force interposes, and election takes place; what is this election so highly vaunted? It is either the combination of a few great men, who decide for the whole, and will allow of no opposition: Or it is the fury of a multitude, that follow a seditious ringleader, who is not known, perhaps, to a dozen among them, and who owes his advancement merely to his own impudence, or to the momentary caprice of his fellows.

Are these disorderly elections, which are rare too, of such mighty authority, as to be the only lawful foundation of all government and allegiance?

In reality, there is not a more terrible event, than a total dissolution of government, which gives liberty to the multitude, and makes the determination or choice of a new establishment depend upon a number, which nearly approaches to that of the body of the people: For it never comes entirely to the whole body of them. Every wise man, then, wishes to see, at the head of a powerful and obedient army, a general, who may speedily seize the prize, and give to the people a master, which they are so unfit to chuse for themselves. So little correspondent is fact and reality to those philosophical notions.

Let not the establishment at the *Revolution* deceive us, or make us so much in love with a philosophical origin to government, as to imagine all others monstrous and irregular. Even that event was far from corresponding to these refined ideas. It was only the succession, and that only in the regal part of the government, which was then changed: And it was only the majority of seven hundred, who determined that change for near ten millions. I doubt not, indeed, but the bulk of those ten millions acquiesced willingly in the determination: But was the matter left, in the least, to their choice? Was it not justly supposed to be, from that moment, decided, and every man punished, who refused to submit to the new sovereign? How otherwise could the matter have ever been brought to any issue or conclusion?

The republic of ATHENS was, I believe, the most extensive democracy, that we read of in history: Yet if we make the requisite allowances for the women, the slaves, and the strangers, we shall find, that that establishment was not, at first, made, nor any law ever voted, by a tenth part of those who were bound to pay obedience to it: Not to mention the islands and foreign dominions, which the ATHENIANS claimed as theirs by right of conquest. And as it is well known, that popular assemblies in that city were always full of licence and disorder, notwithstanding the institutions and laws by which they were checked: How much more disorderly must they prove, where they form not the established constitution, but meet tumultuously on the dissolution of the ancient government, in order to give rise to a new one? How chimerical must it be to talk of a choice in such circumstances?

The ACHÆANS enjoyed the freest and most perfect democracy of all antiquity; yet they employed force to oblige some cities to enter into their league, as we learn from POLYBIUS.[2]

HARRY the IVth and HARRY the VIIth of England, had really no title to the throne but a parliamentary election; yet they never would acknowledge it, lest they should thereby weaken their authority. Strange, if the only real foundation of all authority be consent and promise!

It is in vain to say, that all governments are or should be,

[2] Lib. ii. cap. 38.

at first, founded on popular consent, as much as the necessity of human affairs will admit. This favours entirely my pretension. I maintain, that human affairs will never admit of this consent; seldom of the appearance of it. But that conquest or usurpation, that is, in plain terms, force, by dissolving the ancient governments, is the origin of almost all the new ones, which were ever established in the world. And that in the few cases, where consent may seem to have taken place, it was commonly so irregular, so confined, or so much intermixed either with fraud or violence, that it cannot have any great authority.

My intention here is not to exclude the consent of the people from being one just foundation of government where it has place. It is surely the best and most sacred of any. I only pretend, that it has very seldom had place in any degree, and never almost in its full extent. And that therefore some other foundation of government must also be admitted.

Were all men possessed of so inflexible a regard to justice, that, of themselves, they would totally abstain from the properties of others; they had for ever remained in a state of absolute liberty, without subjection to any magistrate or political society: But this is a state of perfection, of which human nature is justly deemed incapable. Again; were all men possessed of so perfect an understanding, as always to know their own interests, no form of government had ever been submitted to, but what was established on consent, and was fully canvassed by every member of the society: But this state of perfection is likewise much superior to human nature. Reason, history, and experience shew us, that all political societies have had an origin much less accurate and regular; and were one to choose a period of time, when the people's consent was the least regarded in public transactions, it would be precisely on the establishment of a new government. In a settled constitution, their inclinations are often consulted; but during the fury of revolutions, conquests, and public convulsions, military force or political craft usually decides the controversy.

When a new government is established, by whatever means, the people are commonly dissatisfied with it, and pay obedience more from fear and necessity, than from any idea of allegiance or of moral obligation. The prince is watchful and jealous, and must carefully guard against every beginning or appearance of insurrection. Time, by degrees, removes all these difficulties, and accustoms the nation to regard, as their lawful or native princes, that family, which, at first, they considered as usurpers or foreign conquerors. In order to found this opinion, they have no recourse to any notion of voluntary consent or promise, which, they know, never was, in this case, either expected or demanded. The original establishment was formed by violence, and submitted to from necessity. The subsequent administration is also supported by power, and acquiesced in by the people, not as a matter of choice, but of obligation. They imagine not that their consent gives their prince a title: but they willingly consent, because they think, that, from long possession, he has acquired a title, independent of their choice or inclination.

Should it be said, that, by living under the dominion of a prince, which one might leave, every individual has given a *tacit* consent to his authority, and promised him obedience; it may be answered, that such an implied consent can only have place, where a man imagines, that the matter depends on his choice. But where he thinks (as all mankind do who are born under established governments) that by his birth he owes allegiance to a certain prince or certain form of government; it would be absurd to infer a consent or choice, which he expressly, in this case, renounces and disclaims.

Can we seriously say, that a poor peasant or partizan has a free choice to leave his country, when he knows no foreign language or manners, and lives from day to day, by the small wages which he acquires? We may as well assert, that a man, by remaining in a vessel, freely consents to the dominion of the master; though he was carried on board while asleep, and must leap into the ocean, and perish, the moment he leaves her.

What if the prince forbid his subjects to quit his dominions; as in TIBERIUS's time, it was regarded as a crime in a ROMAN knight that he had attempted to fly to the PARTHIANS, in order to escape the tyranny of that emperor?[3] Or as the ancient MUSCOVITES prohibited all travelling under pain of death? And did a prince observe, that many of his subjects were seized with the frenzy of migrating to foreign countries, he would doubtless, with great reason and justice, restrain them, in order to prevent the depopulation of his own kingdom. Would he forfeit the allegiance of all his subjects, by so wise and reasonable a law? Yet the freedom of their choice is surely, in that case, ravished from them.

A company of men, who should leave their native country, in order to people some uninhabited region, might dream of recovering their native freedom; but they would soon find, that their prince still laid claim to them, and called them his subjects, even in their new settlement. And in this he would but act conformably to the common ideas of mankind.

The truest *tacit* consent of this kind, that is ever observed, is when a foreigner settles in any country, and is beforehand acquainted with the prince, and government, and laws, to which he must submit: Yet is his allegiance, though more voluntary, much less expected or depended on, than that of a natural born subject. On the contrary, his native prince still asserts a claim to him. And if he punish not the renegade, when he seizes him in war with his new prince's commission; this clemency is not founded on the municipal law, which in all countries condemns the prisoner; but on the consent of princes, who have agreed to this indulgence, in order to prevent reprisals.

Did one generation of men go off the stage at once, and another succeed, as is the case with silk-worms and butterflies, the new race, if they had sense enough to choose their government, which surely is never the case with men, might voluntarily, and by general consent, establish their own form of civil polity, without any regard to the laws or precedents, which prevailed among their ancestors. But as human society is in perpetual flux, one man every hour going out of the world, another coming into it, it is necessary, in order to preserve stability in government, that the new brood should con-

[r]TACIT. Ann. vi. cap. 14.

form themselves to the established constitution, and nearly follow the path which their fathers, treading in the footsteps of theirs, had marked out to them. Some innovations must necessarily have place in every human institution, and it is happy where the enlightened genius of the age gives these a direction to the side of reason, liberty, and justice: but violent innovations no individual is entitled to make: they are even dangerous to be attempted by the legislature: more ill than good is ever to be expected from them: and if history affords examples to the contrary, they are not to be drawn into precedent, and are only to be regarded as proofs, that the science of politics affords few rules, which will not admit of some exception, and which may not sometimes be controuled by fortune and accident. The violent innovations in the reign of HENRY VIII. proceeded from an imperious monarch, seconded by the appearance of legislative authority: Those in the reign of CHARLES I. were derived from faction and fanaticism, and both of them have proved happy in the issue: But even the former were long the source of many disorders, and still more dangers; and if the measures of allegiance were to be taken from the latter, a total anarchy must have place in human society, and a final period at once be put to every government.

Suppose, that an usurper, after having banished his lawful prince and royal family, should establish his dominion for ten or a dozen years in any country, and should preserve so exact a discipline in his troops, and so regular a disposition in his garrisons, that no insurrection had ever been raised, or even murmur heard, against his administration: Can it be asserted, that the people, who in their hearts abhor his treason, have tacitly consented to his authority, and promised him allegiance, merely because, from necessity, they live under his dominion? Suppose again their native prince restored, by means of an army, which he levies in foreign countries: They receive him with joy and exultation, and shew plainly with what reluctance they had submitted to any other yoke. I may now ask, upon what foundation the prince's title stands? Not on popular consent surely: For though the people willingly acquiesce in his authority, they never imagine, that their consent made him sovereign. They consent; because they apprehend him to be already, by birth, their lawful sovereign. And as to that tacit consent, which may now be inferred from their living under his dominion, this is no more than what they formerly gave to the tyrant and usurper.

When we assert, that all lawful government arises from the consent of the people, we certainly do them a great deal more honour than they deserve, or even expect and desire from us. After the ROMAN dominions became too unwieldly for the republic to govern them, the people, over the whole known world, were extremely grateful to AUGUSTUS for that authority, which, by violence, he had established over them; and they showed an equal disposition to submit to the successor, whom he left them, by his last will and testament. It was afterwards their misfortune, that there never was, in one family, any long regular succession; but that their line of princes was continually broken, either by private assassinations or public rebellions. The *prætorian* bands, on the failure of every family, set up one emperor; the legions in the East a second; those in GERMANY, perhaps, a third: And the sword alone could decide the controversy. The condition of the people, in that mighty monarchy, was to be lamented, not because the choice of the emperor was never left to them; for that was impracticable: But because they never fell under any succession of masters, who might regularly follow each other. As to the violence and wars and bloodshed, occasioned by every new settlement; these were not blameable, because they were inevitable.

The house of LANCASTER ruled in this island about sixty years; yet the partizans of the white rose seemed daily to multiply in ENGLAND. The present establishment has taken place during a still longer period. Have all views of right in another family been utterly extinguished; even though scarce any man now alive had arrived at years of discretion, when it was expelled, or could have consented to its dominion, or have promised it allegiance? A sufficient indication surely of the general sentiment of mankind on this head. For we blame not the partizans of the abdicated family, merely on account of the long time, during which they have preserved their imaginary loyalty. We blame them for adhering to a family, which, we affirm, has been justly expelled, and which, from the moment the new settlement took place, had forfeited all title to authority.

But would we have a more regular, at least a more philosophical, refutation of this principle of an original contract or popular consent; perhaps, the following observations may suffice.

All *moral* duties may be divided into two kinds. The *first* are those, to which men are impelled by a natural instinct or immediate propensity, which operates on them, independent of all ideas of obligation, and of all views, either to public or private utility. Of this nature are, love of children, gratitude to benefactors, pity to the unfortunate. When we reflect on the advantage, which results to society from such humane instincts, we pay them the just tribute of moral approbation and esteem: But the person, actuated by them, feels their power and influence, antecedent to any such reflection.

The *second* kind of moral duties are such as are not supported by any original instinct of nature, but are performed entirely from a sense of obligation, when we consider the necessities of human society, and the impossibility of supporting it, if these duties were neglected. It is thus *justice* or a regard to the property of others, *fidelity* or the observance of promises, become obligatory, and acquire an authority over mankind. For as it is evident, that every man loves himself better than any other person, he is naturally impelled to extend his acquisitions as much as possible; and nothing can restrain him in this propensity, but reflection and experience, by which he learns the pernicious effects of that licence, and the total dissolution of society which must ensue from it. His original inclination, therefore, or instinct, is here checked and restrained by a subsequent judgment or observation.

The case is precisely the same with the political or civil duty of *allegiance,* as with the natural duties of justice and fidelity. Our primary instincts lead us, either to indulge ourselves in unlimited freedom, or to seek dominion over others: And it is reflexion only, which engages us to sacrifice such strong passions to the interests of peace and public order. A small degree of experience and observation suffices to teach us, that society cannot possibly be maintained without the authority of magistrates, and that this authority must soon fall into contempt, where exact obedience is not paid to it. The observation of these general and obvious interests is the source of all allegiance, and of that moral obligation, which we attribute to it.

What necessity, therefore, is there to found the duty of *allegiance* or obedience to magistrates on that of *fidelity* or a regard to promises, and to suppose, that it is the consent of each individual, which subjects him to government; when it appears, that both allegiance and fidelity stand precisely on the same foundation, and are both submitted to by mankind, on account of the apparent interests and necessities of human society? We are bound to obey our sovereign, it is said; because we have given a tacit promise to that purpose. But why are we bound to observe our promise? It must here be asserted, that the commerce and intercourse of mankind, which are of such mighty advantage, can have no security where men pay no regard to their engagements. In like manner, may it be said, that men could not live at all in society, at least in a civilized society, without laws and magistrates and judges, to prevent the encroachments of the strong upon the weak, of the violent upon the just and equitable. The obligation to allegiance being of like force and authority with the obligation to fidelity, we gain nothing by resolving the one into the other. The general interests or necessities of society are sufficient to establish both.

If the reason be asked of that obedience, which we are bound to pay to government, I readily answer, *because society could not otherwise subsist:* And this answer is clear and intelligible to all mankind. Your answer is, *because we should keep our word.* But besides, that no body, till trained in a philosophical system, can either comprehend or relish this answer: Besides this, I say, you find yourself embarrassed, when it is asked, *why we are bound to keep our word?* Nor can you give any answer, but what would, immediately, without any circuit, have accounted for our obligation to allegiance.

But *to whom is allegiance due? And who is our lawful sovereign?* This question is often the most difficult of any, and liable to infinite discussions. When people are so happy, that they can answer, *Our present sovereign, who inherits, in a direct line, from ancestors, that have governed us for many ages;* this answer admits of no reply; even though historians, in tracing up to the remotest antiquity, the origin of that royal family, may find, as commonly happens, that its first authority was derived from usurpation and violence. It is confessed, that private justice, or the abstinence from the properties of others, is a most cardinal virtue: Yet reason tells us, that there is no property in durable objects, such as lands or houses, when carefully examined in passing from hand to hand, but must, in some period, have been founded on fraud and injustice. The necessities of human society, neither in private nor public life, will allow of such an accurate enquiry: And there is no virtue or moral duty, but what may, with facility, be refined away, if we indulge a false philosophy, in sifting and scrutinizing it, by every captious rule of logic, in every light or position, in which it may be placed.

The questions with regard to private property have filled infinite volumes of law and philosophy, if in both we add the commentators to the original text; and in the end, we may safely pronounce, that many of the rules, there established, are uncertain, ambiguous, and arbitrary. The like opinion may be formed with regard to the succession and rights of princes and forms of government. Several cases, no doubt, occur, especially in the infancy of any constitution, which admit of no determination from the laws of justice and equity: And our historian RAPIN pretends,[4] that the controversy between EDWARD the THIRD and PHILIP DE VALOIS was of this nature, and could be decided only by an appeal to heaven, that is, by war and violence.

Who shall tell me, whether GERMANICUS or DRUSUS ought to have succeeded to TIBERIUS, had he died, while they were both alive, without naming any of them for his successor?

[4] Allows: in editions before 1770.

Ought the right of adoption to be received as equivalent to that of blood, in a nation, where it had the same effect in private families, and had already, in two instances, taken place in the public? Ought GERMANICUS to be esteemed the elder son because he was born before DRUSUS; or the younger, because he was adopted after the birth of his brother? Ought the right of the elder to be regarded in a nation, where he had no advantage in the succession of private families? Ought the ROMAN empire at that time to be deemed hereditary, because of two examples; or ought it, even so early, to be regarded as belonging to the stronger or to the present possessor, as being founded on so recent an usurpation?

COMMODUS mounted the throne after a pretty long succession of excellent emperors, who had acquired their title, not by birth, or public election, but by the fictitious rite of adoption. That bloody debauchee being murdered by a conspiracy suddenly formed between his wench and her gallant, who happened at that time to be *Prætorian Præfect*; these immediately deliberated about choosing a master to human kind, to speak in the style of those ages; and they cast their eyes on PERTINAX. Before the tyrant's death was known, the *Præfect* went secretly to that senator, who, on the appearance of the soldiers, imagined that his execution had been ordered by COMMODUS. He was immediately saluted emperor by the officer and his attendants; cheerfully proclaimed by the populace; unwillingly submitted to by the guards; formally recognized by the senate; and passively received by the provinces and armies of the empire.

The discontent of the *Prætorian* bands broke out in a sudden sedition, which occasioned the murder of that excellent prince: And the world being now without a master and without government, the guards thought proper to set the empire formally to sale. JULIAN, the purchaser, was proclaimed by the soldiers, recognized by the senate, and submitted to by the people; and must also have been submitted to by the provinces, had not the envy of the legions begotten opposition and resistance. PESCENNIUS NIGER in SYRIA elected himself emperor, gained the tumultuary consent of his army, and was attended with the secret good-will of the senate and people of ROME. ALBINUS in BRITAIN found an equal right to set up his claim; but SEVERUS, who governed PANNONIA, prevailed in the end above both of them. That able politician and warrior, finding his own birth and dignity too much inferior to the imperial crown, professed, at first, an intention only of revenging the death of PERTINAX. He marched as general into ITALY; defeated JULIAN; and without our being able to fix any precise commencement even of the soldiers' consent, he was from necessity acknowledged emperor by the senate and people; and fully established in his violent authority by subduing NIGER and ALBINUS.[5]

*Inter hæc Gordianus* CÆSAR (says CAPITOLINUS, speaking of another period) *sublatus a militibus,* Imperator *est appellatus, quia non erat alius in præsenti.* It is to be remarked, that GORDIAN was a boy of fourteen years of age.

Frequent instances of a like nature occur in the history of the emperors; in that of ALEXANDER's successors; and of many other countries: Nor can anything be more unhappy than a despotic government of this kind; where the succession is disjoined and irregular, and must be determined, on every vacancy, by force or election. In a free government, the matter is often unavoidable, and is also much less dangerous. The interests of liberty may there frequently lead the people, in their own defence, to alter the succession of the crown. And the constitution, being compounded of parts, may still maintain a sufficient stability, by resting on the aristocratical or democratical members, though the monarchical be altered, from time to time, in order to accommodate it to the former.

In an absolute government, when there is no legal prince, who has a title to the throne, it may safely be determined to belong to the first occupant. Instances of this kind are but too frequent, especially in the eastern monarchies. When any race of princes expires, the will or destination of the last sovereign will be regarded as a title. Thus the edict of LEWIS the XIVth, who called the bastard princes to the succession in case of the failure of all the legitimate princes, would, in

[5] HERODIAN, lib. ii.

such an event, have some authority. [6]Thus the will of CHARLES the Second disposed of the whole SPANISH monarchy. The cession of the ancient proprietor, especially when joined to conquest, is likewise deemed a good title. The general obligation, which binds us to government, is the interest and necessities of society; and this obligation is very strong. The determination of it to this or that particular prince or form of government is frequently more uncertain and dubious. Present possession has considerable authority in these cases, and greater than in private property; because of the disorders which attend all revolutions and changes of government.

We shall only observe, before we conclude, that, though an appeal to general opinion may justly, in the speculative sciences of metaphysics, natural philosophy, or astronomy, be deemed unfair and inconclusive, yet in all questions with regard to morals, as well as criticism, there is really no other standard, by which any controversy can ever be decided. And nothing is a clearer proof, that a theory of this kind is erroneous, than to find, that it leads to paradoxes, repugnant to the common sentiments of mankind, and to the practice and opinion of all nations and all ages. The doctrine, which founds all lawful government on an *original contract*, or consent of the people, is plainly of this kind; nor has the most noted of

---

[6] It is remarkable, that, in the remonstrance of the duke of BOURBON and the legitimate princes, against this destination of LOUIS the XIVth, the doctrine of the *original contract* is insisted on, even in that absolute government. The FRENCH nation, say they, chusing HUGH CAPET and his posterity to rule over them and their posterity, where the former line fails, there is a tacit right reserved to chuse a new royal family; and this right is invaded by calling the bastard princes to the throne, without the consent of the nation. But the Comte de BOULAINVILLIERS, who wrote in defence of the bastard princes, ridicules this notion of an original contract, especially when applied to HUGH CAPET; who mounted the throne, says he, by the same arts, which have ever been employed by all conquerors and usurpers. He got his title, indeed, recognized by the states after he had put himself in possession: But is this a choice or a contract? The Comte de BOULAINVILLIERS, we may observe, was a noted republican; but being a man of learning, and very conversant in history, he knew that the people were never almost consulted in these revolutions and new establishments, and that time alone bestowed right and authority on what was commonly at first founded on force and violence. See *Etat de la France*, Vol. III.

its partizans, in prosecution of it, scrupled to affirm, *that absolute monarchy is inconsistent with civil society, and so can be no form of civil government at all;* and *that the supreme power in a state cannot take from any man, by taxes and impositions, any part of his property, without his own consent or that of his representatives.* What authority any moral reasoning can have, which leads into opinions so wide of the general practice of mankind, in every place but this single kingdom, it is easy to determine.

The only passage I meet with in antiquity, where the obligation of obedience to government is ascribed to a promise, is in PLATO's *Crito*: where SOCRATES refuses to escape from prison, because he had tacitly promised to obey the laws. Thus he builds a *tory* consequence of passive obedience, on a *whig* foundation of the original contract.

New discoveries are not to be expected in these matters. If scarce any man, till very lately, ever imagined that government was founded on compact, it is certain that it cannot, in general, have any such foundation.

The crime of rebellion among the ancients was commonly expressed by the terms νεωτερίζειν, *novas res moliri.*

# OF THE STANDARD OF TASTE

THE GREAT VARIETY of Taste, as well as of opinion, which prevails in the world, is too obvious not to have fallen under every one's observation. Men of the most confined knowledge are able to remark a difference of taste in the narrow circle of their acquaintance, even where the persons have been educated under the same government, and have early imbibed the same prejudices. But those, who can enlarge their view to contemplate distant nations and remote ages, are still more surprized at the great inconsistence and contrariety. We are apt to call *barbarous* whatever departs widely from our own taste and apprehension: But soon find the epithet of reproach retorted on us. And the highest arrogance and self-conceit is at last startled, on observing an equal assurance on all sides, and scruples, amidst such a contest of sentiment, to pronounce positively in its own favour.

As this variety of taste is obvious to the most careless enquirer; so will it be found, on examination, to be still greater in reality than in appearance. The sentiments of men often differ with regard to beauty and deformity of all kinds, even while their general discourse is the same. There are certain terms in every language, which import blame, and others praise; and all men, who use the same tongue, must agree in their application of them. Every voice is united in applauding elegance, propriety, simplicity, spirit in writing; and in blaming fustian, affectation, coldness, and a false brilliancy: But when critics come to particulars, this seeming unanimity vanishes; and it is found, that they had affixed a very different meaning to their expressions. In all matters of opinion and science, the case is opposite: The difference among men is there oftener found to lie in generals than in particulars; and to be less in reality than in appearance. An explanation of the terms commonly ends the controversy; and the disputants are surprized to find, that they had been quarrelling, while at bottom they agreed in their judgment.

Those who found morality on sentiment, more than on reason, are inclined to comprehend ethics under the former observation, and to maintain, that, in all questions, which regard conduct and manners, the difference among men is really greater than at first sight it appears. It is indeed obvious, that writers of all nations and all ages concur in applauding justice, humanity, magnanimity, prudence, veracity; and in blaming the opposite qualities. Even poets and other authors, whose compositions are chiefly calculated to please the imagination, are yet found, from HOMER down to FENELON, to inculcate the same moral precepts, and to bestow their applause and blame on the same virtues and vices. This great unanimity is usually ascribed to the influence of plain reason; which, in all these cases, maintains similar sentiments in all men, and prevents those controversies, to which the abstract sciences are so much exposed. So far as the unanimity is real, this account may be admitted as satisfactory: But we must also allow that some part of the seeming harmony in morals may be accounted for from the very nature of language. The word *virtue,* with its equivalent in every tongue, implies praise; as that of *vice* does blame: And no one, without the most obvious and grossest impropriety, could affix reproach to a term, which in general acceptation is understood in a good sense; or bestow applause, where the idiom requires disapprobation. HOMER's general precepts, where he delivers any such, will never be controverted; but it is obvious, that, when he draws particular pictures of manners, and represents heroism in ACHILLES and prudence in ULYSSES, he intermixes a much greater degree of ferocity in the former, and of cunning and fraud in the latter, than FENELON would admit of. The sage ULYSSES in the GREEK poet seems to delight in lies and fictions, and often employs them without any necessity or even advantage: But his more scrupulous son, in the FRENCH epic writer, exposes himself to the most imminent perils, rather than depart from the most exact line of truth and veracity.

The admirers and followers of the ALCORAN insist on the excellent moral precepts interspersed throughout that wild and absurd performance. But it is to be supposed, that the ARABIC words, which correspond to the ENGLISH, equity, justice, temperance, meekness, charity, were such as, from the constant use of that tongue, must always be taken in a good sense; and it would have argued the greatest ignorance, not of morals, but of language, to have mentioned them with any epithets, besides those of applause and approbation. But would we know, whether the pretended prophet had really attained a just sentiment of morals? Let us attend to his narration; and we shall soon find, that he bestows praise on such instances of treachery, inhumanity, cruelty, revenge, bigotry, as are utterly incompatible with civilized society. No steady rule of right seems there to be attended to; and every action is blamed or praised, so far only as it is beneficial or hurtful to the true believers.

The merit of delivering true general precepts in ethics is indeed very small. Whoever recommends any moral virtues, really does no more than is implied in the terms themselves. That people, who invented the word *charity*, and used it in a good sense, inculcated more clearly and much more efficaciously, the precept, *be charitable*, than any pretended legislator or prophet, who should insert such a *maxim* in his writings. Of all expressions, those, which, together with their other meaning, imply a degree either of blame or approbation, are the least liable to be perverted or mistaken.

It is natural for us to seek a *Standard of Taste*; a rule, by which the various sentiments of men may be reconciled; at least, a decision, afforded, confirming one sentiment, and condemning another.

There is a species of philosophy, which cuts off all hopes of success in such an attempt, and represents the impossibility of ever attaining any standard of taste. The difference, it is said, is very wide between judgment and sentiment. All sentiment is right; because sentiment has a reference to nothing beyond itself, and is always real, wherever a man is conscious of it. But all determinations of the understanding are not right; because they have a reference to something beyond themselves, to wit, real matter of fact; and are not always conformable to that standard. Among a thousand different opinions which different men may entertain of the same subject, there is one, and but one, that is just and true; and the only difficulty is to fix and ascertain it. On the contrary, a thousand different sentiments, excited by the same object, are all right: Because no sentiment represents what is really in the object. It only marks a certain conformity or relation between the object and the organs or faculties of the mind; and if that conformity did not really exist, the sentiment could never possibly have being. Beauty is no quality in things themselves: It exists merely in the mind which contemplates them; and each mind perceives a different beauty. One person may even perceive deformity, where another is sensible of beauty; and every individual ought to acquiesce in his own sentiment, without pretending to regulate those of others. To seek the real beauty, or real deformity, is as fruitless an enquiry, as to pretend to ascertain the real sweet or real bitter. According to the disposition of the organs, the same object may be both sweet and bitter; and the proverb has justly determined it to be fruitless to dispute concerning tastes. It is very natural, and even quite necessary, to extend this axiom to mental, as well as bodily taste; and thus common sense, which is so often at variance with philosophy, especially with the sceptical kind, is found, in one instance at least, to agree in pronouncing the same decision.

But though this axiom, by passing into a proverb, seems to have attained the sanction of common sense; there is certainly a species of common sense which opposes it, at least serves to modify and restrain it. Whoever would assert an equality of genius and elegance between OGILBY and MILTON, or BUNYAN and ADDISON, would be thought to defend no less an extravagance, than if he had maintained a mole-hill to be as high as TENERIFFE, or a pond as extensive as the ocean. Though there may be found persons, who give the preference to the former authors; no one pays attention to such a taste; and we pronounce without scruple the sentiment of these pretended critics to be absurd and ridiculous. The principle of the natural equality of tastes is then totally forgot, and while we admit it on some occasions, where the objects seem near an equality, it appears an extravagant paradox, or rather a palpable absurdity, where objects so disproportioned are compared together.

It is evident that none of the rules of composition are fixed by reasonings *a priori*, or can be esteemed abstract conclusions of the understanding, from comparing those habitudes and relations of ideas, which are eternal and immutable. Their foundation is the same with that of all the practical sciences, experience; nor are they any thing but general observations, concerning what has been universally found to please in all countries and in all ages. Many of the beauties of poetry and even of eloquence are founded on falsehood and fiction, on hyperboles, metaphors, and an abuse or perversion of terms from their natural meaning. To check the sallies of the imagination, and to reduce every expression to geometrical truth and exactness, would be the most contrary to the laws of criticism; because it would produce a work, which, by universal experience, has been found the most insipid and disagreeable. But though poetry can never submit to exact truth, it must be confined by rules of art, discovered to the author either by genius or observation. If some negligent or irregular writers have pleased, they have not pleased by their transgressions of rule or order, but in spite of these transgressions: They have possessed other beauties, which were conformable to just criticism; and the force of these beauties has been able to overpower censure, and give the mind a satisfaction superior to the disgust arising from the blemishes. ARIOSTO pleases; but not by his monstrous and improbable fictions, by his bizarre mixture of the serious and comic styles, by the want of coherence in his stories, or by the continual interruptions of his narration. He charms by the force and clearness of his expression, by the readiness and variety of his inventions, and by his natural pictures of the passions, especially those of the gay and amorous kind: And however his faults may diminish our satisfaction, they are not able entirely to destroy it. Did our pleasure really arise from those parts of his poem, which we denominate faults, this would be no objection to criticism in general: It would only be an objection to those particular rules of criticism, which would establish such circumstances to be faults, and would represent them as universally blameable. If they are found to please, they cannot be faults; let the pleasure, which they produce, be ever so unexpected and unaccountable.

But though all the general rules of art are founded only on experience and on the observation of the common sentiments of human nature, we must not imagine, that, on every occasion, the feelings of men will be conformable to these rules. Those finer emotions of the mind are of a very tender and delicate nature, and require the concurrence of many favourable circumstances to make them play with facility and exactness, according to their general and established principles. The least exterior hindrance to such small springs, or the least internal disorder, disturbs their motion, and confounds the operation of the whole machine. When we would make an experiment of this nature, and would try the force of any beauty or deformity, we must choose with care a proper time and place, and bring the fancy to a suitable situation and disposition. A perfect serenity of mind, a recollection of thought, a due attention to the object; if any of these circumstances be wanting, our experiment will be fallacious, and we shall be unable to judge of the catholic and universal beauty. The relation, which nature has placed between the form and the sentiment, will at least be more obscure; and it will require greater accuracy to trace and discern it. We shall be able to ascertain its influence not so much from the operation of each particular beauty, as from the durable admiration, which attends those works, that have survived all the caprices of mode and fashion, all the mistakes of ignorance and envy.

The same HOMER, who pleased at ATHENS and ROME two thousand years ago, is still admired at PARIS and at LONDON. All the changes of climate, government, religion, and language, have not been able to obscure his glory. Authority or prejudice may give a temporary vogue to a bad poet or orator; but his reputation will never be durable or general.

When his compositions are examined by posterity or by foreigners, the enchantment is dissipated, and his faults appear in their true colours. On the contrary, a real genius, the longer his works endure, and the more wide they are spread, the more sincere is the admiration which he meets with. Envy and jealousy have too much place in a narrow circle; and even familiar acquaintance with his person may diminish the applause due to his performances: But when these obstructions are removed, the beauties, which are naturally fitted to excite agreeable sentiments, immediately display their energy; and while the world endures, they maintain their authority over the minds of men.

It appears then, that, amidst all the variety and caprice of taste, there are certain general principles of approbation or blame, whose influence a careful eye may trace in all operations of the mind. Some particular forms or qualities, from the original structure of the internal fabric, are calculated to please, and others to displease; and if they fail of their effect in any particular instance, it is from some apparent defect or imperfection in the organ. A man in a fever would not insist on his palate as able to decide concerning flavours; nor would one, affected with the jaundice, pretend to give a verdict with regard to colours. In each creature, there is a sound and a defective state; and the former alone can be supposed to afford us a true standard of taste and sentiment. If, in the sound state of the organ, there be an entire or a considerable uniformity of sentiment among men, we may thence derive an idea of the perfect beauty; in like manner as the appearance of objects in day-light, to the eye of a man in health, is denominated their true and real colour, even while colour is allowed to be merely a phantasm of the senses.

Many and frequent are the defects in the internal organs, which prevent or weaken the influence of those general principles, on which depends our sentiment of beauty or deformity. Though some objects, by the structure of the mind, be naturally calculated to give pleasure, it is not to be expected, that in every individual the pleasure will be equally felt. Particular incidents and situations occur, which either throw a false light on the objects, or hinder the true from conveying to the imagination the proper sentiment and perception.

One obvious cause, why many feel not the proper sentiment of beauty, is the want of that *delicacy* of imagination, which is requisite to convey a sensibility of those finer emotions. This delicacy every one pretends to: Every one talks of it; and would reduce every kind of taste or sentiment to its standard. But as our intention in this essay is to mingle some light of the understanding with the feelings of sentiment, it will be proper to give a more accurate definition of delicacy, than has hitherto been attempted. And not to draw our philosophy from too profound a source, we shall have recourse to a noted story in DON QUIXOTE.

It is with good reason, says SANCHO to the squire with the great nose, that I pretend to have a judgment in wine: This is a quality hereditary in our family. Two of my kinsmen were once called to give their opinion of a hogshead, which was supposed to be excellent, being old and of a good vintage. One of them tastes it; considers it; and after mature reflection pronounces the wine to be good, were it not for a small taste of leather, which he perceived in it. The other, after using the same precautions, gives also his verdict in favour of the wine; but with the reserve of a taste of iron, which he could easily distinguish. You cannot imagine how much they were both ridiculed for their judgment. But who laughed in the end? On emptying the hogshead, there was found at the bottom, an old key with a leathern thong tied to it.

The great resemblance between mental and bodily taste will easily teach us to apply this story. Though it be certain, that beauty and deformity, more than sweet and bitter, are not qualities in objects, but belong entirely to the sentiment, internal or external; it must be allowed, that there are certain qualities in objects, which are fitted by nature to produce those particular feelings. Now as these qualities may be found in a small degree, or may be mixed and confounded with each other, it often happens, that the taste is not affected with such minute qualities, or is not able to distinguish all the particular flavours, amidst the disorder, in which they are presented. Where the organs are so fine, as to allow nothing to escape them; and at the same time so exact as to perceive every ingredient in the composition: This we call delicacy of taste, whether we employ these terms in the literal or metaphorical sense. Here then the general rules of beauty are of use; being drawn from established models, and from the observation of what pleases or displeases, when presented singly and in a high degree: And if the same qualities, in a continued composition and in a smaller degree, affect not the organs with a sensible delight or uneasiness, we exclude the person from all pretensions to this delicacy. To produce these general rules or avowed patterns of composition is like finding the key with the leathern thong; which justified the verdict of SANCHO's kinsmen, and confounded those pretended judges who had condemned them. Though the hogshead had never been emptied, the taste of the one was still equally delicate, and that of the other equally dull and languid: But it would have been more difficult to have proved the superiority of the former, to the conviction of every by-stander. In like manner, though the beauties of writing had never been methodized, or reduced to general principles; though no excellent models had ever been acknowledged; the different degrees of taste would still have subsisted, and the judgment of one man been preferable to that of another; but it would not have been so easy to silence the bad critic, who might always insist upon his particular sentiment, and refuse to submit to his antagonist. But when we show him an avowed principle of art; when we illustrate this principle by examples, whose operation, from his own particular taste, he acknowledges to be conformable to the principle; when we prove, that the same principle may be applied to the present case, where he did not perceive or feel its influence: He must conclude, upon the whole, that the fault lies in himself, and that he wants the delicacy, which is requisite to make him sensible of every beauty and every blemish, in any composition or discourse.

It is acknowledged to be the perfection of every sense or faculty, to perceive with exactness its most minute objects, and allow nothing to escape its notice and observation. The smaller the objects are, which become sensible to the eye, the finer is that organ, and the more elaborate its make and composition. A good palate is not tried by strong flavours; but by a mixture of small ingredients, where we are still sensible of each part, notwithstanding its minuteness and its confusion with the rest. In like manner, a quick and acute perception of beauty and deformity must be the perfection of our mental taste; nor can a man be satisfied with himself while he suspects, that any excellence or blemish in a discourse has passed him unobserved. In this case, the perfection of the man, and the perfection of the sense or feeling, are found to be united. A very delicate palate, on many occasions, may be a great inconvenience both to a man himself and to his friends: But a delicate taste of wit or beauty must always be a desirable quality; because it is the source of all the finest and most innocent enjoyments, of which human nature is susceptible. In this decision the sentiments of all mankind are agreed. Wherever you can ascertain a delicacy of taste, it is sure to meet with approbation; and the best way of ascertaining it is to appeal to those models and principles, which have been established by the uniform consent and experience of nations and ages.

But though there be naturally a wide difference in point of delicacy between one person and another, nothing tends further to encrease and improve this talent, than *practice* in a particular art, and the frequent survey or contemplation of a particular species of beauty. When objects of any kind are first presented to the eye or imagination, the sentiment, which attends them, is obscure and confused; and the mind is, in a great measure, incapable of pronouncing concerning their merits or defects. The taste cannot perceive the several excellences of the performance; much less distinguish the particular character of each excellency, and ascertain its quality and degree. If it pronounce the whole in general to be beautiful or deformed, it is the utmost that can be expected; and even this judgment, a person, so unpractised, will be apt to deliver with great hesitation and reserve. But allow him to acquire experience in those objects, his feeling becomes more exact and nice: He not only perceives the beauties and defects of each part, but marks the distinguishing species of each quality, and assigns it suitable praise or blame. A clear and distinct sentiment attends him through the whole survey of the objects; and he discerns that very degree and kind of approbation or displeasure, which each part is naturally fitted to produce. The mist dissipates, which seemed formerly to hang over the object: The organ acquires greater perfection in its operations; and can pronounce, without danger of mistake, concerning the merits of every performance. In a word, the same address and dexterity, which practice gives to the execution of any work, is also acquired by the same means, in the judging of it.

So advantageous is practice to the discernment of beauty, that, before we can give judgment on any work of importance, it will even be requisite, that that very individual performance be more than once perused by us, and be surveyed in different lights with attention and deliberation. There is a flutter or hurry of thought which attends the first perusal of any piece, and which confounds the genuine sentiment of beauty. The relation of the parts is not discerned: The true characters of style are little distinguished: The several perfections and defects seem wrapped up in a species of confusion, and present themselves indistinctly to the imagination. Not to mention, that there is a species of beauty, which, as it is florid and superficial, pleases at first; but being found incompatible with a just expression either of reason or passion, soon palls upon the taste, and is then rejected with disdain, at least rated at a much lower value.

It is impossible to continue in the practice of contemplating any order of beauty, without being frequently obliged to form *comparisons* between the several species and degrees of excellence, and estimating their proportion to each other. A man, who has had no opportunity of comparing the different kinds of beauty, is indeed totally unqualified to pronounce an opinion with regard to any object presented to him. By comparison alone we fix the epithets of praise or blame, and learn how to assign the due degree of each. The coarsest daubing contains a certain lustre of colours and exactness of imitation, which are so far beauties, and would affect the mind of a peasant or Indian with the highest admiration. The most vulgar ballads are not entirely destitute of harmony or nature; and none but a person, familiarized to superior beauties, would pronounce their numbers harsh, or narration uninteresting. A great inferiority of beauty gives pain to a person conversant in the highest excellence of the kind, and is for that reason pronounced a deformity: As the most finished object, with which we are acquainted, is naturally supposed to have reached the pinnacle of perfection, and to be entitled to the highest applause. One accustomed to see, and examine, and weigh the several performances, admired in different ages and nations, can only rate the merits of a work exhibited to his view, and assign its proper rank among the productions of genius.

But to enable a critic the more fully to execute this undertaking, he must preserve his mind free from all *prejudice*, and allow nothing to enter into his consideration, but the very object which is submitted to his examination. We may observe, that every work of art, in order to produce its due effect on the mind, must be surveyed in a certain point of view, and cannot be fully relished by persons, whose situation, real or imaginary, is not conformable to that which is required by the performance. An orator addresses himself to a particular audience, and must have a regard to their particular genius, interests, opinions, passions, and prejudices; otherwise he hopes in vain to govern their resolutions, and inflame their affections. Should they even have entertained some prepossessions against him, however unreasonable, he must not overlook this disadvantage; but, before he enters upon the subject, must endeavour to conciliate their affection, and acquire their good graces. A critic of a different age or nation, who should peruse this discourse, must have all these circumstances in his eye, and must place himself in the same situation as the audience, in order to form a true judgment of the oration. In like manner, when any work is addressed to the public, though I should have a friendship or enmity with the author, I must depart from this situation; and considering myself as a man in general, forget, if possible, my individual being and my peculiar circumstances. A person influenced by prejudice, complies not with this condition; but obstinately maintains his natural position, without placing himself in that point of view, which the performance supposes. If the work be addressed to persons of a different age or nation, he makes no allowance for their peculiar views and prejudices; but, full of the manners of his own age and country, rashly condemns what seemed admirable in the eyes of those for whom alone the discourse was calculated. If the work be executed for the public, he never sufficiently enlarges his comprehension, or forgets his interest as a friend or enemy, as a rival or commentator. By this means, his sentiments are perverted; nor have the same beauties and blemishes the same influence upon him, as if he had imposed a proper violence on his imagination, and had forgotten himself for a moment. So far his taste evidently departs from the true standard; and of consequence loses all credit and authority.

It is well known, that in all questions, submitted to the understanding, prejudice is destructive of sound judgment, and perverts all operations of the intellectual faculties: It is no less contrary to good taste; nor has it less influence to corrupt our sentiment of beauty. It belongs to *good sense* to check its influence in both cases; and in this respect, as well as in many others, reason, if not an essential part of taste, is at least requisite to the operations of this latter faculty. In all the nobler productions of genius, there is a mutual relation and correspondence of parts; nor can either the beauties or blemishes be perceived by him, whose thought is not capacious enough to comprehend all those parts, and compare them with each other, in order to perceive the consistence and uniformity of the whole. Every work of art has also a certain end or purpose, for which it is calculated; and is to be deemed more or less perfect, as it is more or less fitted to attain this end. The object of eloquence is to persuade, of history to instruct, of poetry to please by means of the passions and the imagination. These ends we must carry constantly in our view, when we peruse any performance; and we must be able to judge how far the means employed are adapted to their respective purposes. Besides, every kind of composition, even the most poetical, is nothing but a chain of propositions and reasonings; not always, indeed, the justest and most exact, but still plausible and specious, however disguised by the colouring of the imagination. The persons introduced in tragedy and epic poetry, must be represented as reasoning, and thinking, and concluding, and acting, suitably to their character and circumstances; and without judgment, as well as taste and invention, a poet can never hope to succeed in so delicate an undertaking. Not to mention, that the same excellence of faculties which contributes to the improvement of reason, the same clearness of conception, the same exactness of distinction, the same vivacity of apprehension, are essential to the operations of true taste, and are its infallible concomitants. It seldom, or never happens, that a man of sense, who has experience in any art, cannot judge of its beauty; and it is no less rare to meet with a man who has a just taste without a sound understanding.

Thus, though the principles of taste be universal, and, nearly, if not entirely the same in all men; yet few are qualified to give judgment on any work of art, or establish their own sentiment as the standard of beauty. The organs of internal sensation are seldom so perfect as to allow the general principles their full play, and produce a feeling correspondent to those principles. They either labour under some defect, or are vitiated by some disorder; and by that means, excite a sentiment, which may be pronounced erroneous. When the critic has no delicacy, he judges without any distinction, and is only affected by the grosser and more palpable qualities of the object: The finer touches pass unnoticed and disregarded. Where he is not aided by practice, his verdict is attended with confusion and hesitation. Where no comparison has been employed, the most frivolous beauties, such as rather merit the name of defects, are the object of his admiration. Where he lies under the influence of prejudice, all his natural sentiments are perverted. Where good sense is wanting, he is not qualified to discern the beauties of design and reasoning, which are the highest and most excellent. Under some or other of these imperfections, the generality of men labour; and hence a true judge in the finer arts is observed, even during the most polished ages, to be so rare a character: Strong sense, united to delicate sentiment, improved by practice, perfected by comparison, and cleared of all prejudice, can alone entitle critics to this valuable character; and the joint verdict of such, wherever they are to be found, is the true standard of taste and beauty.

But where are such critics to be found? By what marks are they to be known? How distinguish them from pretenders? These questions are embarrassing; and seem to throw us back into the same uncertainty, from which, during the course of this essay, we have endeavoured to extricate ourselves.

But if we consider the matter aright, these are questions of fact, not of sentiment. Whether any particular person be endowed with good sense and a delicate imagination, free from prejudice, may often be the subject of dispute, and be liable to great discussion and enquiry: But that such a character is valuable and estimable will be agreed in by all mankind. Where these doubts occur, men can do no more than in other disputable questions, which are submitted to the understanding: They must produce the best arguments, that their invention suggests to them; they must acknowledge a true and decisive standard to exist somewhere, to wit, real existence and matter of fact; and they must have indulgence to such as differ from them in their appeals to this standard. It is sufficient for our present purpose, if we have proved, that the taste of all individuals is not upon an equal footing, and that some men in general, however difficult to be particularly pitched upon, will be acknowledged by universal sentiment to have a preference above others.

But in reality the difficulty of finding, even in particulars, the standard of taste, is not so great as it is represented. Though in speculation, we may readily avow a certain criterion in science and deny it in sentiment, the matter is found in practice to be much more hard to ascertain in the former case than in the latter. Theories of abstract philosophy, systems of profound theology, have prevailed during one age: In a successive period, these have been universally exploded: Their absurdity has been detected: Other theories and systems have supplied their place, which again gave place to their successors: And nothing has been experienced more liable to the revolutions of chance and fashion than these pretended decisions of science. The case is not the same with the beauties of eloquence and poetry. Just expressions of passion and nature are sure, after a little time, to gain public applause, which they maintain for ever. ARISTOTLE, and PLATO, and EPICURUS, and DESCARTES, may successively yield to each other: But TERENCE and VIRGIL maintain an universal, undisputed empire over the minds of men. The abstract philosophy of CICERO has lost its credit: The vehemence of his oratory is still the object of our admiration.

Though men of delicate taste be rare, they are easily to be distinguished in society, by the soundness of their understanding and the superiority of their faculties above the rest of mankind. The ascendant, which they acquire, gives a prevalence to that lively approbation, with which they receive any productions of genius, and renders it generally predominant. Many men, when left to themselves, have but a faint and dubious perception of beauty, who yet are capable of relishing any fine stroke, which is pointed out to them. Every convert to the admiration of the real poet or orator is the cause of some new conversion. And though prejudices may prevail for a time, they never unite in celebrating any rival to the true genius, but yield at last to the force of nature and just sentiment. Thus, though a civilized nation may easily be mistaken in the choice of their admired philosopher, they never have been found long to err, in their affection for a favorite epic or tragic author.

But notwithstanding all our endeavours to fix a standard of taste, and reconcile the discordant apprehensions of men, there still remain two sources of variation, which are not sufficient indeed to confound all the boundaries of beauty and deformity, but will often serve to produce a difference in the degrees of our approbation or blame. The one is the different humours of particular men; the other, the particular manners and opinions of our age and country. The general principles of taste are uniform in human nature: Where men vary in their judgments, some defect or perversion in the faculties may commonly be remarked; proceeding either from prejudice, from want of practice, or want of delicacy; and there is just reason for approving one taste, and condemning another. But where there is such a diversity in the internal frame or external situation as is entirely blameless on both sides, and leaves no room to give one the preference above the other; in that case a certain degree of diversity in judgment is unavoidable, and we seek in vain for a standard, by which we can reconcile the contrary sentiments.

A young man, whose passions are warm, will be more sensibly touched with amorous and tender images, than a man more advanced in years, who takes pleasure in wise, philosophical reflections concerning the conduct of life and moderation of the passions. At twenty, OVID may be the favourite author; HORACE at forty; and perhaps TACITUS at fifty. Vainly would we, in such cases, endeavour to enter into the sentiments of others, and divest ourselves of those propensities, which are natural to us. We choose our favourite author as we do our friend, from a conformity of humour and disposition. Mirth or passion, sentiment or reflection; whichever of these most predominates in our temper, it gives us a peculiar sympathy with the writer who resembles us.

One person is more pleased with the sublime; another with the tender; a third with raillery. One has a strong sensibility to blemishes, and is extremely studious of correctness: Another has a more lively feeling of beauties, and pardons twenty absurdities and defects for one elevated or pathetic stroke. The ear of this man is entirely turned towards conciseness and energy; that man is delighted with a copious, rich, and harmonious expression. Simplicity is affected by one; ornament by another. Comedy, tragedy, satire, odes, have each its partizans, who prefer that particular species of writing to all others. It is plainly an error in a critic, to confine his approbation to one species or style of writing, and condemn all the rest. But it is almost impossible not to feel a predilection for that which suits our particular turn and disposition. Such preferences are innocent and unavoidable, and can never reasonably be the object of dispute, because there is no standard, by which they can be decided.

For a like reason, we are more pleased, in the course of our reading, with pictures and characters, that resemble objects which are found in our own age or country, than with those which describe a different set of customs. It is not without some effort, that we reconcile ourselves to the simplicity of ancient manners, and behold princesses carrying water from the spring, and kings and heroes dressing their own victuals. We may allow in general, that the representation of such manners is no fault in the author, nor deformity in the piece; but we are not so sensibly touched with them. For this reason, comedy is not easily transferred from one age or nation to another. A FRENCHMAN or ENGLISHMAN is not pleased with the ANDRIA of TERENCE, or CLITIA of MACHIAVEL; where the fine lady, upon whom all the play turns, never once appears to the spectators, but is always kept behind the scenes, suitably to the reserved humour of the ancient GREEKS and modern ITALIANS. A man of learning and reflection can make allowance for these peculiarities of manners; but a common audience can never divest themselves so far of their usual ideas and sentiments, as to relish pictures which in no wise resemble them.

But here there occurs a reflection, which may, perhaps, be useful in examining the celebrated controversy concerning ancient and modern learning; where we often find the one side excusing any seeming absurdity in the ancients from the manners of the age, and the other refusing to admit this excuse, or at least, admitting it only as an apology for the author, not for the performance. In my opinion, the proper boundaries in this subject have seldom been fixed between the contending parties. Where any innocent peculiarities of manners are represented, such as those above mentioned, they ought certainly to be admitted; and a man, who is shocked with them, gives an evident proof of false delicacy and refinement. The poet's *monument more durable than brass,* must fall to the ground like common brick or clay, were men to make no allowance for the continual revolutions of manners and customs, and would admit of nothing but what was suitable to the prevailing fashion. Must we throw aside the pictures of our ancestors, because of their ruffs and fardingales? But where the ideas of morality and decency alter from one age to another, and where vicious manners are described, without being marked with the proper characters of blame and disapprobation; this must be allowed to disfigure the poem, and to be a real deformity. I cannot, nor is it proper I should, enter into such sentiments; and however I may excuse the poet, on account of the manners of his age, I never can relish the composition. The want of humanity and of decency, so conspicuous in the characters drawn by several of the ancient poets, even sometimes by HOMER and the GREEK tragedians, diminishes considerably the merit of their noble performances, and gives modern authors an advantage over them. We are not interested in the fortunes and sentiments of such rough heroes: We are displeased to find the limits of vice and virtue so much confounded: And whatever indulgence we may give to the writer on account of his prejudices, we cannot prevail on ourselves to enter into his sentiments, or bear an affection to characters, which we plainly discover to be blameable.

The case is not the same with moral principles, as with speculative opinions of any kind. These are in continual flux and revolution. The son embraces a different system from the father. Nay, there scarcely is any man, who can boast of great constancy and uniformity in this particular. Whatever speculative errors may be found in the polite writings of any age or country, they detract but little from the value of those compositions. There needs but a certain turn of thought or imagination to make us enter into all the opinions, which then prevailed, and relish the sentiments or conclusions derived from them. But a very violent effort is requisite to change our judgment of manners, and excite sentiments of approbation or blame, love or hatred, different from those to which the mind from long custom has been familiarized. And where a man is confident of the rectitude of that moral standard, by which he judges, he is justly jealous of it, and will not pervert the sentiments of his heart for a moment, in complaisance to any writer whatsoever.

Of all speculative errors, those, which regard religion, are the most excusable in compositions of genius; nor is it ever permitted to judge of the civility or wisdom of any people, or even of single persons, by the grossness or refinement of their theological principles. The same good sense, that directs men in the ordinary occurrences of life, is not hearkened to in religious matters, which are supposed to be placed altogether above the cognizance of human reason. On this account, all the absurdities of the pagan system of theology must be overlooked by every critic, who would pretend to form a just notion of ancient poetry; and our posterity, in their turn, must have the same indulgence to their forefathers. No religious principles can ever be imputed as a fault to any poet, while they remain merely principles, and take not such strong possession of his heart, as to lay him under the imputation of *bigotry* or *superstition*. Where that happens, they confound the sentiments of morality, and alter the natural boundaries of vice and virtue. They are therefore eternal blemishes, according to the principle above mentioned; nor are the prejudices and false opinions of the age sufficient to justify them.

It is essential to the ROMAN catholic religion to inspire a violent hatred of every other worship, and to represent all pagans, mahometans, and heretics as the objects of divine wrath and vengeance. Such sentiments, though they are in reality very blameable, are considered as virtues by the zealots of that communion, and are represented in their tragedies and epic poems as a kind of divine heroism. This bigotry has disfigured two very fine tragedies of the FRENCH theatre, POLIEUCTE and ATHALIA; where an intemperate zeal for particular modes of worship is set off with all the pomp imaginable, and forms the predominant character of the heroes. "What is this," says the sublime JOAD to JOSABET, finding her in discourse with MATHAN, the priest of BAAL, "Does the daughter of DAVID speak to this traitor? Are you not afraid, lest the earth should open and pour forth flames to devour you both? Or lest these holy walls should fall and crush you together? What is his purpose? Why comes that enemy of God hither to poison the air, which we breathe, with his horrid presence?" Such sentiments are received with great applause on the theatre of PARIS; but at LONDON the spectators would be full as much pleased to hear ACHILLES tell AGAMEMNON, that he was a dog in his forehead, and a deer in his heart, or JUPITER threaten JUNO with a sound drubbing, if she will not be quiet.

RELIGIOUS principles are also a blemish in any polite composition, when they rise up to superstition, and intrude themselves into every sentiment, however remote from any connection with religion. It is no excuse for the poet, that the customs of his country had burthened life with so many religious ceremonies and observances, that no part of it was exempt from that yoke. It must for ever be ridiculous in PETRARCH to compare his mistress LAURA, to JESUS CHRIST. Nor is it less ridiculous in that agreeable libertine, BOCCACE, very seriously to give thanks to GOD ALMIGHTY and the ladies, for their assistance in defending him against his enemies.

# OF SUICIDE

ONE CONSIDERABLE advantage that arises from Philosophy, consists in the sovereign antidote which it affords to superstition and false religion. All other remedies against that pestilent distemper are vain, or at least uncertain. Plain good sense and the practice of the world, which alone serve most purposes of life, are here found ineffectual: History as well as daily experience furnish instances of men endowed with the strongest capacity for business and affairs, who have all their lives crouched under slavery to the grossest superstition. Even gaiety and sweetness of temper, which infuse a balm into every other wound, afford no remedy to so virulent a poison; as we may particularly observe of the fair Sex, who, tho' commonly possest of these rich presents of nature, feel many of their joys blasted by this importunate intruder. But when sound Philosophy has once gained possession of the mind, superstition is effectually excluded; and one may fairly affirm, that her triumph over this enemy is more complete than over most of the vices and imperfections incident to human nature. Love or anger, ambition or avarice, have their root in the temper and affections, which the soundest reason is scarce ever able fully to correct; but superstition being founded on false opinion, must immediately vanish when true philosophy has inspired juster sentiments of superior powers. The contest is here more equal between the distemper and the medicine, and nothing can hinder the latter from proving effectual, but its being false and sophisticated.

It will here be superfluous to magnify the merits of philosophy, by displaying the pernicious tendency of that vice of which it cures the human mind. The superstitious man, says TULLY,[1] is miserable in every scene, in every incident of life; even sleep itself, which banishes all other cares of unhappy mortals, affords to him matter of new terror; while he examines his dreams, and finds in those visions of the night

[1] De Divin. lib. ii. 72, 150.

prognostications of future calamities. I may add, that tho'
death alone can put a full period to his misery, he dares not
fly to this refuge, but still prolongs a miserable existence from
a vain fear lest he offend his maker, by using the power, with
which that beneficent being has endowed him. The presents
of God and nature are ravished from us by this cruel enemy;
and notwithstanding that one step would remove us from the
regions of pain and sorrow, her menaces still chain us down
to a hated being, which she herself chiefly contributes to
render miserable.

'Tis observed by such as have been reduced by the calamities of life to the necessity of employing this fatal remedy,
that if the unseasonable care of their friends deprive them of
that species of Death, which they proposed to themselves,
they seldom venture upon any other, or can summon up so
much resolution a second time, as to execute their purpose.
So great is our horror of death, that when it presents itself,
under any form, besides that to which a man has endeavoured
to reconcile his imagination, it acquires new terrors and
overcomes his feeble courage: But when the menaces of
superstition are joined to this natural timidity, no wonder it
quite deprives men of all power over their lives, since even
many pleasures and enjoyments, to which we are carried by
a strong propensity, are torn from us by this inhuman tyrant.
Let us here endeavour to restore men to their native liberty
by examining all the common arguments against Suicide, and
shewing that that action may be free from every imputation
of guilt or blame, according to the sentiments of all the antient
philosophers.

If Suicide be criminal, it must be a transgression of our
duty either to God, our neighbour, or ourselves.—To prove
that suicide is no transgression of our duty to God, the following considerations may perhaps suffice. In order to govern
the material world, the almighty Creator has established general and immutable laws by which all bodies, from the greatest
planet to the smallest particle of matter, are maintained in
their proper sphere and function. To govern the animal world,
he has endowed all living creatures with bodily and mental

powers; with senses, passions, appetites, memory and judgment, by which they are impelled or regulated in that course of life to which they are destined. These two distinct principles of the material and animal world, continually encroach upon each other, and mutually retard or forward each other's operations. The powers of men and of all other animals are restrained and directed by the nature and qualities of the surrounding bodies; and the modifications and actions of these bodies are incessantly altered by the operation of all animals. Man is stopt by rivers in his passage over the surface of the earth; and rivers, when properly directed, lend their force to the motion of machines, which serve to the use of man. But tho' the provinces of the material and animal powers are not kept entirely separate, there results from thence no discord or disorder in the creation; on the contrary, from the mixture, union and contrast of all the various powers of inanimate bodies and living creatures, arises that surprizing harmony and proportion which affords the surest argument of supreme wisdom. The providence of the Deity appears not immediately in any operation, but governs everything by those general and immutable laws, which have been established from the beginning of time. All events, in one sense, may be pronounced the action of the Almighty; they all proceed from those powers with which he has endowed his creatures. A house which falls by its own weight is not brought to ruin by his providence more than one destroyed by the hands of men; nor are the human faculties less his workmanship, than the laws of motion and gravitation. When the passions play, when the judgment dictates, when the limbs obey; this is all the operation of God, and upon these animate principles, as well as upon the inanimate, has he established the government of the universe. Every event is alike important in the eyes of that infinite being, who takes in at one glance the most distant regions of space and remotest periods of time. There is no event, however important to us, which he has exempted from the general laws that govern the universe, or which he has peculiarly reserved for his own immediate action and operation. The revolution of states and empires depends upon the smallest caprice or passion of single men; and the lives of men are shortened or extended by the smallest accident of air or diet, sunshine or tempest. Nature still continues her progress and operation; and if general laws be ever broke by particular volitions of the Deity, 'tis after a manner which entirely escapes human observation. As, on the one hand, the elements and other inanimate parts of the creation carry on their action without regard to the particular interest and situation of men; so men are entrusted to their own judgment and discretion, in the various shocks of matter, and may employ every faculty with which they are endowed, in order to provide for their ease, happiness, or preservation. What is the meaning then of that principle, that a man who, tired of life, and hunted by pain and misery, bravely overcomes all the natural terrors of death and makes his escape from this cruel scene; that such a man, I say, has incurred the indignation of his Creator by encroaching on the office of divine providence, and disturbing the order of the universe? shall we assert that the Almighty has reserved to himself in any peculiar manner the disposal of the lives of men, and has not submitted that event, in common with others, to the general laws by which the universe is governed? This is plainly false; the lives of men depend upon the same laws as the lives of all other animals; and these are subjected to the general laws of matter and motion. The fall of a tower, or the infusion of a poison, will destroy a man equally with the meanest creature; an inundation sweeps away every thing without distinction that comes within the reach of its fury. Since therefore the lives of men are for ever dependant on the general laws of matter and motion, is a man's disposing of his life criminal, because in every case it is criminal to encroach upon these laws, or disturb their operation? But this seems absurd; all animals are entrusted to their own prudence and skill for their conduct in the world, and have full authority, as far as their power extends, to alter all the operations of nature. Without the exercise of this authority they could not subsist a moment; every action, every motion of a man, innovates on the order of some parts of matter, and diverts from their ordinary course the general laws of motion. Putting together, therefore, these conclusions, we find that human life depends upon the general laws of matter and motion, and that it is no encroachment on the office of providence to disturb or alter these general laws: Has not every one, of consequence, the free disposal of his own life? And may he not lawfully employ that power with which nature has endowed him? In order to destroy the evidence of this conclusion, we must shew a reason, why this particular case is excepted; is it because human life is of so great importance, that 'tis a presumption for human prudence to dispose of it? But the life of a man is of no greater importance to the universe than that of an oyster. And were it of ever so great importance, the order of nature has actually submitted it to human prudence, and reduced us to a necessity in every incident of determining concerning it. Were the disposal of human life so much reserved as the peculiar province of the Almighty that it were an encroachment on his right, for men to dispose of their own lives; it would be equally criminal to act for the preservation of life as for its destruction. If I turn aside a stone which is falling upon my head, I disturb the course of nature, and I invade the peculiar province of the Almighty by lengthening out my life beyond the period which by the general laws of matter and motion he had assigned it.

A hair, a fly, an insect is able to destroy this mighty being whose life is of such importance. Is it an absurdity to suppose that human prudence may lawfully dispose of what depends on such insignificant causes? It would be no crime in me to divert the *Nile* or *Danube* from its course, were I able to effect such purposes. Where then is the crime of turning a few ounces of blood from their natural channel?— Do you imagine that I repine at providence or curse my creation, because I go out of life, and put a period to a being, which, were it to continue, would render me miserable? Far be such sentiments from me; I am only convinced of a matter of fact, which you yourself acknowledge possible, that human life may be unhappy, and that my existence, if further prolonged, would become ineligible: but I thank providence, both for the good which I have already enjoyed, and for the power with which I am endowed of escaping the ill that threatens me.[2] To you it belongs to repine at providence, who foolishly imagine that you have no such power, and who must still prolong a hated life, tho' loaded with pain and sickness, with shame and poverty.—Do you not teach, that when any ill befalls me, tho' by the malice of my enemies, I ought to be resigned to providence, and that the actions of men are the operations of the Almighty as much as the actions of inanimate beings? When I fall upon my own sword, therefore, I receive my death equally from the hands of the Deity as if it had proceeded from a lion, a precipice, or a fever. The submission which you require to providence, in every calamity that befalls me, excludes not human skill and industry, if possibly by their means I can avoid or escape the calamity: And why may I not employ one remedy as well as another?—If my life be not my own, it were criminal for me to put it in danger, as well as to dispose of it; nor could one man deserve the appellation of *hero* whom glory or friendship transports into the greatest dangers, and another merit the reproach of *wretch* or *miscreant* who puts a period to his life from the same or like motives.—There is no being, which possesses any power or faculty, that it receives not from its Creator, nor is there any one, which by ever so irregular an action can encroach upon the plan of his providence, or disorder the universe. Its operations are his works equally with that chain of events, which it invades, and which ever principle prevails, we may for that very reason conclude it to be most favoured by him. Be it animate, or inanimate, rational, or irrational; 'tis all a case: Its power is still derived from the supreme creator, and is alike comprehended in the order of his providence. When the horror of pain prevails over the love of life; when a voluntary action anticipates the effects of blind causes; 'tis

[2] Agamus Deo gratias, quod nemo in vita teneri potest. SEN., Epist. 12.

only in consequence of those powers and principles, which he has implanted in his creatures. Divine providence is still inviolate and placed far beyond the reach of human injuries.[3] 'Tis impious, says the old Roman superstition, to divert rivers from their course, or invade the prerogatives of nature. 'Tis impious, says the French superstition, to inoculate for the small-pox, or usurp the business of providence, by voluntarily producing distempers and maladies. 'Tis impious, says the modern *European* superstition, to put a period to our own life, and thereby rebel against our creator; and why not impious, say I, to build houses, cultivate the ground, or sail upon the ocean? In all these actions we employ our powers of mind and body, to produce some innovation in the course of nature; and in none of them do we any more. They are all of them therefore equally innocent, or equally criminal.—*But you are placed by providence, like a centinel in a particular station, and when you desert it without being recalled, you are equally guilty of rebellion against your almighty sovereign, and have incurred his displeasure.*—I ask, why do you conclude that providence has placed me in this station? For my part I find that I owe my birth to a long chain of causes, of which many depended upon voluntary actions of men. *But Providence guided all these Causes, and nothing happens in the universe without its consent and Co-operation.* If so, then neither does my death, however voluntary, happen without its consent; and whenever pain or sorrow so far overcome my patience, as to make me tired of life, I may conclude that I am recalled from my station in the clearest and most express terms. 'Tis Providence surely that has placed me at this present moment in this chamber: But may I not leave it when I think proper, without being liable to the imputation of having deserted my post or station? When I shall be dead, the principles of which I am composed will still perform their part in the universe, and will be equally useful in the grand fabric, as when they composed this individual creature. The difference to the whole will be no greater than betwixt

[3] Tacit. Ann. lib. i. 79.

my being in a chamber and in the open air. The one change is of more importance to me than the other; but not more so to the universe.

'Tis a kind of blasphemy to imagine that any created being can disturb the order of the world or invade the business of providence! It supposes, that that Being possesses powers and faculties, which it received not from its creator, and which are not subordinate to his government and authority. A man may disturb society no doubt, and thereby incur the displeasure of the Almighty: But the government of the world is placed far beyond his reach and violence. And how does it appear that the Almighty is displeased with those actions that disturb society? By the principles which he has implanted in human nature, and which inspire us with a sentiment of remorse if we ourselves have been guilty of such actions, and with that of blame and disapprobation, if we ever observe them in others.—Let us now examine, according to the method proposed, whether Suicide be of this kind of actions, and be a breach of our duty to our *neighbour* and to *society*.

A man, who retires from life, does no harm to society: He only ceases to do good; which, if it is an injury, is of the lowest kind.—All our obligations to do good to society seem to imply something reciprocal. I receive the benefits of society and therefore ought to promote its interests, but when I withdraw myself altogether from society, can I be bound any longer? But, allowing that our obligations to do good were perpetual, they have certainly some bounds; I am not obliged to do a small good to society at the expence of a great harm to myself; why then should I prolong a miserable existence, because of some frivolous advantage which the public may perhaps receive from me? If upon account of age and infirmities I may lawfully resign any office, and employ my time altogether in fencing against these calamities, and alleviating as much as possible the miseries of my future life: Why may I not cut short these miseries at once by an action which is no more prejudicial to society?—But suppose that it is no longer in my power to promote the interest of society; suppose that

I am a burthen to it; suppose that my life hinders some person from being much more useful to society. In such cases my resignation of life must not only be innocent but laudable. And most people who lie under any temptation to abandon existence, are in some such situation; those, who have health, or power, or authority, have commonly better reason to be in humour with the world.

A man is engaged in a conspiracy for the public interest; is seized upon suspicion; is threatened with the rack; and knows from his own weakness that the secret will be extorted from him: Could such a one consult the public interest better than by putting a quick period to a miserable life? This was the case of the famous and brave *Strozi* of *Florence*.—Again, suppose a malefactor is justly condemned to a shameful death; can any reason be imagined, why he may not anticipate his punishment, and save himself all the anguish of thinking on its dreadful approaches? He invades the business of providence no more than the magistrate did, who ordered his execution; and his voluntary death is equally advantageous to society by ridding it of a pernicious member.

That suicide may often be consistent with interest and with our duty to ourselves, no one can question, who allows that age, sickness, or misfortune may render life a burthen, and make it worse even than annihilation. I believe that no man ever threw away life, while it was worth keeping. For such is our natural horror of death, that small motives will never be able to reconcile us to it; and though perhaps the situation of a man's health or fortune did not seem to require this remedy, we may at least be assured, that any one who, without apparent reason, has had recourse to it, was curst with such an incurable depravity or gloominess of temper as must poison all enjoyment, and render him equally miserable as if he had been loaded with the most grievous misfortunes.—If suicide be supposed a crime, 'tis only cowardice can impel us to it. If it be no crime, both prudence and courage should engage us to rid ourselves at once of existence, when it be-comes a burthen. 'Tis the only way that we can then be useful to society, by setting an example, which, if imitated, would preserve to every one his chance for happiness in life and would effectually free him from all danger or misery.[4]

[4] It would be easy to prove that Suicide is as lawful under the Christian dispensation as it was to the Heathens. There is not a single text of Scripture which prohibits it. That great and infallible rule of faith and practice which must controul all philosophy and human reasoning, has left us in this particular to our natural liberty. Resignation to Providence is indeed recommended in Scripture; but that implies only submission to ills that are unavoidable, not to such as may be remedied by prudence or courage. *Thou shalt not kill*, is evidently meant to exclude only the killing of others over whose life we have no authority. That this precept, like most of the Scripture precepts, must be modified by reason and common sense, is plain from the practice of magistrates, who punish criminals capitally, notwithstanding the letter of the law. But were this commandment ever so express against suicide, it would now have no authority, for all the law of *Moses* is abolished, except so far as it is established by the law of Nature. And we have already endeavoured to prove, that suicide is not prohibited by that law. In all cases Christians and Heathens are precisely upon the same footing; *Cato* and *Brutus*, *Arria* and *Portia* acted heroically; those who now imitate their example ought to receive the same praises from posterity. The power of committing suicide is regarded by *Pliny* as an advantage which men possess even above the Deity himself. "Deus non sibi potest mortem consciscere si velit, quod homini dedit optimum in tantis vitæ pœnis."—Lib. ii. cap. 5.

# DIALOGUES CONCERNING
## NATURAL RELIGION

# Part X

It is my opinion, I own, replied DEMEA, that each man feels, in a manner, the truth of religion within his own breast; and from a consciousness of his imbecility and misery, rather than from any reasoning, is led to seek protection from that Being, on whom he and all nature is dependent. So anxious or so tedious are even the best scenes of life, that futurity is still the object of all our hopes and fears. We incessantly look forward, and endeavour, by prayers, adoration, and sacrifice, to appease those unknown powers, whom we find, by experience, so able to afflict and oppress us. Wretched creatures that we are! what resource for us amidst the innumerable ills of life, did not Religion suggest some methods of atonement, and appease those terrors, with which we are incessantly agitated and tormented?

I am indeed persuaded, said PHILO, that the best and indeed the only method of bringing every one to a due sense of religion, is by just representations of the misery and wickedness of men. And for that purpose a talent of eloquence and strong imagery is more requisite than that of reasoning and argument. For is it necessary to prove, what every one feels within himself? 'Tis only necessary to make us feel it, if possible, more intimately and sensibly.

The people, indeed, replied DEMEA, are sufficiently convinced of this great and melancholy truth. The miseries of life, the unhappiness of men, the general corruptions of our nature, the unsatisfactory enjoyment of pleasures, riches, honours; these phrases have become almost proverbial in all languages. And who can doubt of what all men declare from their own immediate feeling and experience?

In this point, said PHILO, the learned are perfectly agreed with the vulgar; and in all letters, *sacred* and *profane*, the topic of human misery has been insisted on with the most pathetic eloquence that sorrow and melancholy could inspire. The poets, who speak from sentiment, without a system, and whose testimony has therefore the more authority, abound in images of this nature. From HOMER down to DR. YOUNG, the whole inspired tribe have ever been sensible, that no other representation of things would suit the feeling and observation of each individual.

As to authorities, replied DEMEA, you need not seek them. Look round this library of CLEANTHES. I shall venture to affirm, that, except authors of particular sciences, such as chemistry or botany, who have no occasion to treat of human life, there scarce is one of those innumerable writers, from whom the sense of human misery has not, in some passage or other, extorted a complaint and confession of it. At least, the chance is entirely on that side; and no one author has ever, so far as I can recollect, been so extravagant as to deny it.

There you must excuse me, said PHILO: LEIBNITZ has denied it; and is perhaps the first,[1] who ventured upon so bold and paradoxical an opinion; at least, the first, who made it essential to his philosophical system.

And by being the first, replied DEMEA, might he not have been sensible of his error? For is this a subject, in which philosophers can propose to make discoveries, especially in so late an age? And can any man hope by a simple denial (for the subject scarcely admits of reasoning) to bear down the united testimony of mankind, founded on sense and consciousness?

And why should man, added he, pretend to an exemption from the lot of all other animals? The whole earth, believe me, PHILO, is cursed and polluted. A perpetual war is kindled amongst all living creatures. Necessity, hunger, want, stimulate the strong and courageous: Fear, anxiety, terror, agitate the weak and infirm. The first entrance into life gives anguish to the new-born infant and to its wretched parent: Weakness,

---

[1] That sentiment had been maintained by Dr. King and some few others, before LEIBNITZ, though by none of so great fame as that GERMAN philosopher.

impotence, distress, attend each stage of that life: and 'tis at last finished in agony and horror.

Observe too, says PHILO, the curious artifices of Nature, in order to embitter the life of every living being. The stronger prey upon the weaker, and keep them in perpetual terror and anxiety. The weaker too, in their turn, often prey upon the stronger, and vex and molest them without relaxation. Consider that innumerable race of insects, which either are bred on the body of each animal, or flying about infix their stings in him. These insects have others still less than themselves, which torment them. And thus on each hand, before and behind, above and below, every animal is surrounded with enemies, which incessantly seek his misery and destruction.

Man alone, said DEMEA, seems to be, in part, an exception to this rule. For by combination in society, he can easily master lions, tigers, and bears, whose greater strength and agility naturally enable them to prey upon him.

On the contrary, it is here chiefly, cried PHILO, that the uniform and equal maxims of Nature are most apparent. Man, it is true, can, by combination, surmount all his *real* enemies, and become master of the whole animal creation: but does he not immediately raise up to himself imaginary enemies, the dæmons of his fancy, who haunt him with superstitious terrors, and blast every enjoyment of life? His pleasure, as he imagines, becomes, in their eyes, a crime: his food and repose give them umbrage and offence: his very sleep and dreams furnish new materials to anxious fear: and even death, his refuge from every other ill, presents only the dread of endless and innumerable woes. Nor does the wolf molest more the timid flock, than superstition does the anxious breast of wretched mortals.

Besides, consider, DEMEA; this very society, by which we surmount those wild beasts, our natural enemies; what new enemies does it not raise to us? What woe and misery does it not occasion? Man is the greatest enemy of man. Oppression, injustice, contempt, contumely, violence, sedition, war, calumny, treachery, fraud; by these they mutually torment each other: and they would soon dissolve that society which they had formed, were it not for the dread of still greater ills, which must attend their separation.

But though these external insults, said DEMEA, from animals, from men, from all the elements, which assault us, form a frightful catalogue of woes, they are nothing in comparison of those, which arise within ourselves, from the distempered condition of our mind and body. How many lie under the lingering torment of diseases? Hear the pathetic enumeration of the great poet.

> Intestine stone and ulcer, colic-pangs,
> Demoniac frenzy, moping melancholy,
> And moon-struck madness, pining atrophy,
> Marasmus and wide-wasting pestilence.
> Dire was the tossing, deep the groans: DESPAIR
> Tended the sick, busiest from couch to couch.
> And over them triumphant DEATH his dart
> Shook, but delay'd to strike, tho' oft invok'd
> With vows, as their chief good and final hope.[2]

The disorders of the mind, continued DEMEA, though more secret, are not perhaps less dismal and vexatious. Remorse, shame, anguish, rage, disappointment, anxiety, fear, dejection, despair; who has ever passed through life without cruel inroads from these tormentors? How many have scarcely ever felt any better sensations? Labour and poverty, so abhorred by every one, are the certain lot of the far greater number; and those few privileged persons, who enjoy ease and opulence, never reach contentment or true felicity. All the goods of life united would not make a very happy man: but all the ills united would make a wretch indeed; and any one of them almost (and who can be free from every one), nay often the absence of one good (and who can possess all), is sufficient to render life ineligible.

Were a stranger to drop, on a sudden, into this world,

[2] Milton: Paradise Lost, XI.

I would show him, as a specimen of its ills, an hospital full of diseases, a prison crowded with malefactors and debtors, a field of battle strewed with carcases, a fleet floundering in the ocean, a nation languishing under tyranny, famine, or pestilence. To turn the gay side of life to him, and give him a notion of its pleasures; whither should I conduct him? to a ball, to an opera, to court? He might justly think, that I was only showing him a diversity of distress and sorrow.

There is no evading such striking instances, said PHILO, but by apologies, which still farther aggravate the charge. Why have all men, I ask, in all ages, complained incessantly of the miseries of life? . . . They have no just reason, says one: these complaints proceed only from their discontented, repining, anxious disposition. . . . And can there possibly, I reply, be a more certain foundation of misery, than such a wretched temper?

But if they were really as unhappy as they pretend, says my antagonist, why do they remain in life? . . .

Not satisfied with life, afraid of death.

This is the secret chain, say I, that holds us. We are terrified, not bribed to the continuance of our existence.

It is only a false delicacy, he may insist, which a few re-fined spirits indulge, and which has spread these complaints among the whole race of mankind. . . . And what is this delicacy, I ask, which you blame? Is it any thing but a greater sensibility to all the pleasures and pains of life? and if the man of a delicate, refined temper, by being so much more alive than the rest of the world, is only so much more un-happy; what judgment must we form in general of human life?

Let men remain at rest, says our adversary; and they will be easy. They are willing artificers of their own misery. . . . No! reply I; an anxious languor follows their repose: disap-pointment, vexation, trouble, their activity and ambition.

I can observe something like what you mention in some

others, replied CLEANTHES: but I confess, I feel little or nothing of it in myself, and hope that it is not so common as you represent it.

If you feel not human misery yourself, cried DEMEA, I congratulate you on so happy a singularity. Others, seemingly the most prosperous, have not been ashamed to vent their complaints in the most melancholy strains. Let us attend to the great, the fortunate Emperor, CHARLES V, when, tired with human grandeur, he resigned all his extensive dominions into the hands of his son. In the last harangue, which he made on that memorable occasion, he publicly avowed, *that the greatest prosperities which he had ever enjoyed, had been mixed with so many adversities, that he might truly say he had never enjoyed any satisfaction or contentment.* But did the retired life, in which he sought for shelter, afford him any greater happiness? If we may credit his son's account, his repentance commenced the very day of his resignation.

CICERO'S fortune, from small beginnings, rose to the greatest lustre and renown; yet what pathetic complaints of the ills of life do his familiar letters, as well as philosophical discourses, contain? And suitably to his own experience, he introduces CATO, the great, the fortunate CATO, protesting in his old age, that, had he a new life in his offer, he would reject the present.

Ask yourself, ask any of your acquaintance, whether they would live over again the last ten or twenty years of their lives. No! but the next twenty, they say, will be better:

> And from the dregs of life, hope to receive
> What the first sprightly running could not give.[3]

Thus at last they find (such is the greatness of human misery; it reconciles even contradictions) that they complain, at once, of the shortness of life, and of its vanity and sorrow.

And is it possible, CLEANTHES, said PHILO, that after all these reflections, and infinitely more, which might be sug-

[3] Dryden: Aurungzebe, Act IV., sc. i.

gested, you can still persevere in your Anthropomorphism, and assert the moral attributes of the Deity, his justice, benevolence, mercy, and rectitude, to be of the same nature with these virtues in human creatures? His power we allow infinite: whatever he wills is executed: but neither man nor any other animal is happy: therefore he does not will their happiness. His wisdom is infinite: he is never mistaken in choosing the means to any end: but the course of nature tends not to human or animal felicity: therefore it is not established for that purpose. Through the whole compass of human knowledge, there are no inferences more certain and infallible than these. In what respect, then, do his benevolence and mercy resemble the benevolence and mercy of men?

EPICURUS's old questions are yet unanswered.

Is he willing to prevent evil, but not able? then is he impotent. Is he able, but not willing? then is he malevolent. Is he both able and willing? whence then is evil?

You ascribe, CLEANTHES, (and I believe justly) a purpose and intention to Nature. But what, I beseech you, is the object of that curious artifice and machinery, which she has displayed in all animals? The preservation alone of individuals and propagation of the species. It seems enough for her purpose, if such a rank be barely upheld in the universe, without any care or concern for the happiness of the members that compose it. No resource for this purpose: no machinery, in order merely to give pleasure or ease: no fund of pure joy and contentment: no indulgence without some want or necessity accompanying it. At least, the few phenomena of this nature are overbalanced by opposite phenomena of still greater importance.

Our sense of music, harmony, and indeed beauty of all kinds, gives satisfaction, without being absolutely necessary to the preservation and propagation of the species. But what racking pains, on the other hand, arise from gouts, gravels, megrims, tooth-aches, rheumatisms; where the injury to the animal-machinery is either small or incurable? Mirth, laughter, play, frolic, seem gratuitous satisfactions, which have no further tendency: spleen, melancholy, discontent, superstition, are pains of the same nature. How then does the divine benevolence display itself, in the sense of you Anthropomorphites? None but we Mystics, as you were pleased to call us, can account for this strange mixture of phenomena, by deriving it from attributes, infinitely perfect, but incomprehensible.

And have you at last, said CLEANTHES smiling, betrayed your intentions, PHILO? Your long agreement with DEMEA did indeed a little surprise me; but I find you were all the while erecting a concealed battery against me. And I must confess, that you have now fallen upon a subject, worthy of your noble spirit of opposition and controversy. If you can make out the present point, and prove mankind to be unhappy or corrupted, there is an end at once of all religion. For to what purpose establish the natural attributes of the Deity, while the moral are still doubtful and uncertain?

You take umbrage very easily, replied DEMEA, at opinions the most innocent, and the most generally received even amongst the religious and devout themselves: and nothing can be more surprising than to find a topic like this, concerning the wickedness and misery of man, charged with no less than Atheism and profaneness. Have not all pious divines and preachers, who have indulged their rhetoric on so fertile a subject: have they not easily, I say, given a solution of any difficulties, which may attend it? This world is but a point in comparison of the universe; this life but a moment in comparison of eternity. The present evil phenomena, therefore, are rectified in other regions, and in some future period of existence. And the eyes of men, being then opened to larger views of things, see the whole connection of general laws; and trace, with adoration, the benevolence and rectitude of the Deity, through all the mazes and intricacies of his providence.

No! replied CLEANTHES, No! These arbitrary suppositions can never be admitted, contrary to matter of fact, visible and uncontroverted. Whence can any cause be known but from its known effects? Whence can any hypothesis be proved but from the apparent phenomena? To establish one hypothesis upon another, is building entirely in the air; and the utmost we ever attain, by these conjectures and fictions, is to ascertain the bare possibility of our opinion; but never can we, upon such terms, establish its reality.

The only method of supporting divine benevolence (and it is what I willingly embrace) is to deny absolutely the misery and wickedness of man. Your representations are exaggerated: Your melancholy views mostly fictitious: Your inferences contrary to fact and experience. Health is more common than sickness: Pleasure than pain: Happiness than misery. And for one vexation, which we meet with, we attain, upon computation, a hundred enjoyments.

Admitting your position, replied PHILO, which yet is extremly doubtful, you must, at the same time, allow, that, if pain be less frequent than pleasure, it is infinitely more violent and durable. One hour of it is often able to outweigh a day, a week, a month of our common insipid enjoyments: And how many days, weeks, and months are passed by several in the most acute torments? Pleasure, scarcely in one instance, is ever able to reach ecstacy and rapture: And in no one instance can it continue for any time at its highest pitch and altitude. The spirits evaporate: the nerves relax; the fabric is disordered; and the enjoyment quickly degenerates into fatigue and uneasiness. But pain often, good God, how often! rises to torture and agony; and the longer it continues, it becomes still more genuine agony and torture. Patience is exhausted; courage languishes; melancholy seizes us; and nothing terminates our misery but the removal of its cause, or another event, which is the sole cure of all evil, but which, from our natural folly, we regard with still greater horror and consternation.

But not to insist upon these topics, continued PHILO, though most obvious, certain, and important; I must use the freedom to admonish you, CLEANTHES, that you have put this controversy upon a most dangerous issue, and are unawares introducing a total Scepticism, into the most essential articles of natural and revealed theology. What! no method of fixing a just foundation for religion, unless we allow the happiness of human life, and maintain a continued existence even in this world, with all our present pains, infirmities, vexations, and follies, to be eligible and desirable! But this is contrary to every one's feeling and experience: It is contrary to an authority so established as nothing can subvert: No decisive proofs can ever be produced against this authority; nor is it possible for you to compute, estimate, and compare all the pains and all the pleasures in the lives of all men and of all animals: And thus by your resting the whole system of religion on a point, which, from its very nature, must for ever be uncertain, you tacitly confess, that that system is equally uncertain.

But allowing you, what never will be believed; at least, what you never possibly can prove, that animal, or at least, human happiness, in this life, exceeds its misery; you have yet done nothing: For this is not, by any means, what we expect from infinite power, infinite wisdom, and infinite goodness. Why is there any misery at all in the world? Not by chance surely. From some cause then. Is it from the intention of the Deity? But he is perfectly benevolent. Is it contrary to his intention? But he is almighty. Nothing can shake the solidity of this reasoning, so short, so clear, so decisive; except we assert, that these subjects exceed all human capacity, and that our common measures of truth and falsehood are not applicable to them; a topic, which I have all along insisted on, but which you have, from the beginning, rejected with scorn and indignation.

But I will be contented to retire still from this intrenchment: For I deny that you can ever force me in it: I will allow, that pain or misery in man is *compatible* with infinite power and goodness in the Deity, even in your sense of these attributes: What are you advanced by all these concessions? A mere possible compatibility is not sufficient. You must *prove* these pure, unmixed, and uncontrollable attributes from the present mixed and confused phenomena, and from these alone. A hopeful undertaking! Were the phenomena ever so pure and unmixed, yet being finite, they would be insufficient for that purpose. How much more, where they are also so jarring and discordant!

Here, CLEANTHES, I find myself at ease in my argument. Here I triumph. Formerly, when we argued concerning the natural attributes of intelligence and design, I needed all my sceptical and metaphysical subtilty to elude your grasp. In many views of the universe, and of its parts, particularly the latter, the beauty and fitness of final causes strike us with such irresistible force, that all objections appear (what I believe they really are) mere cavils and sophisms; nor can we then imagine how it was ever possible for us to repose any weight on them. But there is no view of human life or of the condition of mankind, from which, without the greatest violence, we can infer the moral attributes, or learn that infinite benevolence, conjoined with infinite power and infinite wisdom, which we must discover by the eyes of faith alone. It is your turn now to tug the labouring oar, and to support your philosophical subtilties against the dictates of plain reason and experience.

# Part XI

I scruple not to allow, said CLEANTHES, that I have been apt to suspect the frequent repetition of the word, *infinite*, which we meet with in all theological writers, to savour more of panegyric than of philosophy, and that any purposes of reasoning, and even of religion, would be better served, were we to rest contented with more accurate and more moderate expressions. The terms, *admirable, excellent, superlatively great, wise,* and *holy*; these sufficiently fill the imaginations of men; and any thing beyond, besides that it leads into absurdities, has no influence on your affections or sentiments. Thus, in the present subject, if we abandon all human analogy, as seems your intention, DEMEA, I am afraid we abandon all religion, and retain no conception of the great object of our adoration. If we preserve human analogy, we must for ever find it impossible to reconcile any mixture of evil in the universe with infinite attributes; much less can we ever prove the latter from the former. But supposing the Author of Nature to be finitely perfect, though far exceeding mankind; a satisfactory account may then be given of natural and moral evil, and every untoward phenomenon be explained and adjusted. A less evil may then be chosen, in order to avoid a greater; Inconveniences be submitted to, in order to reach a desirable end: And in a word, benevolence, regulated by wisdom, and limited by necessity, may produce just such a world as the present. You, PHILO, who are so prompt at starting views, and reflections, and analogies, I would gladly hear, at length, without interruption, your opinion of this new theory; and if it deserve our attention, we may afterwards, at more leisure, reduce it into form.

My sentiments, replied PHILO, are not worth being made a mystery of; and therefore, without any ceremony, I shall deliver what occurs to me with regard to the present subject.

320

It must, I think, be allowed, that, if a very limited intelligence, whom we shall suppose utterly unacquainted with the universe, were assured, that it were the production of a very good, wise, and powerful being, however infinite, he would, from his conjectures, form *beforehand* a different notion of it from what we find it to be by experience; nor would he ever imagine, merely from these attributes of the cause, of which he is informed, that the effect could be so full of vice and misery and disorder, as it appears in his life. Supposing now, that this person were brought into the world, still assured, that it was the workmanship of such a sublime and benevolent Being; he might, perhaps, be surprised at the disappointment; but would never retract his former belief, if founded on any very solid argument; since such a limited intelligence must be sensible of his own blindness and ignorance, and must allow, that there may be many solutions of those phenomena, which will for ever escape his comprehension. But supposing, which is the real case with regard to man, that this creature is not antecedently convinced of a supreme intelligence, benevolent, and powerful, but is left to gather such a belief from the appearances of things; this entirely alters the case, nor will he ever find any reason for such a conclusion. He may be fully convinced of the narrow limits of his understanding; but this will not help him in forming an inference concerning the goodness of superior powers, since he must form that inference from what he knows, not from what he is ignorant of. The more you exaggerate his weakness and ignorance, the more diffident you render him, and give him the greater suspicion, that such subjects are beyond the reach of his faculties. You are obliged, therefore, to reason with him merely from the known phenomena, and to drop every arbitrary supposition or conjecture.

Did I show you a house or palace, where there was not one apartment convenient or agreeable; where the windows, doors, fires, passages, stairs, and the whole œconomy of the building were the source of noise, confusion, fatigue, darkness, and the extremes of heat and cold; you would certainly blame the contrivance, without any farther examination. The architect would in vain display his subtilty, and prove to you, that if this door or that window were altered, greater ills would ensue. What he says, may be strictly true: The alteration of one particular, while the other parts of the building remain, may only augment the inconveniences. But still you would assert in general, that, if the architect had had skill and good intentions, he might have formed such a plan of the whole, and might have adjusted the parts in such a manner, as would have remedied all or most of these inconveniences. His ignorance, or even your own ignorance of such a plan, will never convince you of the impossibility of it. If you find many inconveniences and deformities in the building, you will always, without entering into any detail, condemn the architect.

In short, I repeat the question: Is the world considered in general, and as it appears to us in this life, different from what a man or such a limited Being would, *beforehand*, expect from a very powerful, wise, and benevolent Deity? It must be strange prejudice to assert the contrary. And from thence I conclude, that, however consistent the world may be, allowing certain suppositions and conjectures, with the idea of such a Deity, it can never afford us an inference concerning his existence. The consistence is not absolutely denied, only the inference. Conjectures, especially where infinity is excluded from the Divine attributes, may perhaps be sufficient to prove a consistence; but can never be foundations for any inference.

There seem to be *four* circumstances, on which depend all, or the greatest parts of the ills, that molest sensible creatures; and it is not impossible but all these circumstances may be necessary and unavoidable. We know so little beyond common life, or even of common life, that, with regard to the œconomy of a universe, there is no conjecture, however wild, which may not be just; nor any one, however plausible, which may not be erroneous. All that belongs to human understanding, in this deep ignorance and obscurity, is to be sceptical, or at least cautious; and not to admit of any hypothesis, whatever; much less, of any which is supported by no appearance of probability. Now this I assert to be the case with regard to all the causes of evil, and the circumstances, on which it depends. None of them appear to human reason, in the least degree, necessary or unavoidable; nor can we suppose them such, without the utmost licence of imagination.

The *first* circumstance which introduces evil, is that contrivance or œconomy of the animal creation, by which pains, as well as pleasures, are employed to excite all creatures to action, and make them vigilant in the great work of self-preservation. Now pleasure alone, in its various degrees, seems to human understanding sufficient for this purpose. All animals might be constantly in a state of enjoyment; but when urged by any of the necessities of nature, such as thirst, hunger, weariness; instead of pain, they might feel a diminution of pleasure, by which they might be prompted to seek that object, which is necessary to their subsistence. Men pursue pleasure as eagerly as they avoid pain; at least, might have been so constituted. It seems, therefore, plainly possible to carry on the business of life without any pain. Why then is any animal ever rendered susceptible of such a sensation? If animals can be free from it an hour, they might enjoy a perpetual exemption from it; and it required as particular a contrivance of their organs to produce that feeling, as to endow them with sight, hearing, or any of the senses. Shall we conjecture, that such a contrivance was necessary, without any appearance of reason? and shall we build on that conjecture as on the most certain truth?

But a capacity of pain would not alone produce pain, were it not for the *second* circumstance, viz. the conducting of the world by general laws; and this seems nowise necessary to a very perfect being. It is true; if every thing were conducted by particular volitions, the course of nature would be perpetually broken, and no man could employ his reason in the conduct of life. But might not other particular volitions remedy this inconvenience? In short, might not the Deity exterminate all ill, wherever it were to be found; and produce all good, without any preparation or long progress of causes and effects?

Besides, we must consider, that, according to the present œconomy of the world, the course of Nature, though supposed exactly regular, yet to us appears not so, and many events are uncertain, and many disappoint our expectations. Health and sickness, calm and tempest, with an infinite number of other accidents, whose causes are unknown and variable, have a great influence both on the fortunes of particular persons and on the prosperity of public societies: and indeed all human life, in a manner, depends on such accidents. A being, therefore, who knows the secret springs of the universe, might easily, by particular volitions, turn all these accidents to the good of mankind, and render the whole world happy, without discovering himself in any operation. A fleet, whose purposes were salutary to society, might always meet with a fair wind: Good princes enjoy sound health and long life: Persons, born to power and authority, be framed with good tempers and virtuous dispositions. A few such events as these, regularly and wisely conducted, would change the face of the world; and yet would no more seem to disturb the course of Nature or confound human conduct, than the present œconomy of things, where the causes are secret, and variable, and compounded. Some small touches, given to CALIGULA's brain in his infancy, might have converted him into a TRAJAN: one wave, a little higher than the rest, by burying CAESAR and his fortune in the bottom of the ocean, might have restored liberty to a considerable part of mankind. There may, for aught we know, be good reasons, why Providence interposes not in this manner; but they are unknown to us: and though the mere supposition, that such reasons exist, may be sufficient to *save* the conclusion concerning the divine attributes, yet surely it can never be sufficient to *establish* that conclusion.

If every thing in the universe be conducted by general laws, and if animals be rendered susceptible of pain, it scarcely seems possible but some ill must arise in the various shocks of matter, and the various concurrence and opposition of general laws: But this ill would be very rare, were it not for the *third* circumstance, which I proposed to mention, viz. the great frugality with which all powers and faculties are distributed to every particular being. So well adjusted are the organs and capacities of all animals, and so well fitted to their preservation, that, as far as history or tradition reaches, there appears not to be any single species, which has yet been extinguished in the universe. Every animal has the requisite endowments; but these endowments are bestowed with so scrupulous an œconomy, that any considerable diminution must entirely destroy the creature. Wherever one power is increased, there is a proportional abatement in the others. Animals, which excel in swiftness, are commonly defective in force. Those, which possess both, are either imperfect in some of their senses, or are oppressed with the most craving wants. The human species, whose chief excellency is reason and sagacity, is of all others the most necessitous, and the most deficient in bodily advantages; without clothes, without arms, without food, without lodging, without any convenience of life, except what they owe to their own skill and industry. In short, Nature seems to have formed an exact calculation of the necessities of her creatures; and like a *rigid master*, has afforded them little more powers or endowments, than what are strictly sufficient to supply those necessities. An *indulgent parent* would have bestowed a large stock, in order to guard against accidents, and secure the happiness and welfare of the creature, in the most unfortunate concurrence of circumstances. Every course of life would not have been so surrounded with precipices, that the least departure from the true path, by mistake or necessity, must involve us in misery and ruin. Some reserve, some fund would have been provided to ensure happiness; nor would the powers and the necessities have been adjusted with so rigid an œconomy. The author of Nature is inconceivably powerful: his force is supposed great, if not altogether inexhaustible: nor is there any reason, as far as we can judge, to make him observe this strict frugality in his dealings with his creatures. It would have been better, were his power extremely limited, to have created fewer animals, and to have endowed these with more faculties for their happiness and preservation. A builder is never esteemed prudent, who undertakes a plan, beyond what his stock will enable him to finish.

In order to cure most of the ills of human life, I require not that man should have the wings of the eagle, the swiftness of the stag, the force of the ox, the arms of the lion, the scales of the crocodile or rhinoceros; much less do I demand the sagacity of an angel or cherub. I am contented to take an increase in one single power or faculty of his soul. Let him be endowed with a greater propensity to industry and labour; a more vigorous spring and activity of mind; a more constant bent to business and application. Let the whole species possess naturally an equal diligence with that which many individuals are able to attain by habit and reflection; and the most beneficial consequences, without any alloy of ill, is the immediate and necessary result of this endowment. Almost all the moral, as well as natural evils of human life arise from idleness; and were our species, by the original constitution of their frame, exempt from this vice or infirmity, the perfect cultivation of land, the improvement of arts and manufactures, the exact execution of every office and duty, immediately follow; and men at once may fully reach that state of society, which is so imperfectly attained by the best-regulated government. But as industry is a power, and the most valuable of any, Nature seems determined, suitably to her usual maxims, to bestow it on men with a very sparing hand; and rather to punish him severely for his deficiency in it, than to reward him for his attainments. She has so contrived his frame, that nothing but the most violent necessity can oblige him to labour; and she employs all his other wants to overcome, at least in part, the want of diligence, and to endow him with some share of a faculty, of which she has thought fit naturally to bereave him. Here our demands may be allowed very humble, and therefore the more reasonable If we required the endowments of superior penetration and judgment, of a more delicate taste of beauty, of a nicer sensibility to benevolence and friendship; we might be told, that we impiously pretend to break the order of Nature, that we want to exalt ourselves into a higher rank of being, that the presents which we require, not being suitable to our state and condition, would only be pernicious to us. But it is hard; I dare to repeat it, it is hard, that being placed in a world so full of wants and necessities; where almost every being and element is either our foe or refuses us their assistance, . . . we should also have our own temper to struggle with, and should be deprived of that faculty, which can alone fence against these multiplied evils.

The *fourth* circumstance, whence arises the misery and ill of the universe, is the inaccurate workmanship of all the springs and principles of the great machine of nature. It must be acknowledged, that there are few parts of the universe, which seem not to serve some purpose, and whose removal would not produce a visible defect and disorder in the whole. The parts hang all together; nor can one be touched without affecting the rest in a greater or less degree. But at the same time, it must be observed, that none of these parts or principles, however useful, are so accurately adjusted, as to keep precisely within those bounds, in which their utility consists; but they are, all of them, apt, on every occasion, to run into the one extreme or the other. One would imagine, that this grand production had not received the last hand of the maker; so little finished in every part, and so coarse are the strokes, with which it is executed. Thus, the winds are requisite to convey the vapours along the surface of the globe, and to assist men in navigation: but how oft, rising up to tempests and hurricanes, do they become pernicious? Rains are necessary to nourish all the plants and animals of the earth: but how often are they defective? how often excessive? Heat is requisite to all life and vegetation; but is not always found in the due proportion. On the mixture and secretion of the humours and juices of the body depend the health and prosperity of the animal: but the parts perform not regularly their proper function. What more useful than all the passions of the mind, ambition, vanity, love, anger? But how oft do they break their bounds, and cause the greatest convulsions in society? There is nothing so advantageous in the universe, but what frequently becomes pernicious by its excess or defect; nor has Nature guarded, with the requisite accuracy, against all disorder or confusion. The irregularity is never, perhaps, so great as to destroy any species; but is often sufficient to involve the individuals in ruin and misery.

On the concurrence, then, of these *four* circumstances does all, or the greatest part of natural evil depend. Were all living creatures incapable of pain, or were the world administered by particular volitions, evil never could have found access into the universe: and were animals endowed with a large stock of powers and faculties, beyond what strict necessity requires; or were the several springs and principles of the universe so accurately framed as to preserve always the just temperament and medium; there must have been very little ill in comparison of what we feel at present. What then shall we pronounce on this occasion? Shall we say, that these circumstances are not necessary, and that they might easily have been altered in the contrivance of the universe? This decision seems too presumptuous for creatures, so blind and ignorant. Let us be more modest in our conclusions. Let us allow, that, if the goodness of the Deity (I mean a goodness like the human) could be established on any tolerable reasons *a priori*, these phenomena, however untoward, would not be sufficient to subvert that principle; but might easily, in some unknown manner, be reconcilable to it. But let us still assert, that as this goodness is not antecedently established, but must be inferred from the phenomena, there can be no grounds for such an inference, while there are so many ills in the universe, and while these ills might so easily have been remedied, as far as human understanding can be allowed to judge on such a subject. I am Sceptic enough to allow, that the bad appearances, notwithstanding all my reasonings, may be compatible with such attributes as you suppose: But surely they can never prove these attributes. Such a conclusion cannot result from Scepticism; but must arise from the phenomena, and from our confidence in the reasonings, which we deduce from these phenomena.

Look round this universe. What an immense profusion of

beings, animated and organized, sensible and active! You admire this prodigious variety and fecundity. But inspect a little more narrowly these living existences, the only beings worth regarding. How hostile and destructive to each other! How insufficient all of them for their own happiness! How contemptible or odious to the spectator! The whole presents nothing but the idea of a blind Nature, impregnated by a great vivifying principle, and pouring forth from her lap, without discernment or parental care, her maimed and abortive children!

Here the MANICHÆAN system occurs as a proper hypothesis to solve the difficulty: and no doubt, in some respects, it is very specious, and has more probability than the common hypothesis, by giving a plausible account of the strange mixture of good and ill, which appears in life. But if we consider, on the other hand, the perfect uniformity and agreement of the parts of the universe, we shall not discover in it any marks of the combat of a malevolent with a benevolent being. There is indeed an opposition of pains and pleasures in the feelings of sensible creatures: but are not all the operations of Nature carried on by an opposition of principles, of hot and cold, moist and dry, light and heavy? The true conclusion is, that the original source of all things is entirely indifferent to all these principles, and has no more regard to good above ill than to heat above cold, or to drought above moisture, or to light above heavy.

There may *four* hypotheses be framed concerning the first causes of the universe: *that* they are endowed with perfect goodness, *that* they have perfect malice, *that* they are opposite and have both goodness and malice, *that* they have neither goodness nor malice. Mixed phenomena can never prove the two former unmixed principles. And the uniformity and steadiness of general laws seem to oppose the third. The fourth, therefore, seems by far the most probable.

What I have said concerning natural evil will apply to moral, with little or no variation; and we have no more reason to infer, that the rectitude of the Supreme Being resembles human rectitude than that his benevolence resembles the human. Nay, it will be thought, that we have still greater cause to exclude from him moral sentiments, such as we feel them; since moral evil, in the opinion of many, is much more predominant above moral good than natural evil above natural good.

But even though this should not be allowed, and though the virtue, which is in mankind, should be acknowledged much superior to the vice; yet so long as there is any vice at all in the universe, it will very much puzzle you Anthropomorphites, how to account for it. You must assign a cause for it, without having recourse to the first cause. But as every effect must have a cause, and that cause another; you must either carry on the progression *in infinitum*, or rest on that original principle, who is the ultimate cause of all things . . .

Hold! hold! cried DEMEA: Whither does your imagination hurry you? I joined in alliance with you, in order to prove the incomprehensible nature of the Divine Being, and refute the principles of CLEANTHES, who would measure every thing by a human rule and standard. But I now find you running into all the topics of the greatest libertines and infidels; and betraying that holy cause, which you seemingly espoused. Are you secretly, then, a more dangerous enemy than CLEANTHES himself?

And are you so late in perceiving it? replied CLEANTHES. Believe me, DEMEA; your friend PHILO, from the beginning, has been amusing himself at both our expense; and it must be confessed, that the injudicious reasoning of our vulgar theology has given him but too just a handle of ridicule. The total infirmity of human reason, the absolute incomprehensibility of the Divine Nature, the great and universal misery and still greater wickedness of men; these are strange topics surely to be so fondly cherished by orthodox divines and doctors. In ages of stupidity and ignorance, indeed, these principles may safely be espoused; and perhaps, no views of things are more proper to promote superstition, than such as encourage the blind amazement, the diffidence, and melancholy of mankind. But at present . . .

Blame not so much, interposed PHILO, the ignorance of

these reverend gentlemen. They know how to change their style with the times. Formerly it was a most popular theological topic to maintain, that human life was vanity and misery, and to exaggerate all the ills and pains, which are incident to men. But of late years, divines, we find, begin to retract this position, and maintain, though still with some hesitation, that there are more goods than evils, more pleasures than pains, even in this life. When religion stood entirely upon temper and education, it was thought proper to encourage melancholy; as indeed, mankind never have recourse to superior powers so readily as in that disposition. But as men have now learned to form principles, and to draw consequences, it is necessary to change the batteries, and to make use of such arguments as will endure, at least some scrutiny and examination. This variation is the same (and from the same causes) with that which I formerly remarked with regard to Scepticism.

Thus PHILO continued to the last his spirit of opposition, and his censure of established opinions. But I could observe, that DEMEA did not at all relish the latter part of the discourse; and he took occasion soon after, on some pretence or other, to leave the company.

# INDEX

# Index

The main purpose of this index is to enable cross-reference to be made between the *Enquiry* and Hume's other philosophical writings. Names of philosophers are cited in a list under *Authors* and not separately; other names are entered alphabetically.